Current Morphology

D1706972

This book aims to provide a thorough and wide-ranging introduction to approaches to morphology within linguistic theory over the last twenty years. This comprehensive survey covers the generative linguistic mainstream, including the 'lexicalist' morphology initiated by Chomsky, phonologically inspired developments, and the syntactically orientated approaches that have developed in the 1980s. It also covers some European approaches that are less fashionable or relatively unknown among English-speaking linguists.

The author not only identifies the issues tackled within each approach, but also analyses each approach critically from the point of view of its success in resolving these issues.

The book will be useful both for students and for practising linguists such as syntacticians, phonologists and other specialists requiring an overview of a neighbouring branch of linguistic theory.

Andrew Carstairs-McCarthy teaches linguistics at the University of Canterbury, Christchurch, New Zealand. He is the author of *Allomorphy in Inflexion* and is a regular contributor to linguistic journals.

Linguistic Theory Guides
General Editor Richard Hudson

Current Morphology

Andrew Carstairs-McCarthy

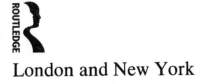

London and New York

First published 1992
by Routledge
11 New Fetter Lane, London EC4P 4EE

Simultaneously published in the USA and Canada
by Routledge
a division of Routledge, Chapman and Hall Inc.
29 West 35th Street, New York, NY 10001

Set in 10/12pt Times by Selectmove
Printed and bound in Great Britain by
Clays Ltd, St Ives plc.

British Library Cataloguing in Publication Data
Carstairs-McCarthy, Andrew
  Current morphology.
  1. English language. Morphology (Grammar)
  I. Title
  415

Library of Congress Cataloging in Publication Data
Carstairs-McCarthy, Andrew
  Current morphology/Andrew Carstairs-McCarthy.
  p.   cm. — (Linguistic theory guides)
  Includes bibliographical references and index.
  1. Grammar, Comparative and general—Morphology—History.
  I. Title.   II. Series.
  P241.C3   199/2
  415—dc20   91–16164

ISBN 0–415–00998–7
ISBN 0–415–07118–6 pbk

To Jeremy

Contents

x

Series editor's preface

The Linguistic Theory Guides have been commissioned with a rather special readership in mind – the typical linguist, who knows a good deal about a small number of theories in his or her area of specialism, but is baffled by the problem of keeping up with other theories even in that area, to say nothing of other areas. There just aren't enough hours in the day to read more widely, and even if there were it wouldn't help much because so much of the literature is simply incomprehensible except to the initiated. The result is that most of us cultivate our own garden reasonably conscientiously, but have very little idea of what is happening in other people's gardens.

This theoretical narrowing is a practical problem if you are expected to teach on a broad front – say, to give a course of lectures on syntactic theory – when you only know one theory of syntax. Honesty demands that one should tell students about alternative approaches, but how can you when you have at best a hazy idea of what most theories have to say? Another practical problem is the danger of missing pearls of wisdom which might be vitally important in one's research, because they happen to have been formulated in terms of some unfamiliar theory. There can be very few linguists who have not rediscovered some wheel in their area of specialism, out of ignorance about work in other theories.

However, there is an even more serious problem at the research level, because one of the main goals of our joint research effort is to work towards the best possible theory (or set of theories), and this can only be done if we constantly compare and evaluate all the available theories. From this perspective, it is simply pointless to spend one's life developing one theory, or some part of it, if it is already outclassed by some other theory. It is true that evaluation of theories is quite a subjective matter, and is far too complex for any kind of absolute certainty to be arrived at. All we can do is to make a reasonably dispassionate, though subjective, assessment of the strengths and weaknesses of the alternatives, in the full expectation that our colleagues may disagree radically with our verdict. Total ignorance of the alternative theories is clearly not a good basis for evaluating them – though it is arguably better than the misinformation that can be used to bolster one's confidence in one's favourite theory.

It is with these problems in mind, then, that we have planned the Linguistic Theory Guides. Each book in the series will focus on one theory that is currently prominent in the literature (or in a few special cases, on a range of such theories). The list of titles is open-ended, and new titles will be added as new theories come into prominence. The aim will be both to inform and to evaluate – to provide enough information to enable the reader to appreciate whatever literature presupposes the theory concerned, and to highlight its strengths and weaknesses. The intention is emphatically not to sell the theory, though the valuation will naturally be sufficiently positive to explain why the theory is worth considering seriously. Several of the theories are already well provided with textbooks which say a great deal about their strengths and very little about their weaknesses. We assume that our typical reader finds such books irritating at best. What they want is clear exposition at the right level of sophistication (i.e. well above first-year undergraduate level), and wise evaluation, both internally and in relation to other theories.

It is not easy to write a book with these qualities, and we have selected our authors with great care. What we have looked for in each case is essentially someone who is a sympathetic outsider, rather than a devotee of the theory – someone who has experience of working within other theories, but who is well-disposed to the theory concerned, and reasonably well-informed about it. We hope that this recipe will produce books which will be acceptably non-partisan in tone, but we have also taken steps to make them factually reliable as descriptions of the theories concerned. Each book has benefited from detailed comment by at least one prominent devotee (a term which we do not apply disparagingly – without their devotees theories would not come into being, still less develop, and there would be no theoretical linguistics), as well as by an outside reader. Needless to say, the authors have been allowed to stick to their evaluations if the protests of their devotee readers have failed to change their minds.

It is our sincere hope that these books will make a significant contribution to the growth and development of our subject, as well as being helpful to those who read them.

Richard Hudson

Acknowledgements

This work was done mainly when I was on study leave from the University of Canterbury during 1989–90, as a visiting fellow at Corpus Christi College, Cambridge, and a Christensen Visiting Fellow at St Catherine's College, Oxford. I am very grateful to both colleges for their hospitality, which gave me access to bigger library resources than I would have had at home (although the University of Canterbury Library was most helpful too). For discussion, comments and criticism on parts of the book I am grateful to Bob Beard, Richard Hudson and Andy Spencer. They are, of course, not responsible for the many faults which remain.

I would like to thank my partner Jeremy for his patience and encouragement during many late nights and days of frustration.

University of Canterbury
Christchurch, New Zealand

31 January 1991

Part I
Introduction

1 Aims and scope

1.1 MORPHOLOGY WITHIN LINGUISTIC THEORY: CENTRAL OR PERIPHERAL?

The revival of morphology as a subject of study by theoretical linguists has been announced more than once in recent years. In fact, it has become something of a cliché for collections of papers on morphology to begin with an editorial statement hailing the bright new dawn (Hammond and Noonan 1988; Booij and van Marle 1988). But this new atmosphere has not affected the status of morphology as an 'optional extra' in most linguistics degree programmes. As the published output in linguistics has expanded and new specialisms have proliferated, pressure on the time available in the average linguistics programme has grown correspondingly. Morphology has to compete for space in the syllabus with topics such as pragmatics, cognitive science, language acquisition and sign language, which scarcely existed as 'teachable' specialisms twenty years ago. So, even in linguistics programmes with a 'theoretical' orientation, phonology and syntax maintain their sway as the two indispensable core requirements, and morphology has not generally managed to establish itself alongside them.

It is true that all linguists know something about morphology. In most introductory courses, 'morpheme' follows close on the heels of 'phoneme' in the first batch of technical terms to which beginners are exposed. In most such courses, too, students are invited to inspect an array of verb forms from a language such as Swahili or Turkish, insert morpheme boundaries, and identify the lexical or grammatical 'meanings' of the morphemes thus isolated. There will also be some discussion of the contrast between the 'regular' forms of English noun plurals such as *cats*, *dogs* and *horses* and the 'irregular' forms of *sheep*, *oxen* and *mice*, though the instructor's definition of 'morpheme' may leave it frustratingly unclear whether *sheep* and *mice* consist of one morpheme or two. In later courses, where budding theoretical linguists are taught the importance of constraining the power of syntactic rules, they may learn of the reasons which persuaded Chomsky (1970) that at least some word formation should be relegated to the 'lexicon' (what Bloomfield (1933: 274) called the 'list of basic irregularities') rather than handled syntactically. In phonology, they will be invited to pay attention to those morphological alternations which can be accounted for in terms of phonological processes and to ignore those which cannot. This kind of training is likely to create the impression that, because words are more idiosyncratic in their structure and meaning than phrases and clauses are, the constraints which govern morphological behaviour must be fewer and looser than those which govern syntax, and the search for these constraints is bound to be relatively unrewarding to the linguistic theorist or student of Universal Grammar.

This book is addressed mainly to linguists who have had only the perfunctory morphological training just outlined but who are willing to be persuaded that the resultant pessimistic impression may be misleading. It is also addressed to linguists who are already expert in one approach to morphology but who are inquisitive about other 'schools'. The first-order aims are to summarise various approaches which are current or which directly influence current work, to discuss their main strengths and weaknesses, and (in chapter 9) to point to wider aspects of linguistic theory and linguistic methodology on which morphology has a special bearing. But there is a second-order aim: to persuade more linguists to take up morphological issues. Naturally I will be pleased if some readers share my assessments of the approaches discussed; but I will be equally pleased if I encourage new researchers into morphology, whatever conclusions they come to.

1.2 EARLIER ATTITUDES TO MORPHOLOGY

In pregenerative twentieth-century linguistics, both European and American, much attention was paid to morphological issues.[1] In America, the emphasis was on the criteria for identifying morphemes and the conditions for recognising 'discontinuous', 'zero', 'replacive' and 'portmanteau morphs', while some European linguists debated how (if at all) the relationship between grammatical properties was reflected in the relationship between their morphological expressions. In nineteenth-century linguistics, with its mainly historical orientation, inflectional paradigms and the operation of 'analogy' shared centre stage with the debate on the exceptionlessness of 'sound laws'. So the Saussurean revolution, unlike the Chomskyan one, did not affect the central position of morphology in linguistic theory. The dramatic shift in theoretical linguistic priorities after Chomsky's *Syntactic Structures* appeared in 1957 is well known and has been amply chronicled by Newmeyer (1980). Initially, some shift was inevitable, given that the new theoretical framework provided ways of tackling exciting new questions in the previously neglected domain of sentence structure. But the growing emphasis on aspects of grammar which are innate rather than learned seemed to supply a more substantial reason for continuing to sideline morphology, because the ratio of what is learned to what is innate appeared higher in morphology than in syntax. (We will return to this issue in chapter 9.) Even so, several linguists kept the morphological flame alive in the years between 1957 and the mid-1970s, including several who would call themselves 'generative'.

English is notoriously poor in inflectional morphology, and it is tempting, though pointless, to speculate on the course which generative theory might have taken in its first two decades if most of its practitioners had been native speakers of (say) Russian rather than English. Not surprisingly, most pioneers of generative morphology in the 1960s and early 1970s were Europeans, who saw that morphology had to be 'done' somehow if accounts of morphologically complex languages were to be descriptively adequate, even if from the point of view of Universal Grammar it should turn out to be a relatively unconstrained and therefore uninteresting domain. Work of this kind was done on, for example, German (Bierwisch 1967; Wurzel 1970), Swedish (Kiefer 1970), modern Greek (Warburton 1973) and Hungarian (Mel'čuk 1973). All these writers were concerned mainly with inflectional morphology, and all located it somewhere 'between' lexically interpreted surface structures and the phonological component – roughly where Chomsky and Halle (1968) located 'readjustment rules' such as the rule which ensures that the verb *sing* undergoes vowel change rather than suffixation in the past tense. Among linguists writing in English, Matthews (1972) was virtually unique in pursuing morphological interests which were independent of contemporary generative concerns, expounding the advantages of a 'word-based' rather than a 'morpheme-based' approach to morphology (what Hockett 1954 and Robins 1959 called the 'Word-and-Paradigm' model).

Paradoxically, none of this work contributed much at the time to the rehabilitation of morphology within Chomskyan generative grammar. This had to wait for the implications of Chomsky's (1970) study of

English nominalisation to sink in. But, since then, the relevance of this earlier work to current debates has been increasingly realised. For example, Wurzel's work on German influenced Lieber's account of morphological alternation (chapter 2), Bierwisch's approach to inflectional homonymy has influenced Zwicky's (chapter 7), and Matthews's Word-and-Paradigm framework has even inspired a nickname ('Extended Word-and-Paradigm') for S.R. Anderson's framework (chapter 7). In fact, as 1957 and 1970 recede, they seem in retrospect less and less significant as watersheds in morphological research. Is this evidence of a laudable readiness to build on past achievements, or of theoretical stagnation? Unfortunately, that kind of question has no objective answer!

1.3 TOPICS COVERED AND TOPICS EXCLUDED

This book is not a beginner's introduction to morphology, such as is offered by Matthews (1974), Bergenholtz and Mugdan (1979) and Bauer (1988). Nor is it specifically an introduction to generative work, as offered by Scalise (1984) or Spencer (1991), although such work inevitably looms large in it. Rather, this book attempts to survey the most influential developments in theoretical linguistic approaches to morphology in North America, Europe and Australasia over the last twenty years or so, as well as some developments which deserve to be more influential than they have been so far, in such a way as to help the reader to get to grips with the primary material.

The author of a survey such as this has to decide whether to organise the material around 'schools' (with the drawback that one issue may be discussed in several places) or around 'issues' (so that discussion of individual scholars is scattered). I have settled for a compromise. Part II (chapters 2–4) is 'school-oriented' in that it covers the Chomskyan impetus – work developing or reacting against ideas found in Chomsky and Halle's *The Sound Pattern of English* (1968) or Chomsky's 'Remarks on nominalization' (1970). Within part II, the chapters are issue-oriented, focusing in turn on morphology's relationship with the lexicon, phonology and syntax. Part III (chapters 5–8) covers work whose impetus is not Chomskyan. This does not mean that all this work is nongenerative (much less 'anti-generative'), merely that the relevant issues are substantially independent of those raised by Chomsky and Halle. Chapter 8 focuses on the Natural Morphology 'school' and some related work, but chapters 5–7 are issue-oriented; the result is that discussion of Bybee and of Carstairs[2] is divided between chapters, but it is easy to identify the sections concerned. In part IV (chapter 9) I offer my own suggestions about where the study of morphology might go from here and about its relevance to wider issues.

On the phonological side, I take morphology to include morphophonology, which figures in chapters 3 and 8 especially. On the syntactic side, I have included incorporation but I have not attempted a full survey of recent work on clitics, limiting myself to aspects of their behaviour which have been linked to specifically morphological issues (chapter 4). As for morphosyntactic properties or features (accusative case, past tense and so on), I concentrate on their morphological aspect (how they are structured and realised) rather than on their syntactic aspect (how they are distributed among syntactic constituents, and how 'agreement' and 'government' operate). This implies that I think that the two aspects are sufficiently independent in general to allow separate discussion; but they are almost certainly not independent entirely, and on the extent and nature of their mutual influence the reader should consult Corbett (1983; 1987; 1988). The interface between derivational morphology and lexical semantics has not received much attention in recent years, so there is little to report there; but I argue in chapters 2 and 6 that this is a serious deficiency.

The import of the restriction to 'theoretical linguistic approaches' is that I do not attempt to cover psycholinguistic and computational studies in morphology, except where they are cited in discussion by some theoretical morphologist. This is certainly not meant to imply that I believe that such studies are irrelevant to 'linguistic' morphology. I acknowledge that, in omitting them, I could be accused of perpetuating a habit of neglect and of communication failure. My only excuse is that the book is long enough as it is, and I doubt my own competence to do justice to these areas. I strongly urge readers to make good the deficiency for themselves. Entrées to recent psycholinguistic work on morphology are provided by Aitchison (1987), de Bleser and Bayer (1988) and Stemberger and MacWhinney (1988), as well as in a collection of papers from the Conference on Linguistic and Psychological Approaches to Morphology held at Cambridge in 1987, published as *Linguistics* 26.4 (1988).

This book does not provide a single coherent network of definitions of terms such as 'morpheme', 'inflection', 'morphosyntactic category' and so on, because all these terms are used more or less differently by different linguists.[3] Where appropriate I quote individual linguists' definitions; but my emphasis is on illustrating the kinds of facts which different morphological approaches seek to account for rather than on comparing and contrasting their terminologies.

Part II

The Chomskyan impetus in morphological research

2 Morphology and the lexicon

2.1 INTRODUCTION

Although generative work on morphology has advanced greatly in scope and sophistication in the last twenty years, the morphological agenda for generative linguists is still conditioned to a remarkable extent by the problems originally addressed by Chomsky in *Aspects of the Theory of Syntax* (1965) and 'Remarks on nominalization' (1970) and by Halle in 'Prolegomena to a theory of word-formation' (1973). Our approach will be selective and critical; we will concentrate on those aspects of what they said or did not say which seem most relevant to subsequent developments. In section 2.1.5 we will list the questions which Chomsky's and Halle's work provoked, and in later sections discuss what answers to them (if any) have been proposed in more recent work.[1]

2.1.1 Chomsky's *Aspects of the Theory of Syntax*

Bloomfield (1933: 274) called the lexicon 'an appendix of the grammar, a list of basic irregularities'. On this view, the lexicon is irredeemably untidy, so it is bound to be that aspect of any language which is of least interest to the linguistic theorist. In Chomsky's *Aspects* (1965), a tidying-up process begins; we find there the first outline of a generative theory of the lexicon, with proposals on how lexical entries are structured and organised.

Each lexical item is to be supplied with syntactic, semantic and phonological information. The syntactic information for each item includes its **category** (Noun, Verb, etc.) and perhaps **subcategory** (Proper Noun, Intransitive Verb, etc.), as well as **selection restrictions**, which relate to syntactic or semantic characteristics of other items in the immediate syntactic context. In addition, lexical entries may be abbreviated by appeal to **lexical redundancy rules**. Let us apply these notions to the following examples:

(1)   John admires sincerity grudgingly.
(2)   John admires sincerity.
(3)   *John weighs 70 kilos grudgingly.
(4)   John weighs 70 kilos.
(5)   *John admires.
(6)   *John elapses sincerity.
(7)   *Sincerity admires John.

The well-formedness of (1) and (2) demonstrates that the verb *admire* must be subcategorised to allow either a following noun phrase plus manner adverbial, as in (1), or a following noun phrase alone, as in (2). But these two subcategorisations are not independent; any verb which can appear with a manner adverbial can also appear without one (Chomsky claims), although the converse is not true, as (3) and (4) illustrate (at least if it is John's own weight that is at issue). We can therefore ascribe to the lexicon something which is not itself a lexical entry but rather a generalisation about lexical entries, namely the lexical redundancy rule (8):

(8) $[+\underline{\quad}\emptyset\hat{}\,\text{Manner}]\rightarrow[+\underline{\quad}\emptyset]$

Here, $\emptyset$ stands for any constant string (possibly null), and $\hat{}$ indicates concatenation. *Admire* is a transitive verb, a fact which is represented in *Aspects* notation by means of the lexical feature $[+\underline{\quad}\text{NP}]$; therefore the absence of a noun phrase following *admires* in (5) violates its subcategorisation. The intransitive verb *elapse*, conversely, is lexically marked $[-\underline{\quad}\text{NP}]$, so it cannot tolerate the presence of the noun phrase *sincerity* in (6). Finally, (7) is ill-formed because it violates the selectional feature which requires that the subject of *admire* should be [+Human] (or, at any rate, [+Animate]).

The lexicon interacts with the syntactic component through **lexical insertion**, that is the process whereby the terminal nodes of phrase markers come to be filled by lexical items of the appropriate category and subcategory and with the appropriate selectional features. This process takes place at deep structure, after the operation of the phrase-structure rules but before any transformations have applied. Within the *Aspects* framework, no other point in the derivation of a sentence is suitable, since subcategorisation features for lexical items reflect only the deep-structure contexts in which these items may occur, not the contexts in which they may appear after deep-structure phrase markers have been altered by transformations.

So far we have looked only at lexical items which are unanalysable wholes, such as *John, sincere* and *admire*. But there exist also: (a) items which one is inclined to regard as single lexical items on semantic grounds but which have an internal syntactic structure, such as the idioms *take for granted* and *take offence at* and the phrasal verbs *take off* or *look up*; and (b) items (words or word-forms) which are in one way or another morphologically complex, such as *sincerity, admired, admiration, telegraph* and *horrify*. We will consider Chomsky's attitude to each of these in turn.

Chomsky regards idioms and phrasal verbs as single lexical items. However, they are hard to reconcile with his theory of the lexicon in that some of them at least must apparently be inserted under nonterminal (phrasal) nodes rather than terminal ones, or even under discontinuous sets of nodes. For example, *take for granted* must presumably be inserted at deep structure in the double-slotted configuration [____$_V$ NP [____]$_{PP}$]$_{VP}$. Chomsky notes the problem without offering a solution; he links it with other 'poorly understood quasi-productive processes' on which 'all presently known theories of language have failed to provide any substantial insight' (1965: 235).

The morphologically complex word-forms that Chomsky considers in *Aspects* fall into three classes: (a) inflected forms; (b) derived words which are not deverbal or deadjectival nominalisations (e.g. *telegraph, horrify*); and (c) deverbal and deadjectival nominalisations (e.g. *destruction, refusal, sincerity*). Although he handles these three classes in what at first sight seem quite different ways, there is a common factor; Chomsky is reluctant to recognise as lexically distinct any two or more items which have a large proportion of their syntactic, semantic or phonological characteristics in common.

Distinct inflected forms of the same word are treated in something like the fashion of traditional grammar rather than that of twentieth-century structuralist morphological analysis; that is, morphosyntactic properties such as Masculine, Accusative and Plural are treated not as morphemes but as values (not necessarily binary) for features such as Gender, Case and Number. The difference between the German Masculine Accusative Plural word-form *Brüder* 'brothers' and the Dative Plural word-form *Brüdern*, for example, lies in the fact that, although they are both specified lexically as being of Masculine Gender and specified in deep structure as being Plural in Number, they differ as to Case, which is determined by surface structure; but they are still forms of the same lexical item, whose Case difference is manifested in the interpretation provided for them by the phonological component.

Words such as *telegraph* and *horrify* puzzle Chomsky considerably.

The processes which form them are only 'quasi-productive', because we find gaps (*horror, horrid, horrify; terror, *terrid, terrify; candor, candid, *candify; telescope, phonograph, *phonoscope*). This points towards entering these items in the lexicon directly. But, in Chomsky's view, that overlooks the extent to which their meaning and phonological behaviour are predictable on the basis of their internal structure. One alternative that Chomsky suggests is to treat at least some of the gaps as accidental, and 'incorporate in the grammar overly general rules that allow for nonoccurring as well as actual cases' (1965: 187). Such rules would presumably be transformational, analogous to those which produce deverbal nouns, discussed below; a lexical item like *horror* or *terror* would in the appropriate adjectival context be transformed to *horrid* or *terrid*, though Chomsky does not explain how the nonexistence of *terrid* would be handled under this analysis. A second alternative would be to treat both stems such as *horr-* and *terr-* and suffixes such as *-id* and *-ify* as separate lexical items, with the theory of the lexicon extended to allow some 'internal computation' (the 'scare quotes' are Chomsky's) whereby stems and affixes are combined; these computation rules would be somehow restricted so as not to generate nonexistent items.

In *Aspects*, nouns derived from verbs, such as *destruction* and *refusal*, and nouns derived from adjectives, such as *sincerity*, are regarded as much more straightforward than words like *telegraph* and *horrify*, because the processes concerned are regarded as being entirely productive. Phrases such as *their destruction of the property, their refusal to participate* and *John's sincerity* are derived by **nominalisation transformations** from sentences such as *they destroy the property, they refuse to participate* and *John is sincere*. Chomsky explicitly denies that words such as *destruction, refusal* and *sincerity* are entered in the lexicon as such; instead, the lexical entries for the verbs *destroy* and *refuse* and the adjective *sincere* will contain information about the phonological shape which they assume when they have undergone nominalisation.

Five years later, in 'Remarks on nominalization', Chomsky explicitly abandoned nominalisation transformations, at least in accounting for morphologically more or less idiosyncratic derived nominals such as *destruction* and *refusal*. This change of mind represents the most significant difference between Chomsky's positions in *Aspects* and 'Remarks', and it was extremely influential. But, before considering the reasons for it, we need to look at the view of the lexicon which characterised the 'generative semantic' approach to syntax against which Chomsky was reacting in 1970.

2.1.2 The lexicon in generative semantics

As we have seen, not all lexical items are unanalysable wholes. *Pig* and (British English) *piglet* are clearly related to each other both in meaning (PIG and YOUNG PIG) and in shape (*piglet* consisting of a base *pig* and a suffix *-let*). And, since this relationship is evident to native speakers, it must be somehow captured in any adequate description of British English. Even in American English, where monomorphemic *shoat* is more usual than *piglet*, the semantic relationship between *pig* and *shoat* is the same as that between *pig* and *piglet*, despite their dissimilarity in shape.[2] And the background against which Chomsky wrote 'Remarks on nominalization' was one in which many linguists (those espousing **generative semantics**) claimed that the proper way to capture both kinds of relationship (semantic and morphological) was through a much wider repertoire of lexical insertion possibilities than was envisaged by Chomsky in *Aspects*.[3]

For present purposes, the two most important tenets of the generative semanticists are the following:

(a) The terminal nodes of phrase-structure trees, which in the *Aspects* model are either empty ('before' lexical insertion) or occupied by lexical items ('after' lexical insertion), may be occupied by semantic components, or features, such as YOUNG and PIG. These features are not to be confused with English words such as *young* and *pig*. Although for convenience we may label the features with English names in small capitals, they are part of an inventory which is at least partly, and may be wholly, universal (just as the inventory of phonological features posited by generative phonological theory is held to be universal).

(b) Lexical items may be inserted not only at terminal nodes but also at nonterminal nodes (for example, phrase or clause nodes), replacing the subtrees that these nodes dominate.

Insertion of lexical items at nonterminal (or indeed, terminal) nodes in phrase markers was seen by the generative semanticists as essentially the same kind of operation as the manipulation of phrase markers by syntactic transformations. In fact, they so extended the role of transformations in linguistic theory as to abandon the modular approach to linguistic description enshrined in *Aspects*, with a distinct syntactic component, semantic component and lexicon interacting only in certain limited ways. Rather, for the generative semanticist, the generation of any sentence involves a succession of phrase markers related by transformations within one seamless semantic-syntactic component, becoming progressively less 'semantic' and more 'lexical' as structures whose terminal nodes dominated only semantic features are progressively replaced by lexical items. Correspondingly, instead of a lexical entry for each lexical item, the generative semanticists in effect posit a special **lexical insertion transformation** for each item, specifying what phrase marker, dominating what semantic features, that lexical item can optionally or obligatorily replace. Thus, to take one well-known (or notorious) example, the lexical insertion transformation for *kill* would permit 'X *kill* Y' to replace a phrase marker roughly of the form shown at (9):

(9)

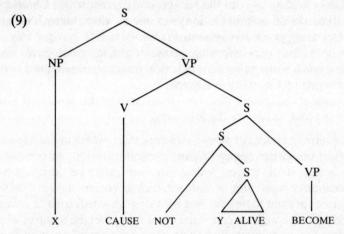

The details of the structure in (9) do not matter here. The important points are that the most 'abstract' syntactic structure for a sentence comes to be equivalent to a representation of its logical and semantic structure, and that the transformations which replace phrase markers with lexical items must be capable of effecting multiple operations of movement, deletion and substitution simultaneously.

A generative semantic analysis might assume for both British *piglet* and American *shoat* the 'deep structure' in (10):

(10)

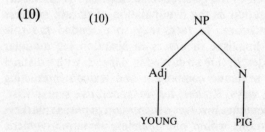

In American English there will exist a lexical insertion transformation replacing this whole tree by the item *shoat*; in British English, however, transformations will in this context replace YOUNG by *-let* and PIG by *pig*, with subsequent obligatory inversion of *-let pig* to yield *piglet*. The *shoat* and *-let* transformations will be optional, however, because in both varieties of English we must also allow the deep structure in (10) to surface straightforwardly as *young pig*.

In 'Remarks on nominalization' Chomsky strongly attacked the syntactic assumptions under which this kind of analysis is possible, and proposed a radically different way of representing the kind of relationship which exists between *pig* and *piglet*, for example. It is worth remembering, however, that he had nothing to say about the kind of relationship that exists between *pig* and *shoat*. Chomsky's response to the generative semanticists in this area was therefore, in a sense, one-sided; he instigated an approach to the lexicon within which relationships in shape overshadow relationships in meaning. We will have more to say about this one-sidedness later.

2.1.3 Chomsky's 'Remarks on nominalization'

In *Aspects* Chomsky took it for granted that 'derived nominals' such as *destruction* and *refusal* are related to their corresponding verbs transformationally. In 'Remarks' he rejects this assumption. He points out that, with the framework for lexical entries introduced in *Aspects*, it is an empirical question whether the similarities between, for example, *John refused to come* and *John's refusal to come* are better accounted for by transformations (deriving the latter from the syntactic structure underlying the former, essentially) or lexically, by appeal to the subcategorization and selectional and semantic features of a single lexical item *refuse* which is neutral between nominal and verbal status. Within the lexical entries for category-neutral items of this kind, the difference between verbs and their corresponding derived nominals will show up mainly in the phonological information; more or less idiosyncratically, the entries will specify *refuse, destroy, reside* and so on as spellings for the items concerned when they surface as verbs, and *refusal, destruction, residence* and so on as their spellings when they surface as nouns.

Chomsky's answer to the empirical question is that the evidence favours on balance the lexicalist over the transformationalist position. His arguments fall into two classes: syntactic and semantic-morphological. The main syntactic argument hinges on the relative 'productivity' of **gerundive nominals** such as *being eager, being easy* in (11) over derived nominals such as *eagerness, easiness* in (12), and their relationship to simple sentences such as (13):

(11) a.   John's being eager to please
      b.   John's being easy to please

(12) a.   John's eagerness to please
      b.   *John's easiness to please

(13) a.   John is eager to please.
      b.   John is easy to please.

Chomsky's use of the term 'productivity' here, although it recalls the *Aspects* distinction between 'productive' and 'semi-productive' derivational processes, is potentially confusing. He is not referring to productivity in any of the senses which are usual in discussions of morphology (for instance, the sense in which *-ness*, as in *shallowness*, can be said to be a more productive noun-forming suffix than *-th*, as in *depth*). Rather, he is referring to the fact that, when one attempts to form nominalisations on the analogy of acceptable simple sentences such as (13), one finds that gerundive nominalisations are nearly always acceptable (as in (11)), but that derived nominalisations show an at first sight rather perplexing pattern, with some being acceptable and others not (as with (12a) versus (12b)). Chomsky explains this discrepancy in a fashion which relies crucially on the assumption, carried over from *Aspects*, that lexical insertion takes place at deep structure. He argues that, if *eager, easy, eagerness* and *easiness* are all four inserted at deep structure, then the acceptability distribution illustrated at (12)–(13) follows directly from their subcategorisation requirements – or rather from the subcategorisation requirements of the two category-neutral items *eager*$_{N,A}$ and *easy*$_{N,A}$, which acquire nominal or adjectival shape according to context. On the other hand, if *eagerness* and *easiness* are derived from *eager* and *easy* by a nominalisation transformation, there is no obvious reason for the unacceptability of (12b); one could perhaps account for it by ordering transformations in some way, or by building restrictions into them, but any such solution would be *ad hoc* by comparison with the lexicalist solution. In contrast, the gerundive nominalisations of (11), being generated transformationally, are not subject to restrictions imposed by the need to satisfy subcategorisation requirements.

    Chomsky's semantic-morphological reasons for preferring the lexicalist analysis are of a more traditional kind. If we look at a range of derived nominals such as *laughter, marriage, belief, doubt, conversion, residence*, we observe both a variety of different formal (usually suffixal) manifestations of their derived status, and also a variety of different semantic relationships; typically a derived nominal reflects some but not all possible meanings of its corresponding verb. This 'range of variation and its rather accidental character are typical of lexical structure' (1970: 189). On the other hand, if one were to derive the nominals transformationally, one would have to make the operation of these transformations dependent on the meaning of the base form. Here Chomsky retains at least one aspect of Bloomfield's view, quoted earlier; even if the lexicon has some structure (by way of both general specifications on the form of lexical entries and lexical redundancy rules), still it is the place in the grammar where idiosyncrasies are to be expected, whereas in the syntax (including its transformational subcomponent) idiosyncrasies are unusual.

Although Chomsky's focus is on nominalisations, clearly many of the same issues arise in connection with derived words of other categories, such as deverbal adjectives (*readable, attractive*) and deadjectival nouns (*readability, attractiveness*); and the lexicalist solution for derived nominals cannot be considered fully satisfactory unless it can be extended in appropriate ways to derivatives such as these. Chomsky claims that this extension is possible. He does not, however, discuss its implications for his view that lexical entries may be neutral between categories. Under this view, *attract* and *attraction*, for example, both belong to a common lexical item *attract*$_{V,N}$, 'spelled' *attract* when it is a verb and *attraction* when it is a noun. It seems plausible, perhaps, to assign *attractive* to the same lexical item (*attract*$_{V,N,A}$) as a third, adjectival, spelling. But then how are we to analyse *attractiveness*? It is surely unsatisfactory to regard *attraction* and *attractiveness* as distinct rival nominal manifestations of the same lexical item. This question is not discussed in 'Remarks', however.

2.1.4 Halle's 'Prolegomena to a theory of word formation'

As its name implies, Halle's 'Prolegomena to a theory of word formation' (1973) is primarily concerned with the internal structure of morphologically complex words. Even so, Halle's view of word formation still assigns a crucial role to the lexicon, in something like Chomsky's sense. Word formation is not an extension of syntax 'below' the level of the word; indeed, Halle is at pains to emphasise differences between word structure and sentence structure which militate against any such view. The buffer between word formation and syntax is the **dictionary**, which is a list of all actually occurring words; and lexical insertion is a matter of selecting words (not morphemes) appropriate for the phrase markers into which they are to be inserted. To this extent, Halle does not depart from Chomsky's position. What is new is Halle's attempt to confront the process of 'internal computation' which Chomsky skirts nervously around in *Aspects*.

Halle's starting point is the observation that part of what speakers know about their language is that the morphemes within a word cannot be strung together in random order; *trans-form-at-ion-al* is a possible (indeed, an actual) word in English, but *ion-trans-al-at-form* is not. Grammars must therefore contain **word-formation rules** (WFRs), one of whose functions is to specify how the morphemes are to be arranged in sequence to form actual words. The word-formation rules that Halle cites as examples fall into two groups: those which specify possible linear strings of morphemes, and those which derive words from other words. For the first group, Halle gives examples as in (15), which are motivated by the examples in (14):

(14)   serendip+i+ty tot+al be+lieve
(15)   [STEM+i+ty]$_N$ [STEM+al]$_A$ [be+STEM]$_V$

The fact that not all stems can appear in all the frames of (15) (there is no*totity* or *beserendip*, for example) is taken care of by ensuring that 'the stems in the list of morphemes' are 'appropriately marked so that a given stem will be substitutable only in certain frames and not in others' (1973: 10). For the second group, Halle's examples include those in (16) and (17):

(16)   profan+i+ty arriv+al black+en
(17)   [ADJ(+i)+ty]$_N$ [VERB+al]$_N$ [ADJ+en]$_V$

As can be seen from (15) and (17), both kinds of WFR supply information about the syntactic category of the words generated. They also generally say something about the meaning of these words. For example, the WFR for the suffix *–hood* will specify that it applies to nouns designating human beings (such as *boy*) in order to produce abstract nouns designating a corresponding state or quality (*boyhood*).

The word to which a WFR applies may, of course, be itself derived from another word or stem. And, given that each of the WFRs in (15) and (17) imposes a labelled bracketing on the morphemes which it combines, successive WFRs will produce not just complex words but a nested structure of labelled brackets, much like a syntactic phrase marker. Thus, the successive application of the rules [STEM+al]$_A$

and $[ADJ(+i)+ty]_N$ to the stem *tot-* will yield not just *totality* but $[[tot+al]_A+i+ty]_N$. Implicit in Halle's framework, then, is the claim not just that speakers can distinguish words in their language from nonwords, but that their competence includes 'knowledge' of the internal structure of complex words.

Not everything that complies with the word-formation rules is an actual word, however; *arrival, derivation, refusal, confusion* exist, but not **arrivation, *derival, *refusion, *confusal*. This fact is taken care of by means of a **filter** interposed between the word-formation rules and the dictionary. The nonexistent but productively formed words just listed would enter the filter and be provided there with the feature [−Lexical Insertion], which would ensure that they could not appear in any actual sentence, 'in spite of the fact that that they are neither semantically nor syntactically or phonologically anomalous' (1973: 5). Other functions of the filter are to take care of semantic unpredictability (the fact that *recital* and *recitation* have distinct meanings, for instance, even though both are derived from *recite*) and phonological anomalies (for example, the fact that *obesity*, pronounced *ob*[i]*sity*, is an exception to the phonological rule of Trisyllabic Laxing, which ought to yield **ob*[e]*sity*, just like *sev*[e]*rity* alongside *severe*).

Whereas Chomsky in *Aspects* treated inflectional morphology as a matter of providing phonological interpretation for bundles of morphosyntactic features, Halle treats it in the same way that he treats derivational morphology: 'I know of no reason why the list of morphemes should not also include the *inflectional affixes* or *desinences*, or why the rules of word formation should not also include rules for positioning the inflectional affixes appropriately or for handling such other inflectional phenomena as reduplication, stem Ablaut, etc.' (1973: 6). What combination of morphosyntactic properties a given item is to be inflected for will, as ever, be mainly determined by its syntactic context; but the realisation of those properties will be at least partly a matter of choosing a suitable word-form derived by WFRs in the lexicon, rather than of taking the phonological representation for the stem (assumed to be unique) and 'readjusting' it or modifying it phonologically. This poses a problem, however; for Halle as well as for Chomsky, lexical insertion takes place at deep structure, yet some of the syntactic properties relevant to inflection (such as case, and perhaps also tense in those languages with 'sequence of tenses') are not determined until surface structure. Halle solves this problem by proposing that it is not single items which are inserted but rather 'partial or entire paradigms, i.e. certain or all inflected forms of a given "word" ' (1973: 9); the inflectionally inappropriate members of the paradigm are then filtered out at the level of surface structure. He supports this proposal by appeal to the phenomenon of 'paradigm pressure', whereby some forms within an inflectional paradigm change their shape in order to conform more closely to other members of the paradigm; 'if paradigms can influence the evolution of language then there is every reason to expect that paradigms must appear as entities in their own right somewhere in a grammar', such as in the dictionary. In this respect, the dictionary is more than a mere function of the operation of the WFRs and the filter on the list of morphemes.[4]

An odd feature of Halle's framework is that the word-formation rules which operate on individual morphemes (such as [STEM+ $i+ty]_N$) are apparently distinct from those which operate on words (such as $[ADJ(+i)+ty]_N$); yet individual rules of the two types can resemble each other closely, as these examples show. Halle's reason for keeping the two types apart seems to be a reluctance to assign syntactic categories to bound stems, as opposed to words; since *serendip* is not a word, it cannot be an adjective, and so cannot be subject to a WFR which derives nouns from adjectives. This reluctance is consistent in spirit with Chomsky's proposal that category-neutral lexical items such as $refuse_{N,V}$ may be realised as a verb (*refuse*) or a noun (*refusal*) according to syntactic context. However, it forces Halle to increase the power of word-formation rules in a fashion that might not otherwise be necessary; they must be allowed to pay attention not only to the syntactic category of their input but also to idiosyncratic markings on stems. If, on the other hand, the bound stem *tot-*, for instance, were allowed to be classified as a noun (so that *total* could be derived by the WFR which is independently needed to generate *cultural, organisational, ornamental* and so on), then it would automatically escape the suffixation of *-ity* and there would be no need to mark it as idiosyncratically not subject to the rule [STEM+i+ty].

Independently of this problem, the power of WFRs must be such that they can refer to phonological as well as syntactic characteristics of their bases – even to phonological characteristics which the bases do not acquire until after the operation of some phonological rules. Halle cites in this connection the de-adjectival verbs in *-en*, which apparently require monosyllabic bases ending in one obstruent optionally preceded by a sonorant: *blacken, whiten, toughen, dampen* versus **dyen, *dimmen, *greenen, *laxen*; the fact that *soften* and *moisten* are acceptable, even though their bases end in two obstruents underlyingly (/ft/ and /st/), shows that the phonological condition for the -*en* WFR is not applied until after the final /t/ of the stem has been deleted by a phonological rule.[5]

We quoted above Bloomfield's view of the lexicon as the list of the basic irregularities in the grammar of any language. Halle's 'Prolegomena', however, posits not one list but three:

(a) the list of morphemes, containing unanalysable stems (e.g. *dog, think, tot-, serendip-*) and affixes;
(b) the dictionary, containing actual words;
(c) the filter, containing possible words which are not actual (such as **arrivation*), marked [−Lexical Insertion]; words whose meanings are not fully determinable from their component morphemes and WFRs (such as *recital* and *recitation*); and words with phonological idiosyncrasies (such as *obesity*).

To see how this works, consider the actual words *childhood* and *brotherhood* and the nonword **wifehood*. *Child, wife* and (strange as it may seem!) *bro-* and -*ther* are contained in the list of morphemes, with some indication of the meaning of the first three; the first two are words already and the last two are combined into a word by the WFR [STEM+ther]$_N$ (1973: 10). All the words thus formed are then combined with the suffix -*hood* (also listed among the morphemes) by means of the following WFR:

(18) [NOUN$_{+\text{Human}}$ +hood]$_{N, +\text{Abstract}}$

The outputs of this WFR are not simply listed in the dictionary, however. *Brotherhood* must be listed in the filter, along with the information that, rather than the expected literal meaning 'state of being a male sibling' it has either the metaphorical meaning 'feeling of warmth and solidarity' or the meaning 'collectivity of male members of a religious or secret society'; it is also listed in the dictionary, along with these meanings. **Wifehood* must be marked in the filter as [−Lexical Insertion] and of course omitted from the dictionary. Even *childhood*, seemingly the most well behaved of the three, does not pass through the filter completely unscathed, since there must presumably be some indication there that its most usual meaning is not 'state of being a child' but 'period during which one is a child'.

2.1.5 Issues arising from Chomsky's and Halle's work

A variety of questions arise from the pioneering works summarised so far. These questions can be grouped roughly into six categories, as follows:

I   *The nature of the entities listed.* Chomsky appears to think of the lexicon as a single list; Halle, as we have seen, has three lists. Is this proliferation necessary? If not, what sort of entities should be listed, and how is the list to be organised?

II   *Productivity and meaning relationships.* For Chomsky, what makes derivational morphology particularly perplexing is the fact that different derivational processes vary in their productivity in a fashion scarcely parallelled in syntax, and the words that result often depart from their 'expected' meaning. How are these facts to be handled? And what about meaning relationships which have no morphological reflex, such as that between *pig* and *shoat*?

III *The internal structure of words.* For Halle, words have an internal structure imposed by the word-formation rules which produce them. Do WFRs constitute the best mechanism to account for this, and what alternatives are available in frameworks without WFRs?

IV   *Variations in shape.* Pairs such as *destroy* and *destruct(ion)* *belief* and *believe, man* and *men* illustrate the kinds of variation in shape that stems can exhibit, and sets such as *(dog)s*, *(formul)ae*, *(ox)en* and *teeth* illustrate similarly the diversity of possible phonological interpretations for what, for Chomsky at least, is a single inflectional feature (Plural). How are these kinds of variation to be handled?

V   *Inflection and derivation.* These are treated as quite distinct by Chomsky, yet Halle (1973) combines them. Which approach is preferable?

VI   *Idioms.* Items larger than words whose meaning is unpredictable share some obvious features with words whose meanings are different from what their constituent morphemes would lead us to expect. Should the lexicon treat these two classes of item in the same way?

VII *Morphology and syntax.* Much of Chomsky's argument against the transformationalist treatment of derived nominals hinged on difficulties which these nominals would pose for current syntactic theory if they were created by means of a nominalisation transformation. How serious are these difficulties now, in view of the fact that the Standard Theory of syntax presupposed by Chomsky in 1965 and 1970 is considerably different from any of the syntactic frameworks assumed by generativists today? In general, is there a line to be drawn at all between syntax and morphology, and, if so, where?

Of these topics, VI goes beyond the ambit of morphological theory, though we will touch on it; and VII is the subject-matter of chapter 4 below. The rest will be dealt with in the remaining sections of this chapter. Most of these topics are not 'theory-bound' in the sense of being of interest only to generativists; however, we will be concentrating here on their treatment by generative linguists explicitly developing or reacting against the ideas of Chomsky and Halle on the lexicon. We will in fact concentrate on how these topics are dealt with in the following works:

> Jackendoff's 'Morphological and semantic regularities in the lexicon' (1975);
> Aronoff's *Word-Formation in Generative Grammar* (1976);
> Lieber's *On the Organization of the Lexicon* (1981b);
> Di Sciullo and Williams's *On the Definition of Word* (1987);
> Corbin's *Morphologie dérivationnelle et structuration du lexique* (1987).

I do not intend to imply that this exhausts the relevant work inspired by Chomsky and Halle's proposals. References to other works will in fact be found in the sections which follow.[6] The works I have just listed do, however, cover the full range of generative reactions to the issues listed as I–V, and any such issue not addressed in one or other of these works is (so far as I know) not addressed in the Chomsky–Halle tradition anywhere.

2.2 THE NATURE OF THE ENTITIES LISTED IN THE LEXICON

Halle proposes in his 'Prolegomena' that word formation involves three lists: a list of morphemes, a dictionary of actual words and a filter consisting of a list of all items which are regularly formed but are either nonexistent or in some way idiosyncratic. But there is an uncomfortable amount of duplication between the morpheme list and the dictionary; and it seems strange to suggest that speakers have command of not only a dictionary but, in effect, an 'anti-dictionary' containing all words which might be in the dictionary but are not. Not surprisingly, subsequent scholars have looked for ways to reduce this apparent duplication. One obvious target is to reduce the three lists to one, whether a list of words, a list of morphemes or a mixed list of morphologically disparate items. Of these three options, something like the first has been proposed by Jackendoff and Aronoff, the second by Lieber and the third by Di Sciullo and Williams. Corbin retains two lists, but within a framework considerably different from Halle's.[7]

Jackendoff's starting point is the problem that confronted Chomsky in 1970: if *refuse* and *refusal* (and similar verb-noun pairs) are related lexically rather than transformationally, how is their evident morphological and semantic kinship to be represented? Chomsky's tentative solution was to propose a single category-neutral lexical entry for both; the phonological portion of this single entry would specify different 'spellings' according to whether the item was inserted in a verbal or a nominal context. But this in turn creates problems. As we have already noted, there would often be motivation for adjectival as well as verbal and nominal spellings, as with *attractive* alongside *attract* and *attraction*; how then would we represent the deadjectival noun *attractiveness*? And, even if we restrict our attention to deverbal nouns, problems abound. Some verbs, such as *commit*, have more than one corresponding noun (*commission, committal* and *commitment*); conversely, some nouns which look like nominalisations, such as *aggression* and *perdition*, have no corresponding verbs in general use (**aggress, *perdite*).

Jackendoff's solution is to extend a mechanism that Chomsky had proposed in *Aspects*: the lexical redundancy rule. In *Aspects*, this mechanism was applied to syntactic subcategorisation, as in (8) (repeated here for convenience):

(8) $[+ \underline{\quad} \emptyset \text{ ^Manner}] \rightarrow [+\underline{\quad}\emptyset]$

This redundancy rule is envisaged as applying without exception, so that it can be used to abbreviate lexical entries, reducing their cost by helping to ensure that a characteristic which holds of a syntactically definable class of lexical items is not repeated in the lexical entry of each one; the specification to the right of the arrow can simply be omitted from any entry which contains the specification to the left of the arrow. Jackendoff's redundancy rules have the same purpose of reducing the cost to individual lexical entries of characteristics which they share with other items of a specifiable kind. There are two important differences between Jackendoff's rules and Chomsky's, however, quite apart from the fact that Jackendoff is concerned with morphological rather than syntactic regularities. Firstly, his redundancy rules operate between, rather than within, lexical entries; secondly, they do not abbreviate lexical entries.

Let us consider a Jackendovian treatment of the pair *refuse* and *refusal*. These will both be listed as items in the lexicon, each with a full entry, including the semantic and phonological information that they share, roughly as in (19) and (20):

$$(19) \begin{bmatrix} /\text{ri=fuz}/ \\ +\text{V}] \\ +[\text{NP}_1\underline{}\text{NP}_2 \\ \text{NP}_1 \text{ REFUSE NP}_2 \end{bmatrix} \qquad (20) \begin{bmatrix} /\text{ri=fuz+al}/ \\ +\text{N} \\ +\text{NP}_1\text{'s}\underline{}\text{of NP}_2 \\ \text{ABSTRACT RESULT OF ACT} \\ \text{OF NP}_1\text{'s REFUSING NP}_2 \end{bmatrix}$$

But there will also be contained in the lexicon a redundancy rule to capture the fact that the relationship between the two is regular in some degree, both semantically and morphologically. This rule can be formulated provisionally as in (21) (a revised version will be discussed in the next section); y represents an arbitrary phonological specification and Z represents an arbitrary semantic one:

$$(21) \begin{bmatrix} /y/ \\ +\text{V} \\ +[\text{NP}_1\underline{}(\text{P})\text{ NP}_2] \\ \text{NP}_1 Z \text{ NP}_2 \end{bmatrix} \longleftrightarrow \begin{bmatrix} /y+\text{al}/ \\ +\text{N}] \\ +\text{NP}_1\text{'s}\underline{}(\text{P})\text{ NP}_2 \\ \text{ABSTRACT RESULT OF ACT} \\ \text{OF NP}_1\text{'s } Z\text{-ING NP}_2 \end{bmatrix}$$

We say 'regular in some degree' because, of course, it is not the case that every verb, or even every Latin-derived verb, has a corresponding noun in *-al*. That is why the rule is not framed as a straightforward implication, like Chomsky's syntactic redundancy rule. Rather, it is a bidirectional statement of a recurring lexical pattern, in virtue of which *refusal* and *refuse* are allowed to share some of their cost; the fact that the noun corresponding to *refuse* is *refusal* means that the lexicon is less 'expensive' than it would be if the noun corresponding to *refuse* were morphologically completely unrelated (say, **sneeb*). The amount of the cost that *refuse* and *refusal* share (or, in general, the degree to which the lexical burden is lightened by the existence of rule (21)) is a matter more relevant to topic II, and will be discussed in section 2.3. For present purposes, what is important is that Jackendoff's extension of the Chomskyan notion of a lexical redundancy rule makes it possible to list all derived words as separate items in the lexicon without treating all the information in each entry as equally idiosyncratic. Adapting Bloomfield's dictum, we can say that the lexicon incorporates information about certain regularities of a morphological and semantic kind alongside the 'list of basic irregularities'.

An important corollary of Jackendovian redundancy rules is that the meanings of morphemes of all traditional kinds (free forms, bound stems and affixes) can be represented without their having to be listed in the lexicon. Instead, their meaning will emerge from the redundancy rules which record their patterns of occurrence. Thus, we do not have to list an adjectival prefix *un-* with the meaning 'not'; rather, a semantic redundancy rule reflecting the pattern of pairs of listed items such as *happy* and *unhappy*, *breakable* and *unbreakable* and so on will reduce the cost of those adjectives in which *un-* is a prefix with negative force. We are still perfectly entitled to claim that *un-* has a meaning, and indeed quite a precise meaning; but this does not commit us to supplying it with a lexical entry.

I have suggested so far that Jackendoff's lexicon contains only words. Strictly, this is not true; it also contains semantically idiosyncratic items larger than words, such as *kick the bucket* 'die'. Syntactically, this item behaves in most respects like the homophonous verb phrase with compositional (nonidiomatic) meaning; for example, when inflected for past tense, it is the verb *kick* which carries the suffix *-ed*. Jackendoff takes care of this parallelism by listing *kick the bucket* in the lexicon, but with an internal structure which is syntactic rather than morphological; the role of redundancy rule is played here by the syntactic principles (whatever they are) which determine the structure of verb phrases. This redundancy rule ensures that *kick the bucket* 'costs' less than syntactically more or less anomalous idioms such as *run full tilt* or *bring to book*. But Jackendoff himself does not consider the treatment of idioms in any detail; for him, as for Chomsky, the prototypical lexical item is a word.

Aronoff, working at about the same time as Jackendoff, also proposes a single lexicon of words, not morphemes. For Aronoff, word-formation rules (somewhat like Halle's in 'Prolegomena') take the place of lexical redundancy rules; but they share with Jackendoff's redundancy rules the characteristic that they apply to words rather than morphemes: 'A new word is formed by applying a regular rule to a single already existing word' (1976: 21). Affixes do not exist independently of the WFRs which introduce them, so (just as in Jackendoff's framework) they do not need to be listed. Where Aronoff and Jackendoff differ is over whether the lexicon lists all words or only some. For Jackendoff, all actual words are listed, whether their formation is regular or irregular, their meaning transparent or idiosyncratic. For Aronoff, however, 'all and *only* those words which are exceptional, i.e. arbitrary in at least one of their various features, will be entered in the lexicon' (1976: 43). The lexicon will therefore contain, for example, the words *height* and *transmission* but not *lowness* or *emission*. *Height* must be listed because its suffix *-t* is idiosyncratic, while *transmission* has an unpredictable meaning ('gearbox of a car'); *lowness* and *emission* need not be listed, however, because both in shape and meaning they represent the expected outcome of the application of productive WFRs (for *-ness* and *-ion*) to *low* and *emit* respectively. The Aronovian lexicon is therefore a subset of the Jackendovian. In the next section we will look in more detail at Aronoff's criteria for distinguishing listed words from nonlisted ones.

Lieber's answer (1981b) to the question of what is listed is quite different. She envisages a lexicon consisting of all 'unanalyzable morphological elements', also referred to as **lexical terminal elements**; these are essentially morphemes in the traditional, concrete sense (stems and affixes). The lexical entries for bound morphemes (including affixes) differ in principle from those for free morphemes only in that entries for bound morphemes contain subcategorisation frames stipulating the kind of morphological material that they must be bound to, whereas entries for free morphemes do not. For example, the adjectival prefix *un-*, which forms adjectives from adjectives, will have in its lexical entry the subcategorisation frame $[_A$___$[_A$, and the suffix *-ise* (or *-ize*), which forms verbs from nouns, will be subcategorised $]_N$___$]_V$. In contrast to Halle, who assigns no lexical category to bound stems, Lieber assumes that all lexical items (bound or free, stems or affixes) may have lexical categories. Indeed, she regards as a strong point in favour of her analysis the fact that a typical affix habitually forms words of one and only one of the classes to which morphologically simple words belong; for example, *-ise* forms only verbs, *-ment* forms only nouns, and so on. This behaviour of affixes is captured naturally if they are listed alongside stems in the lexicon, with the same expectation that their lexical entry should specify a lexical category. Some affixes may be unspecified for category, such as the prefix *counter-*, for reasons discussed in section 2.4 below; but these are in a minority.

If affixes are in the lexicon alongside stems, we will also expect that their lexical entries will contain more or less clear meanings. There must be scope for vagueness and polysemy, of course; nevertheless, Lieber's proposal of a common list arouses an expectation that, so far as semantic behaviour is concerned, affixes should resemble stems more closely than they resemble nonaffixal morphological processes such as ablaut, reduplication or stress alternation. Whereas affixes have lexical entries, nonaffixal processes do not; so there is no natural place in the grammar for the meaning of a nonaffixal process to be recorded, and we will therefore expect nonaffixal processes to differ from affixes in lacking consistent meanings. Lieber claims that this expectation is borne out by umlaut in German and reduplication in Tagalog, both of which lack any single identifiable meaning. However, it is quite easy to find *prima facie* counterexamples of both kinds, that is nonaffixal processes with consistent meanings and affixes without consistent meanings. In Ancient Greek, reduplication has one consistent 'meaning' or function, namely the formation of Perfective verb stems (e.g. *lu-* 'untie', *paideu-* 'train'; Perfective *le-lu-k-*, *pe-paideu-k-*). Conversely, the German suffix -*(e)n* has a wide variety of functions, both derivational and inflectional (denominal adjective formation in *gold-en* 'golden'; verbal infinitive in *sprech-en* 'to speak'; past participle in *gesproch-en* 'spoken'; plural in *Held-en* 'heroes'; etc.). One could, of course, posit a number of distinct but homonymous -*(e)n* suffixes; but by such a means one could invariably ensure that Lieber's expectation is met, thus rendering it vacuous. So it is questionable whether this particular consequence of Lieber's framework is empirically supported.[8]

Lieber's approach raises an obvious question. If morphologically complex items such as derived words are not listed in the lexicon and there is no filter of the kind that Halle envisages, where in the grammar is the unpredictable meaning of *transmission* and the nonexistence of **arrivation* represented? We return to this in the next section.

All the scholars that we have discussed so far assume an intimate connection between, on the one hand, the principles of word structure and, on the other hand, the principles which distinguish between what needs to be listed and what does not. This assumption is rejected by Di Sciullo and Williams and by Corbin, though in other respects their approaches diverge considerably.

For Di Sciullo and Williams, as for Aronoff, the main criterion for being listed is arbitrariness or unpredictability. Unlike Aronoff, however, they do not insist that all listed items (**listemes**) should be of the same kind; in fact, a major novelty of their approach within the lexicalist tradition is that they see no necessary connection between listedness (the property of being in the lexicon) and wordhood. Most words are indeed in the lexicon, because most words have idiosyncratic properties of various kinds; but words are not special in this respect. All morphemes are listed – necessarily so, since they have no internal structure from which their grammatical or semantic behaviour could be predicted – but so are most noncompound words, many compound words, some phrases and just a few sentences. Morphology, which is 'strictly the science of word-forms' (1987: 69), is no more concerned with the lexicon than syntax is. 'A listeme is generally a short encoding of a complicated but quite specific idea' (1987:14), and the fact that listedness is commoner among smaller units than among larger is simply a consequence of the fact that we naturally prefer 'short encodings' which really are short.

Di Sciullo and Williams see the lexicon as 'simply a collection of the lawless' (1987: 4), 'of no interest to the grammarian' (ibid., 1). In this respect it resembles what Corbin calls the **conventional lexicon** (*lexique conventionnel*). She subdivides the **lexical component** of the grammar into a **base component**, a **derivational component** and a **conventional component**, of which the conventional lexicon forms part.[9] Within the base component is Corbin's first list, containing individual morphemes (free and bound stems and affixes) as well as a certain number of 'complex non-derived' words such as French *royaume* 'kingdom', which is clearly related morphologically as well as semantically to *roi* 'king' but which contains no independently motivated affix; English examples might be *hatred* and *laughter*, clearly related to *hate* and *laugh* but not relatable to them by any WFR of the derivational component. It is the derivational component which contains possible derived words generated by the application of WFRs, and in principle any possible derived word is available for lexical insertion. But possible derived words are not listed or even finite in number, since there is nothing in the derivational component to impose an upper bound on word length; for example, *institutionalisationalisation* 'the action of rendering institutionalisational' breaks no rules of derivational competence even if pragmatic or performance factors may make it unlikely ever to be used. In Corbin's conventional component, a **selecter** (*sélectionneur*) weeds out well-formed derivatives which are not used (such as English *arrivation*), and various minor rules take care of the idiosyncrasies that well-formed derivatives may acquire before entering her second list, the conventional lexicon. This lexicon is part of 'lexical competence', but a more fluid and, to the linguist, less interesting part than the derivational component.

Corbin introduces a useful notation for distinguishing different kinds of nonexistent words; the asterisk is used for words which are morphologically ill formed, that is which break the rules of derivational competence (e.g. **run-ly*, **ish-green*, **al-ation-transform*), while a raised circle identifies words which are morphologically well formed but which do not happen to be in the conventional lexicon (e.g. °*arrivation*, °*committance*, °*institutionalisationalisation*). Corbin's claim that nonexistent words of the second type are available for lexical insertion implies that one may occasionally find oneself using a form such as °*abolishment* or °*adaption* even if the appropriate 'correct' forms from one's conventional lexicon are *abolition* and *adaptation*.

Corbin's conventional component and selecter look at first sight very much like Halle's (1973) dictionary and filter respectively; and indeed, so far as the question of what is listed is concerned, her position is close to Halle's. But her treatment of actual versus possible words rests on a more sophisticated notion of productivity than anything earlier in the lexicalist tradition. This will be discussed in the next section.

2.3 PRODUCTIVITY AND MEANING RELATIONSHIPS

Chomsky and Halle point out two aspects of word formation which have no obvious analogue in syntax; the nonexistence of not only clearly ill-formed words (**ion-trans-al-at-form*) but also some apparently well-formed ones (**arrivation, *derival, *committance, *ridiculosity*); and the unpredictability of the meanings of some words which do exist (for example, *recital* versus *recitation*, and *transmission* in the sense 'car gearbox'). These aspects are often summed up by saying that word-formation processes may be less than fully **productive**. In discussing how subsequent generative linguists have handled the issue of productivity, it will be useful to keep in mind a distinction introduced by Corbin (1987: 212) between what she calls **associative** and **dissociative** theories of the lexicon. Associative theories are those in which meaning and morphological structure are seen as intimately associated, so that the mechanisms which account for a word's structure must also determine (or at any rate suggest) what its meaning should be;[10] dissociative theories are ones in which the meaning and structure of derived words are handled separately.

Aronoff's theory is associative. Recall that, for him, affixes have no existence apart from the word formation rules which introduce them. Now, two essential components of any WFR are the **phonological operation** (specifying the shape of any affix which is added and any change to the shape of the base) and the **semantic reading** (which is a function of the semantic reading of the base on which the rule operates) (1976: 22). One WFR cannot (or cannot normally) have more than one semantic reading. It follows that, if an affix has two distinct meanings, it must be the product of two distinct WFRs; the phonological identity which allows us to speak of 'one affix' is, in Aronoff's terms, a mere accident, on a par with the phonological identity of *beer* and *bier*. Thus, for example, the prefix *un-* which forms negative adjectives from adjectives (e.g. *unhappy, unwise*) and the prefix *un-* which forms 'reversive' verbs from verbs (*untie, unwrap*) must be analysed as entirely distinct. Moreover, WFRs 'are rules by which *new* words are formed' (1976: 31; my emphasis). Although (as Halle points out) native speakers 'know' something about the structure of 'old' or existing words and must therefore be able in some degree to analyse them, nevertheless 'rules for analyzing words are essentially degenerate versions of the rules for forming new ones' (1976: 34). Aronoff thus distinguishes sharply between word-formation processes which are still alive in the sense that neologisms can be formed with them, and processes which, however regular semantically, are now dead, in this sense. The suffixation of *-ness* to form abstract nouns from adjectives is alive, and so is taken care of by a word-formation rule; on the other hand, the suffixation of *-th* with the same function (as in *depth*, *width*, *breadth*) is dead, and so enjoys in Aronoff's framework at best a shadowy recognition as a 'degenerate' rule of word analysis rather than word formation. Aronoff thus recognises far fewer word-formation rules than Halle, who (as we have seen) tolerates even a WFR so limited in application as $[STEM+ther]_N$, which forms just the three words *mother*, *father* and *brother*.

The upshot of Aronoff's insistence on the semantic consistency and living productivity of his WFRs is that a large proportion of complex words must count for him as not formed by rule at all; instead, these words must be lexically listed. Any deviation from a living WFR condemns a word to this status; 'all and only those words which are exceptional, i.e. arbitrary in at least one of their features, will be entered in the lexicon' (1976: 43). Here Aronoff differs from Jackendoff, whose lexicon contains unexceptional, nonarbitrary words too. But Aronoff claims in his own favour the phenomenon of **blocking**. He observes that some nonexistent but possible words have morphologically related synonyms. At first sight, it seems just an accident that *curiosity* exists (related to the adjective *curious*) but **gloriosity* does not, even though *glorious* exists as an obvious base for it. But Aronoff points out that there is already a noun *glory* with precisely the meaning that **gloriosity* would have if it were formed by a WFR for *-ity*. **Gloriosity* does not exist, he suggests, because *glory* blocks it; within the lexicon, *glory* fills the semantic slot that **gloriosity* would need to occupy. On the other hand, the noun *gloriousness*, because it is formed by the living WFR which derives nouns in *-ness* from adjectives, is not lexically listed; it therefore cannot be blocked by *glory*, and ought to exist alongside it, according to Aronoff. And this prediction indeed seems to be correct. In Jackendoff's lexicon, by contrast, *gloriousness* is listed

as well as *glory*, so a 'blocking' explanation for the nonexistence of
*gloriosity is not available.[11]

Two features of Aronoff's argument are worth noticing. First, it
involves lexical semantics. Synonymy is not generally regarded as
impermissible is natural languages, and plenty of pairs of items can
be found which are *prima facie* cognitive synonyms (*bucket* and *pail*,
buy and *purchase*, *aubergine* and *eggplant*). Why should synonyms
which are derivationally related be particularly offensive? In order to
escape a taint of adhocness, blocking needs to be located within some
independently motivated theory of meaning relationships within the
vocabulary; but Aronoff does not attempt this. (Some implications of
the habitual neglect of lexical semantics by generative morphologists
will be discussed in section 2.7.) Secondly, the claim that **gloriosity*
would have to be lexically listed entails the claim that *curiosity* is
lexically listed, which in turn entails that at least some nouns ending in
-ity are not the product of any word-formation rule. But which nouns?
The suffix *-ity* does seem to be alive in the formation of new nouns from
at least some adjectives, particularly ones in *-ive* and *-able/-ible*. On this
issue, Aronoff (1980) and Anshen (Anshen and Aronoff 1989) have
looked at informant reactions and historical evidence. For present
purposes, however, what matters is not the outcome of this work
but the recognition that it is necessary, given Aronoff's insistence on
WFRs as rules for forming new words.

By contrast, Lieber's approach to these problems is squarely
dissociative. She sees lexical gaps and semantic idiosyncrasies either
as matters of usage rather than grammar, or else as belonging to a
separate component of the the grammar dealing with lexical semantics.
'The fact that a given speaker does not use the form **ridiculosity*
has nothing to do with the productivity of *-ity*, or in fact with the
well-formedness of the word, but rather might be a function of the
speaker's educational background, or the fact that *ridiculousness* is
heard frequently, or some other factor not to be accounted for in the
morphological component' (1981b: 115). Similarly, discussing umlaut
in German adjectives, Lieber acknowledges that her analysis does not
predict whether an umlauted or a non-umlauted form of the stem will
be chosen for a given adjective exhibiting one of the suffixes *-lich*
and *-ig*, which tolerate both types of stem.[12] 'But', she says, 'this is
exactly as it should be; the grammar of German generates possible
forms from which individual speakers and dialects choose, thus adding
texture to the language' (1981b: 182). Lieber thus rejects Aronoff's
view that the structure and meaning of derived words are generally
speaking isomorphic. When in Lieber's framework morphemes are

inserted into binary branching tree structures in conformity with their subcategorisation frames (see section 2.4 below), nothing happens comparable to the derivation of a semantic reading for a derived word through the operation of an Aronovian WFR on its base. Lieber justifies this neglect of semantics partly on grounds to do with 'bracketing paradoxes' (discussed in chapter 4 below) and partly because of words such as Russian *dušitel'nij* 'suffocating', in which the usual agentive sense of the suffix *-tel'*, evident in the noun *dušitel'* 'strangler' and the adjective *dušitel'skij* 'of a strangler', is overridden (so to speak) by the presence of the adjective-forming suffix *-n-* (Pesetsky 1979). But, whatever the force of these arguments, it is clear that some such dissociation of structure and meaning is essential if Lieber's lexicon is to be restricted to 'terminal elements' consisting of just affixes and unanalysable stems. Since the idiosyncrasies of morphologically complex items have no place in such a lexicon, they must be relegated to some other component.

Aronoff, Lieber, and Di Sciullo and Williams (1987) are far apart in their attitudes to meaning, but, unlike Jackendoff, they all find ways of sidestepping the issue of morphological productivity. In Lieber's case this involves invoking a (still shadowy) lexical semantic component and nonlinguistic factors such as the speaker's educational background. In Aronoff's case it involves subordinating the analysis of existing words to the formation of new ones; complex words which are idiosyncratic to any extent, whether greater or lesser, are all listed in the lexicon alike. Di Sciullo and Williams (1987: 7–10) do acknowledge differences in morphological productivity, but claim that morphology is no different from syntax in this respect; among verb-particle combinations, for example, *throw down* exists and is semantically compositional (productively formed in one sense, therefore), while *give up* and *throw up* are semantically noncompositional and *give down* does not exist at all. So, even if productivity is a problem, it is not one which the morphologist as such is called upon to tackle.

Jackendoff, by contrast, bravely tries to untie the Gordian knot rather than cut it. He attempts to quantify the extent to which a given morphological redundancy rule reduces the cost of the lexical entries which it relates. Recall that Jackendoff's redundancy rules relate lexical entries, so as to reduce the 'cost' of that part of an individual lexical entry which it shares with other entries. This reduction has to be set against the 'cost' of referring to the rule itself, however. So, in Jackendoff's terms, what one wants is a formula whereby the more widely a redundancy rule applies, the cheaper it is to refer to. The formula he in fact proposes is the following (1975: 666):

(22) The cost of referring to redundancy rule R in evaluating a lexical entry W is $I_{R,W} \times P_{R,W}$, where $I_{R,W}$ is the amount of information in W predicted by R, and $P_{R,W}$ is a number between 0 and 1 measuring the regularity of R in applying to the derivation of W.

An extremely general redundancy rule (Jackendoff's example is the rule for the past-tense forms in *-ed* of 'regular' English verbs) will have a value for $P_{R,W}$ close to zero, so that reference to it will be almost cost-free; on the other hand, for a rule of extremely limited applicability (an example might be Halle's rule $[\text{STEM}+\text{ther}]_N$), $P_{R,W}$ will have a value close to one, so that the cost of referring to it will be almost as high as the cost of that part of the lexical entry which it 'predicts'.[13] Jackendoff admits that establishing a value for $P_{R,W}$ may be difficult in intermediate situations; but the fact that he is in principle willing to tackle the problem shows that he rejects the all-or-nothing attitude to morphological productivity.

One important difference between Jackendoff's redundancy rules and Aronoff's word-formation rules lies in the fact that a redundancy rule may refer to phonological shape alone or to meaning alone, not necessarily to both. In fact, Jackendoff suggests that a rule such as (21), which deals with both phonology and meaning, should be split into separate phonological and semantic rules, on the lines of (23) (1975: 650):

(23) a. $\begin{bmatrix} /y/ \\ +V \end{bmatrix} \longleftrightarrow \begin{bmatrix} /y + al/ \\ +N \end{bmatrix}$

b. $\begin{bmatrix} +V \\ NP_1\ Z\ NP_2 \end{bmatrix} \longleftrightarrow \begin{bmatrix} +N \\ \text{ABSTRACT RESULT OF ACT} \\ \text{OF } NP_1\text{S } Z\text{-ING } NP_2 \end{bmatrix}$

The purpose of this separation is to capture the fact that a number of pairs of words may share a semantic relationship but not a phonological one (e.g. *refuse/refusal*; *destroy/destruction*; *accept/acceptance*) or, at least in principle, vice versa. Jackendoff's framework cannot therefore be classified as consistently associative or dissociative, in Corbin's terms. More importantly, this kind of separation also has implications for the productivity issue. An example of a Jackendovian redundancy rule which refers to shape alone is the rule which relates to one another verbs with the Latinate stems *-mit*, *-fer*, *-cede*, etc. and prefixes *de-*, *con-*, *per-*, etc. (1975: 653–4). This rule will have a $P_{R,W}$ somewhere above zero, because there are numerous gaps among words of this pattern, such as *demit, *percede, *transtend. But the possibility nevertheless exists within Jackendoff's framework of a redundancy rule which says nothing about meaning but which has a $P_{R,W}$ at or close to zero. Such a rule would be fully productive in one sense, even though the meanings of the words related by it might show no consistent pattern.

Corbin's contribution here is to provide a terminology for this state of affairs (1987: 177). A morphological process may be more or less **regular** (*régulier*), that is, the shape and, more especially, the meaning of its products may be more or less predictable on the basis of the shape and meaning of the bases to which it applies; it may be more or less **available** (*disponible*) for the creation of new derivatives, so as to fill gaps in the attested lexicon; and it may be more or less **profitable** (*rentable*), that is, it may apply to a greater or lesser number of bases or produce a greater or lesser number of attested derivatives.[14] These three types of productivity are independent of one another. For example, a process may be maximally available in that it applies to all the bases which fulfil the appropriate conditions (syntactic, phonological or semantic), but may still be relatively unprofitable just because those bases are few in number. An example might be the suffix *-et*, meaning '(piece of chamber music to be played by) a group of *n* musicians', where *n* ranges for pragmatic reasons between two and nine. This suffix is almost maximally available, since of the eight possible derivatives seven are attested as words (*duet, quartet, quintet, sextet, septet, octet, nonet*); on the other hand, the verbal suffix *-ify* is much more profitable (*amplify, clarify, specify, classify, petrify, terrify, horrify, gentrify, qualify, magnify*, etc.), even though its availability is thrown into doubt by the difficulty of specifying straightforwardly the kinds of base to which it can be applied. Corbin exploits these distinctions within a framework which allows her more scope than Aronoff to classify a word as the product of a WFR despite its idiosyncrasies. For example, the noun *transmission* in its totally unpredictable sense 'gearbox' will be subject to an **idiosyncrasy assigner** (*applicateur d'idiosyncrasies*) within the conventional component which will supply its irregular meaning without vitiating its formation by a WFR in the derivational component. For partly rather than totally irregular meanings, what comes into play is not the idiosyncrasy assigner but the selecter, already encountered in section 2.2; for example, the selecter will deal with the fact that *cooker, writer* and *printer* differ unpredictably in that the first is [−Human], the second [+Human] and the third [±Human].

Corbin thus allows herself a generous repertoire of devices for tidying up discrepancies between the output of the derivational component and the content of the conventional lexicon. It is not surprising, therefore, that she classifies her own approach as associative, alongside Aronoff's and in contrast to Lieber's. But, in doing so, she implicitly rules out one possibility that her distinction between availability and regularity helps us to describe: the possibility that a 'rule' may score high on availability but not be regular, simply because it is semantically empty. A model of the lexicon which permits such a possibility will be at least partly dissociative. Is Corbin right to exclude it? The question is a factual one. Recall the Jackendovian redundancy rule which relates to one another the English Latinate verbs consisting of a prefix and a bound stem. If this were reformulated as a word-formation rule, it would be a rule of this type. So is Jackendoff's rule spurious? A more general version of this question is: are there any word-formation processes which involve no consistent semantic relationship at all between bases and outputs? But to answer that question properly one must consider the nature and extent of semantic relationships within the lexicon, independently of morphological processes. Some tentative suggestions on this issue will be offered in section 2.7, in the belief that it may provide an important new angle from which to examine the relationship between morphology and the lexicon.

2.4 THE INTERNAL STRUCTURE OF DERIVED WORDS

Chomsky and Halle assume the internal structure of words to be a labelled bracketing, much like the internal structure of sentences. For example, a complex word such as *unhelpfulness* will have a structure such as:

(24) $[_N[_A un[_A[_N help_V]ful]]ness]$

In Jackendoff's and Aronoff's frameworks, complex words have this kind of internal structure too, even though it is arrived at in different ways. For Jackendoff, the relationship between *unhelpfulness* and *unhelpful*, the relationship between *unhelpful* and *helpful*, that between *helpful* and *help_N*, and that between *help_N* and *help_V* will all be expressed by redundancy rules like (21). For Aronoff, the mechanism will be a series of word-formation rules, each operating on the output of the last.

For Lieber, by contrast, as we saw in section 2.2, affixes are neither introduced by WFRs nor 'detached' by redundancy rules from the words to which they belong, but are listed in the lexicon in their own right. At first sight, therefore, she faces a considerable difficulty; if neither of these kinds of rule is available either to combine morphemes linearly or to assign structure to complex words, how are these tasks to be performed? Lieber's solution is disarmingly simple: there is 'a single context-free rewrite rule' which generates unlabelled binary branching tree structures (although nothing hinges on the claim that the branching is binary); 'lexical terminal elements [morphemes] are inserted into these tree structures subject to their subcategorisation restrictions' (1981b: 47).[15] Lieber does not actually formulate this rewrite rule, but it is clearly the tree structures rather than the rule itself which are important. As an example of how this works, consider the noun *griminess*. This contains three terminal elements, *grime*, *-y* and *-ness*. For any string of three morphemes, two binary branching tree configurations are conceivable, as at (25) and (26):

(25)   (26)

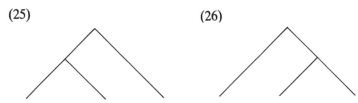

How are we to choose between these? In fact, the choice of (25) over (26) is guaranteed by the subcategorisation frame of the suffix *-y*, together with a requirement that Lieber evidently assumes although she does not state it explicitly: the subcategorisation restrictions of all the morphemes within a word must be satisfied not only within the tree as a whole but also within all subtrees within it. The suffix *-y* forms adjectives from nouns, so its lexical entry will contain the frame]$_N$——]$_A$. But if we try to fit *griminess* to the tree (26), we find that there is a subtree dominating just *-iness* (or *-y-ness*); and within this subtree the subcategorisation of *-y* is not satisfied, because it has no noun to its left. In tree (25), however, the necessary requirements are satisfied, as shown in (27):

(27)

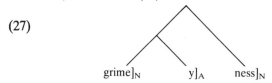

grime]$_N$ y]$_A$ ness]$_N$

In the subtree dominating *grime-y*, *-y* does have a noun to its left; and the requirement of the suffix *-ness* for an adjective to its left is satisfied too. In similar fashion, the subcategorisation requirements of the affixes in *unhelpfulness* will, in Lieber's framework, guarantee for it the tree structure corresponding to the labelled bracketing in (24).

The structures assigned by this means still need to be labelled; we need to represent the fact that *grimy* is an adjective and *griminess* is a noun. Lieber takes care of this by means of **feature-percolation conventions**, which ensure that features of individual morphemes (including category labels) 'percolate' upwards to the appropriate nodes. The conventions are formulated so that, generally speaking, where an affix has a value for some feature which is inconsistent with the value for that feature belonging to its sister constituent in the tree, it is the affix's value which wins; thus, it is the category label A on *-y* rather than the label N on *grime* which percolates up to the node dominating *grimy*, and it is the N from *-ness* rather than the A from *grimy* that percolates up to dominate *griminess*. This is illustrated in (28):

(28)

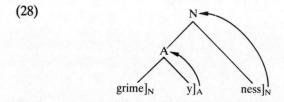

If, on the other hand, an affix is unmarked for some feature (or lexical category), then the mother node must acquire its value for that feature from the affix's sister. The examples that Lieber cites involve the prefix *counter-*, which in English attaches to verbs (e.g. *countersign*), adjectives (*counterintuitive*) and nouns (*counterweight*); *counter-* is entered in the lexicon without any lexical category, so it is the category feature of its sister which pecolates upwards by default.

In general, as in the word *griminess*, there is no conflict between the internal structure suggested by formal considerations, such as the subcategorisation requirements of affixes, and the structure suggested by the word's meaning. In some words, however, there is such a conflict. These words are said to display bracketing paradoxes. The existence of bracketing paradoxes is one of the reasons that Lieber cites for adopting a dissociative view of the relationship between morphological structure and meaning. But it is in recent discussion of the relationship between morphology and syntax that these paradoxes have figured most prominently, so we will defer consideration of them until chapter 4.

2.5 VARIATIONS IN SHAPE

What mechanisms should linguistic theory provide to handle differences in shape such as that between the stems in *destroy* and *destruction*, and between the suffixes in *consumption*, *rebellion* and *reservation*? One possible answer consistent with generative traditions is: phonological rules, subject to more or less narrow lexical or morphological restrictions. The implications and influence of that kind of answer will be discussed in chapter 3. Another answer is: **readjustment rules**, which alter or tidy up in some respects the underlying phonological representations of lexically interpreted syntactic structures before the phonological component gets to work on them. For example, in Chomsky and Halle's *The Sound Pattern of English* (1968), readjustment rules play a part in determining the pattern of vowel alternation in strong verbs (e.g. *sing, sang, sung*) and in accounting for the voiced fricative which (in some varieties of English) appears at the end of the stem in the noun *subversion* by contrast with the adjective *subversive*. Yet a third answer is: these differences may be simply recorded in the lexicon as differences in the phonological portions of related lexical entries. This answer was added to the repertoire by Chomsky (1970). The three mechanisms are not mutually exclusive, so any one grammatical description may in principle exploit all three. Subsequent workers on the lexicon have singled out different ones for emphasis, however; the readjustment-rule mechanism has been developed by Aronoff and Corbin, while Jackendoff and Lieber favour lexicon-internal solutions.

The main focus in Aronoff's work is on how stems and affixes are combined rather than on how they vary in shape. A typical WFR effects just one phonological operation (1976: 63), usually in English the addition of a suffix. But sometimes the string of morphological elements which results from the application of successive WFRs to a given base is not quite what is required as input to the phonology. For example, the WFR which forms abstract nouns in *-ion* has as its unique phonological operation 'add *-ation*', since *-ation* is the commonest variant of the suffix and the only one which is not restricted to bases with certain phonological characteristics (1976: 100). This yields strings such as *educ+ate+ation, consume+ation, rebel+ation, decide+ation*. But *educ+ate+ation* is converted to *education* by means of a **truncation rule** which deletes *-ate* before *-ation*, and the other three are tidied up by an **allomorphy rule** which converts *-ation* to *-tion* after some lexically marked noncoronal stems (*consumption*) and to *-ion* after some lexically marked coronal stems (*rebellion, decision*).

Similar truncation and allomorphy rules are posited by Corbin; but her framework is more flexible than Aronoff's in that one WFR is not limited to a single phonological operation. For example, French has a variety of deverbal suffixes forming nouns with the meaning 'action of V', where V is the base: *-age, -ment, -tion, -ure, -erie, -ade*, etc. In French as in English, *-tion* has certain variant shapes (*-ation, -ition, -ution, -ion*), which can be taken care of by an allomorphy rule; but the choice between *-tion* and its other rivals (*-age, -ment*, etc.) is, for Corbin, not a choice between different lexically restricted WFRs but between different phonological operations of the same WFR. This analysis raises issues relating to the paradigmatic dimension of derivational morphology, which will be discussed in chapter 6. For present purposes, the salient point is that Corbin's theory provides a generous repertoire of devices for handling derivational allomorphy, so implicitly claims that it is not a tightly constrained phenomenon.

Chomsky (1970) does not discuss how the phonological portions of the distinct lexical entries for *destroy* and *destruction* may be related. In Jackendoff's (1975) framework, however, morphological redundancy rules of the kind discussed in sections 2.2 and 2.3 provide the obvious answer. Where there is a consistent but phonologically unpredictable stem alternation between, say, a set of verbs and a set of corresponding nouns, as with the verbs in *-sume* and the nouns in *-sumption*, Jackendoff will posit a redundancy rule which will not allude to meaning – that will be a matter for the more general rule applying to all *-ion* nominals and their bases – but only to the consistent correspondence in shape. For *destroy* and *destruction* one can devise a rule too; but, since the alternation is unique, the formula quoted at (22) ensures that the cost of referring to it is as high as the cost of simply leaving the two alternants unrelated. What is not so clear is how in Jackendoff's framework one might distinguish between, on the one hand, sets of rival allomorphs, in Aronoff's terms (such as *-ion, -tion, -ation*), and, on the other hand, sets of distinct rival affixes (such as *-ion, -ment, -al*). Discussing the latter (1975: 650), Jackendoff separates the semantic rule (or rules) from the morphological rules for the relevant verb-noun pairs, so that the same semantic information is not replicated in the morphological redundancy rule for each suffix. But what does 'each suffix' consist of, in this context? Jackendoff cites *commission, perdition, retribution* and *copulation* all as examples of words with the '+ion' suffix, which suggests a kind of nesting of redundancies; *adoption* and *adaptation*, for example, would both be subject to the same '+ion' redundancy rule, but *adaptation* would presumably be subject to a further rule shared with *deportation*, *revelation, accusation*, etc. However, Jackendoff does not discuss how distinct morphological (as opposed to semantic) redundancy rules can interact in their application to the same word.

In a framework like Lieber's, in which morphemes rather than words are listed in the lexicon, variations in shape cannot be accounted for either by allomorphy rules operating on the output of WFRs or by lexical redundancy rules which relate words. Instead, Lieber introduces **morpholexical rules**, which she illustrates most extensively with data from German. Wurzel (1970) suggested that much of the apparent diversity in the inflectional behaviour of German nouns can be attributed to differences in the incidence and distribution of **stem-formation elements** (*Stammbildungselemente*) rather than to differences in inflectional affixation. So, for example, the *-en* which appears throughout the Plural of *Staat* 'state' and *Bär* 'bear' as well as in the oblique Singular cases of the latter is a stem-formation element, not an inflection; forms such as non-Dative Plural *Staaten* and the superficially identical Dative Plural *Staaten* involve the inflectional affixes /e/ and /n/ respectively added to this stem-formation element, and the underlying representations /staːt+ n +e/ and /staːt+ n + n / both emerge as *Staaten* via phonological rules of schwa-epenthesis, schwa-deletion and degemination. Adopting Wurzel's analysis of the boundary between stem and inflection, Lieber accounts for the relationship between /staːt+ n / and /staːt/ (stems with and without stem-forming /n/) in terms of a morpholexical rule. The two stems are distinct lexical items (with lexical entries sharing the same information on meaning and syntactic category), but they are related by the morpholexical rule X~Xn, where X stands for an arbitrary stem. Rules of the same type are $C_o u C_o \sim C_o \ddot{u} C_o$ (where *u* represents an arbitrary back vowel or diphthong), which links the stems *Gast* and *Gäst-* 'guest', and X~Xr, which links *Bild* and *Bilder* 'picture'. One noun may be subject to more than one morpholexical rule, as for example *Mann* 'man' with its Plural stem *Männer*, involving both $C_o u C_o \sim C_o \ddot{u} C_o$ and X~Xr.

These examples involve inflection rather than derivation, a fact which we will return to in the next section; but, apart from that, morpholexical rules may look so far remarkably like Jackendovian lexical redundancy rules. Lieber is at pains to emphasise the difference, however. The fact that a given lexical item X is related by a Jackendovian redundancy rule to some other item Y is, as it were, an 'optional extra' characteristic of X; item Y could disappear from the lexicon without item X being affected. On the other hand, morpholexical rules are obligatory; they 'state absolutely that lexical items X are related to lexical items Y' (Lieber 1981b: 40). Another crucial difference is that morpholexical rules say nothing about syntactic category, subcategorisation or semantic content; 'they merely define the limits of a class of items [namely the items related by a given rule] and specify relatedness between pairs of those items', and they are inherently arbitrary in their application, although they may 'mimic' the sorts of relationships defined by 'more productive morphological processes' (1981b: 42). Lieber's idea here seems to be that if, for example, the stem-forming element -*n* were consistently added to (say) all masculine nouns or all human nouns in German, then we would be entitled to detach -*n* from the stems concerned and enter it in the lexicon as an item on its own, with a precise meaning or syntactic function; what prevents us from treating it in this way is precisely the alleged arbitrariness of its distribution. Similarly, if some phonological characteristic of alternating stems (such as umlaut) appears in precisely identifiable phonological contexts, we will want to account for it by means of a phonological rather than a morpholexical rule.

An obvious question is: how far apart phonologically can two stems be and still be related by a morpholexical rule? It seems clear from Lieber's discussion that she does not see morpholexical rules as the mechanism for handling irredeemably suppletive alternations such as between the stems of *go* and *went*, or *good* and *better*. The phonological side of the relationship between morpholexically related stems is not discussed further by Lieber (1981b), but is taken up by Spencer (1988b), who uses the machinery of autosegmental phonology (see section 3.2) in an attempt to characterise more precisely the phonological aspect of morpholexical rules.[16]

The empirical consequences of what Lieber says about morpholexical rules emerge most clearly in connection with her treatment of inflection and derivation, to which we turn in the next section.

2.6 INFLECTION AND DERIVATION

Aronoff (1976) and Corbin (1987) explicitly omit inflectional morphology from consideration, so they do not address the issue of whether any or all inflected word-forms should be lexically listed.[17] But Halle (1973), as we have seen, saw no reason not to list inflected forms as well as derivatives; the only difference between them was that inflected forms were grouped in the dictionary into paradigms. It seems fair to say that this was an unusual view when Halle propounded it, running counter to the assumptions of Chomsky (1957; 1965). Did this unusual view gain ground among those generative students of the lexicon who aimed to treat inflectional as well as derivational morphology? The answer is yes.

Jackendoff (1975: 665) explicitly agrees with Halle in treating relationships like those between *wait* and *waited* or between *buy* and *bought* as, in principle, of the same kind as those between *decide* and *decision* or between *refuse* and *refusal*. *Wait/waited* and *buy/bought* are related by redundancy rules which agree in their semantic portion ('+[V+pres]⟷+[V+past]') but disagree in their phonological portion. This semantic portion can therefore be hived off as a separate rule, just as at (23b) we separated from the *refuse/refusal* rule (21) the semantic portion which it shares with the *destroy/destruction* and *accept/acceptance* rules. *Waited* is a distinct lexical item from *wait* in just the same way that *acceptance* is a distinct item from *accept*. Derivation does differ from inflection, however, in that inflected forms are organised into paradigms; 'the lexical insertion rules must insert partial or complete paradigms into deep structures, and the rules of concord must have the function of filtering out all but the correct forms' (1975: 665). The qualification 'partial or complete' probably indicates discomfort on Jackendoff's part about the idea of lexically inserting complete paradigms in languages such as Latin, Russian, Finnish or Zulu, where many words have far more inflected forms than nouns or verbs do in English.

For Lieber, too, both inflection and derivation are 'in the lexicon'.[18] What this means in her framework is that inflectional affixes, just like derivational ones, have lexical entries of their own, including subcategorisation frames specifying what kinds of stems (or other affixes) they are allowed to attach to. Inflection is relevant to syntax, of course; but this is taken care of by ensuring that, when words are inserted into syntactic phrase markers, not only their category and subcategorisation features but also their inflectional features are appropriate to the syntactic context. Feature-percolation conventions will ensure that the relevant features are straightforwardly 'visible' for syntactic purposes, having percolated to the top of the word tree.

Lieber goes further than Halle or Jackendoff in rejecting any theoretical distinction between inflection and derivation. This rejection commits her to certain claims about how they interact. One of the traditional arguments for distinguishing between inflection and derivation has to do with the alleged fact that 'derivational' affixes appear regularly inside, or closer to the stem than, 'inflectional' ones.[19] If true, this tends to suggest that inflectional morphology should be handled 'after' derivation, perhaps in a separate component of the grammar. Lieber's position allows her no straightforward explanation for that alleged fact. But, on the positive side, she cites evidence which relates not to affixes but to stems. If inflection and derivation are not distinguished by morphological theory, then we will expect any stem which appears in inflected forms of a word to be available also for the formation of derivatives, and vice versa. She claims that this expectation is borne out by evidence from German, Old English and Latin; there is at least substantial overlap between the stems that are used in inflection and those that are used in compounding and derivation (for example, German *Männer* 'men', analysed by Lieber as a stem with no overt suffix, related morpholexically to *Mann*, can also crop up in compounds: *Männer-chor* 'male voice choir'). The fact that verbal Perfective stems in Latin (e.g. *tetig-* alongside Imperfective *tang-* 'touch') do not crop up in compounds and derivatives has to be considered an accidental gap. But this is not a serious difficulty, so long as not too many such gaps are found; her framework permits any stem alternant to be used for both inflection and derivation, but does not insist that it must be.

Lieber's refusal to distinguish between inflection and derivation commits her to denying the role that Halle and Jackendoff attribute to inflectional paradigms. However, she makes a virtue of necessity by suggesting that the traditional paradigm, in the sense of an arbitrary declension or conjugation type, is a superfluous notion. She claims that the inflectional behaviour of a word – its choice of inflectional expressions for the various relevant combinations of inflectional properties – is entirely, or to a very large extent, predictable on the basis of stem allomorphy, so that if we know what morpholexical rules a given stem is subject to, we do not need any further specification (such as a diacritic [+1st conjugation] or [+2nd declension]).

This is a strong claim which, if correct, counts strongly in favour of Lieber's way of handling morpholexical alternation. Unfortunately, however, it must be said that Lieber is led into making the claim partly through misinterpretation of Wurzel's (1970) analysis of German. In Wurzel's analysis, there are nouns which share the same pattern of stem alternation, namely none at all, but which take different sets of inflectional affixes; for example, *Tisch* 'table', Plural *Tische* and *Streik* 'strike', Plural *Streiks*. Lieber, however, mistakenly attributes to Wurzel an analysis of the *-s* of *Streiks* as stem-forming element, not an inflectional suffix, and therefore posits a morpholexical rule X~Xs to which *Streik* is said to be subject (1981b: 11; 1982: 39). With such an analysis, one can indeed render the inflectional differences between *Streik* and *Tisch* predictable on the basis of stem alternation. The trouble is that there is no independent motivation for assigning the *-s* in question to the stem rather than the inflectional ending. Yet, if we do not insist on such independent motivation, we will always be able to reconcile Lieber's apparently strong claim with any conceivable pattern of inflectional behaviour, simply by assigning any unpredictable morphological material to the stem, as a stem-forming element. The empirical force of Lieber's claim that there is no need in grammatical theory for the notion 'inflectional paradigm' is therefore substantially undermined.

2.7 A MISSING ELEMENT: LEXICAL SEMANTICS

The generative semantic approach to morphology against which Chomsky (1970) was reacting invoked syntactic transformations to account for not only morphological relationships (e.g. between *destroy* and *destruction*, or between *kill* and *killer*) but also semantic relationships between morphologically simple items (e.g. *kill* and *die*). Thus, we suggested in section 2.1.2 that a generative semantic analysis might posit the same underlying structure for both *piglet* and *shoat*, with terminal elements consisting of semantic components, something like PIG and YOUNG, which would eventually be transformed into stems and affixes. So, when we listed in section 2.1.5 the issues arising from Chomsky's and Halle's work, we included under issue II ('Productivity and meaning relationships') the question: 'What about meaning relationships which have no morphological reflex, such as that between *pig* and *shoat*?' But no answer to this question has so far been suggested in this chapter.

The omission is not an oversight on our part. It is natural that Lieber, whose theory of the lexicon is dissociative, should ignore the question as irrelevant. On the other hand, even Aronoff and Corbin, who see word formation as having an essential semantic dimension, explicitly restrict themselves to those meaning relationships which have morphological correlates. Aronoff states (1976: 33):

> There are cases in which we can define only formal relationships, as with *possible* [which is related by the WFR for *-able/-ible* to a bound stem *poss-* with no independently identifiable meaning], but in no case are we able to define only semantic relationships. Semantics . . . cannot be called into play until we have laid the formal foundation.

Similarly, Corbin (1987: 229) says:

Une relation sémantique entre deux mots ne peut être qualifiée de dérivationnelle *que* si elle est *associée régulièrement* à une relation morphologique. . . . Inversement, une relation dérivationnelle implique nécessairement une relation morphologique *et* une relation sémantique.'

(A semantic relationship between two words can be classed as derivational *only* if it is *associated in a regular fashion* with a morphological relationship. . . . Conversely, a derivational relationship necessarily implies a morphological relationship *and* a semantic relationship. [My translation.])

A study of word-relationships embracing meaning as well as form would be a daunting enterprise, and it is natural that Aronoff and Corbin should want to limit their task. But there is evidence that the meaning of some morphologically complex words has at least as much to do with their place within a 'grid' of semantically related items as it has to do with the meanings of their components, so a decision at the outset to consider only the second of these two factors is bound to distort one's conclusions. This in turn suggests that there may be a kind of semantic productivity which is independent of strictly morphological (or formal) productivity; and this suggestion is reinforced by the complementary discovery, foreshadowed in Jackendoff's framework, of a kind of formal productivity which ignores meaning.

The meaning relationship between *shoat* and *pig* is not unique; it is paralleled by the relationships between *foal* and *horse*, *lamb* and *sheep*, and so on for other domestic animals. In fact, one can construct a grid of such terms on the following lines:

(29) SPECIES		horse	pig	cow	sheep	dog
ADULT:	MALE	stallion	hog	bull	ram	dog
	FEMALE	mare	sow	cow	ewe	bitch
YOUNG		foal	shoat	calf	lamb	pup

The meaning of each of these terms is precisely defined by its position in the lexical-semantic matrix, presented here in a provisional and pre-theoretical fashion in terms of semantic 'components' in small capitals. Of course, varieties of English may differ in the terms used as fillers for individual cells in the matrix; for example, *tup* replaces *ram* in parts of Britain, and *piglet* replaces *shoat* in many dialects. Varieties may also differ in the level of semantic detail incorporated in the matrix; for example, further differentiation under YOUNG may be needed to accommodate terms such as *colt*, *steer* and *hogget* in those rural varieties where these terms have precise connotations of age. But the crucial fact for present purposes is that *piglet* and *shoat* may occupy exactly the same cell. This demonstrates that it is misguided to try to elucidate the meaning of *piglet* solely in terms of the meanings of its morphological components *pig* and *-let*, no matter how straightforwardly compositional the semantics of *piglet* may appear to be. Similarly, the meaning of the word *electorate* may seem to be straightforwardly compositional, with *-ate* meaning 'group of (human beings)' (cf. *directorate* and *episcopate*), if one analyses its internal structure as [[[elect]or]ate]. Yet for New Zealand and Australian varieties of English, this cannot be the whole story, since in those varieties *electorate* is the term for a geographical area which returns one member to parliament, and so fills the lexical-semantic cell occupied in Canadian and British English by the stubbornly noncompositional (or idiomatic) terms *riding* and *constituency* respectively. In other words, the constitutional arrangements of these countries define a 'meaning' which exists independently of its lexical expressions, and which is therefore an inescapable factor in determining the meanings of the words concerned, whether the formation of these words is 'regular' in Corbin's sense or not.[20]

The matrix of semantic features in (29) was described as 'provisional and pretheoretical'. This is certainly a drawback. But all that needs to be established for present purposes is that the meanings of words, both complex and simple, can be related in ways independent of their morphological structure. Precisely how these semantic relationships work, how they are related to morphology and how far they can differ from one language to another remain open questions. Meanwhile, however, the existence of such relationships suggests a new perspective on productivity. The fact that *piglet* has a firm position in the matrix at (29) ensures that it has one of the characteristics of productive derivation; its meaning is relatively firmly established. This characteristic is akin to, though not identical with, Corbin's 'regularity', which involves semantic predictability. From other points of view, however, *piglet* is not productively formed. The *-let* suffix is not profitable, in Corbin's terms, because there are relatively few words in the conventional lexicon which contain it (*booklet* is probably the only one in frequent use), and it may or may not score high on availability, depending on whether or not one classifies nonexistent words such as °*treelet*, °*letterlet*, °*tablelet* as morphologically well formed.

Discussing Jackendoff's lexical redundancy rules, we noted that, unlike Aronoff, Jackendoff permits purely morphological and purely semantic redundancies to be assigned to separate rules. An example of a purely morphological redundancy rule without any semantic counterpart is the rule which relates to each other the lexical entries for Latin-derived prefix-plus-stem verbs such as *confer* and *remit*. One can think of this rule as a sort of word-formation template which reduces the cost of those verbs which comply with it. As we saw, it is not a fully productive rule (in Jackendoff's terms), because there are conceivable prefix-stem combinations which do not exist as words. But are there any such purely morphological rules which are fully productive?

The answer seems to be yes. If one considers the well-formed nominalisations of the verbs which share the stem *-mit* (*admit, permit, commit, remit,* etc.) and the verbs with the stem *-fer* (*transfer, confer, refer, prefer,* etc.), one finds at first sight an entirely haphazard pattern. The conventional lexicon contains *admittance* but not °*permittance, commitment* but not °*remitment, referral* but not °*preferral,* ¹*transfer* (with stress shift) but not °¹*confer,* and so on. Yet two generalisations do emerge; all verbs in *-mit* have a corresponding noun in *-mission* (*admission, permission, commission, remission,* etc.), and all verbs in *-fer* have a corresponding noun in *-ference,* with stress shifted to the prefix (*transference, conference, reference, preference,* etc.). These generalisations can readily be stated as Jackendovian redundancy rules:

(30) a. $\begin{bmatrix} \text{/Prefix + fer/} \\ + \text{V} \end{bmatrix}$ $\longleftrightarrow$ $\begin{bmatrix} \text{/Prefix + fer + ence/} \\ + \text{N} \end{bmatrix}$

  b. $\begin{bmatrix} \text{/Prefix + mit/} \\ + \text{V} \end{bmatrix}$ $\longleftrightarrow$ $\begin{bmatrix} \text{/Prefix + mit + ion/} \\ + \text{N} \end{bmatrix}$

But these redundancy rules, though fully productive, must be classified as purely morphological, because the meanings of the nouns concerned are not predictable from those of the verbs. Usually, though not always, the meaning of a noun in *-mission* or *-ference* corresponds to some meaning of the corresponding verb, but this may not be the verb's commonest meaning. The commonest meaning of *defer* is 'postpone', yet *deference* never means 'postponement' but only 'courtliness, respectful yielding', corresponding to a meaning of *defer* now virtually restricted to the cliché *defer to X's opinion.* The many meanings of *commission* include some (e.g. 'reward to salesman for making a sale', 'official committee') which have no evident synchronic connection with any meaning of *commit,* while conversely several of the meanings of *commit* are reflected in nominalisations other than *commission* (e.g. *committal* 'sending for trial', *commitment* 'dedication to a cause'). And academics may confer degrees or confer about the award of grades for a course, but neither of these activities normally takes place at an academic conference.

Because of Jackendoff's willingness to admit morphological redundancy rules with no semantic correlate, one might have expected him to admit also semantic redundancy rules with no morphological correlate. Rules of this kind might handle the network of relationships illustrated by the domestic animal terms in (29), for example. Yet, like Aronoff and Corbin, Jackendoff explicitly denies this possibility (1975: 651): 'A semantic relation between two words without a morphological relationship cannot be counted as redundancy. . . . Hence we must require a morphological relationship before semantic redundancy can be considered.' Jackendoff's framework therefore allows the formulation of a rule relating *pig* with *piglet* (and *book*, *star*, *drop* with *booklet*, *starlet*, *droplet*) but not one relating *pig* with *shoat* (or *cow*, *sheep*, *horse* with *calf*, *lamb*, *foal*), even though the first of these two sets of words is semantically much less coherent than the second. Jackendoff's reluctance probably stems from a feeling that to recognise purely semantic 'redundancies' would be to open the door again to the free-and-easy manipulation of semantic and syntactic structures that gave generative semantics a bad name. But the fact that semantic relationships were not handled successfully by generative linguists in the past does not prove that they must be subordinate to morphological structure in organising the lexicon. If generative morphologists had realised this earlier, they might have not only handled better the complex of issues grouped under the heading of productivity, but also avoided more successfully the temptation to equate the study of morphology with the study of the lexicon.

3 Morphology and phonology

3.1 ISSUES ARISING FROM *THE SOUND PATTERN OF ENGLISH*

In Chomsky and Halle's *The Sound Pattern of English* (*SPE*) (1968), the task of accounting for morphological alternations is ascribed almost entirely to the phonological component of the grammar, and is the most prominent function that that component performs. Among graduate students at Massachusetts Institute of Technology (MIT) around 1970, it was common to hear a language described as 'having no phonology' when what was meant was that it had no alternations of the kind that most of the phonological rules of *SPE* were devoted to describing. Today the phonological landscape has changed vastly. Phonology is seen as having many tasks in areas which were neglected in early generative work; conversely, few generative phonologists would now see all morphological alternations as falling within the scope of phonology proper.

Even in *SPE*, however, not all alternations were dealt with in the phonological component. Suppletive alternations, such as between *go* and *went* or *good* and *better*, were always seen as outside its scope. Quite apart from these, a number of more or less irregular or unproductive alternations were handled outside the phonological component proper by means of **readjustment rules**. These rules could alter the phonological shape of a lexical item as specified in the lexicon (its 'lexical representation') before it entered the phonological component, or mark it with a diacritic so as to require it to undergo some 'minor' phonological rule. For example, one readjustment rule marks the verb *sing* in Past Tense contexts so as to undergo vowel lowering and emerge as *sang*; another alters the final /t/ of the stem of verbs such as *convert* and *subvert* before the suffix *-ion* so as to ensure that it emerges as [ʒ] in *subversion* (US pronunciation), alongside [s] in *subversive.* Clearly, at least some of the work done by readjustment rules is relevant to morphology. But no clear criteria are offered in *SPE* to distinguish alternations to be handled by these rules from ones which should be handled phonologically. This omission might seem an obvious focus for further work.[1] In fact, however, readjustment rules were almost completely ignored by phonologists in the aftermath of *SPE*; they resurfaced in the allomorphy and truncation rules of Aronovian word formation (see chapter 2), but have re-emerged as a focus of serious attention only in recent work on morphological theory by Bromberger and Halle (unpublished at the time of writing).

Of the issues which have dominated discussion of the *SPE* framework, the most relevant ones morphologically are:

(a) the abstractness of phonological representations;
(b) the distinction between different kinds of boundary (particularly morpheme boundary and word boundary);
(c) the importance ascribed to the cyclic application of rules.

We will consider these issues in the next two sections.

3.1.1 Abstractness: Natural Generative Phonology and the Alternation Condition

Before *SPE* was published, its contents were broadly known among the linguists in touch with MIT, and a reaction had already begun to set in against the power that the *SPE* framework ascribes to phonological rules and the corresponding remoteness of many underlying phonological representations from the phonetic surface. Paul Kiparsky's paper 'How abstract is phonology?' (1968) posed explicitly in its title a question which exercised many phonologists in the late 1960s and early 1970s. At the opposite extreme from *SPE*, Theo Vennemann and Joan Bybee Hooper developed an approach to phonology known as **Natural Generative Phonology** (NGP), which imposed severe limits on both underlying phonological representations and the rules linking them with the phonetic surface.[2] For the morphologist, the importance of NGP lies in its implications for the analysis of morphological alternations. The constraints that NGP imposed on phonology entailed that many alternations which would in *SPE* have been handled by deriving distinct surface forms by phonological rules from a single underlying phonological representation had to be handled in some other way. There were two alternatives (not mutually exclusive); the rules concerned must be at least partly nonphonological, or the distinct surface forms must have more than one underlying representation, just as *go* and *went* have. Both these alternatives were explored by practitioners of NGP.

Hooper in her *Introduction to Natural Generative Phonology* (1976) lists three kinds of rule which share the tasks performed by phonological rules in the *SPE* model: phonetically conditioned rules (P-rules), **morphophonemic rules** (MP-rules), and **via-rules**. P-rules are subject to tight restrictions which in effect limit their role to exceptionless low-level allophony; they are said to be phonetically 'natural' and to belong to a universal inventory of phonological processes which infants have to 'unlearn' rather than learn, in the tradition of Stampe's 'Natural Phonology' (Donegan and Stampe 1979). But it is MP-rules and via-rules which are of most interest to the morphologist.

MP-rules are rules which change phonological features in environments which are specified in terms which are at least partly morpho-syntactic (involving, say, past tense or plural number) or lexical. An example involving both kinds of specification is the rule governing the voicing of fricatives in the plural of English nouns such as *wife* and *house*. This is restricted lexically (it does not apply to *fife* or *horse*) and morphosyntactically (it applies only before the plural -*s*, not the possessive -*'s*). Unlike P-rules, MP-rules are language-specific and may be phonologically arbitrary. Via-rules express nonproductive phonological relationships between distinct lexical items, such as that between Spanish *leche* 'milk', *ocho* 'eight' and *noche* 'night', on the one hand, and *láctico*, *octavo* 'eighth' and *nocturno*, on the other. Both *leche* and *láctico* are entered in the lexicon, and the two entries contain a special statement to the effect that they are related to one another by a via-rule of the form /kt⟷č/. Via-rules clearly resemble closely the morphological redundancy rules of Jackendoff discussed in chapter 2.

But how do we decide which alternations should be handled by MP-rules and which by via-rules? Hooper does not answer this question directly, but two answers emerge from her discussions: (a) MP-rules are relatively more productive (or more available, in Corbin's terms) than via-rules, and (b) via-rules involve derivational morphology, relating distinct lexical items, whereas MP-rules involve inflectional morphology, relating different forms of the same lexical item (since, for Hooper, inflected forms are not separate items). An important factual claim is implicit here, namely that derivational morphology is always phonologically more arbitrary than inflectional morphology is. An embarrassment to Hooper's framework would be a language in which the phonological relationships between derived words and their sources are entirely regular while the phonological relationships between inflected forms are more haphazard. Is Hooper's implicit claim correct, then? This issue is not addressed within Natural Generative Phonology, but it is touched on in Bybee's more recent work, discussed in chapter 6 below, and is related to the question of level-ordering, discussed in the next section.

A problem arises concerning MP-rules and suppletion. Suppletion is traditionally seen as operating within inflectional paradigms; that is, two items are traditionally regarded as suppletive alternants only if they are related inflectionally, like the English *go* (Present) and *went* (Past), or the Russian *rebënok* 'child' and *deti* 'children'. So, since MP-rules also operate within inflectional paradigms, the question arises how we distinguish, in principle, alternants related by MP-rules from suppletive alternants. At first sight, this should usually present little difficulty; *wife* and *wive-*, which were cited above as being related by an MP-rule, are clearly much more similar phonologically than *go* and *went*. But what should we say about, for example, *fly* and *flew*? They share the initial consonant cluster /fl/, but the vocalic alternation /ai~u/ is unique in English inflectional morphology, so an MP-rule to account for it would be restricted in its application to a single item. Faced with this dilemma, Grover Hudson (1975) proposed the radical solution of treating all morphophonemic alternations (more precisely, all alternations within inflectional paradigms not attributable to P-rules) as suppletive; the lexical entry for *wife* would include two partially distinct phonological representations /waif/ and /waiv/, just as the lexical entry for *go* would include two wholly distinct representations /gou/ and /went/ (or perhaps /wen-/).[3] More formally, the two lexical entries will look something like (1):

(1)   a. $/\left\{ \begin{matrix} \text{gou} \\ \text{wen} \end{matrix} \right\}/$ b. $/\text{wai} \left\{ \begin{matrix} \text{f} \\ \text{v} \end{matrix} \right\}/$

The difference in degree of suppletion is represented in the fact that the two phonological shapes in (1a) share no segments, whereas in (1b) they share all but one segment. In this framework, there is no MP-rule deriving /waiv/ from /waif/, or vice versa; rather, there is a distribution rule stating the context in which each allomorph is chosen ('/-v/ in the plural, /-f/ elsewhere').

At first sight, the suppletion analysis has the disadvantage that lexical entries must be more complex than in the MP-rule analysis, without any saving in rules. Not only *wife* but *knife, house, path* and sundry other nouns must have lexical entries with two phonological representations differing just in the voicing of their final spirant; and to account for their distribution there is still need for a rule (generalisable as '[+voice] in the plural, [−voice] elsewhere'). Yet Hooper eventually opts for suppletion in preference to MP-rules. Part of the reason for her choice is methodological or aesthetic rather than empirical; the MP-rule analysis requires the lexical entries for *wife* and so on to contain a special diacritic indicating that they are subject to the fricative-voicing rule, whereas in the suppletion analysis no diacritic is necessary because the listing of the voiceless and voiced fricatives suffices by itself to show that the voicing takes place. But she claims factual support as well. No morphophonemic (as opposed to phonetic) alternation is ever totally productive in the sense that all new words (loan-words, for example) are required to conform to it; and the diachronic tendency towards reduction in allomorphy ('Humboldt's Universal') affects regular or partially regular morphophonemic alternations to just the same extent as it affects instances of total suppletion. This pattern of behaviour in morphological change is just what we expect if partially regular alternations are handled in the lexicon by the same mechanism as suppletions are; so these claims, if true, constitute evidence in favour of the suppletion analysis. Assessing the NGP view of morphology therefore crucially involves investigating morphological change, particularly loan-word morphophonology and the process of paradigmatic levelling.

There is another, more technical, consequence of Hooper's suppletion preference. Let us imagine a language (call it 'E2') which, like English, has two nouns *wife* and *knife*, each with two stem alternants /waif~waiv/ and /naif~naiv/; E2 differs from English, however, in that *knife* appears in the shape /naiv/ before not only the Plural suffix but also the Possessive -'s. This distribution of stems is illustrated in (2):

(2)			
Singular		waif	naif
Singular Possessive		**waif**	**naiv**
Plural		waiv	naiv
Plural Possessive		waiv	naiv

The state of affairs in E2 is more complex than in actual English, but, given the MP-rule approach, it is easy enough to describe. In actual English, we must mark *wife* and *knife* lexically with a diacritic (call it [+D]), distinguishing them from *fife*, which will trigger the MP-rule of fricative voicing in the plural. In E2 we will need the same diacritic and MP-rule, but in addition a second MP-rule to voice fricatives before the possessive marker, applicable to *knife* but not to *wife* in virtue of a second diacritic (say, [+D']) for which *knife* will be marked but *wife* will not. But with the suppletion approach, since *wife* and *knife* each has two stem allomorphs differing in the voicing of the final segment, there is no obvious way of achieving the effect of the two diacritics. A distribution statement to take care of the two alternants of *knife* will need to say that the /___[+voice]/ stem appears in both Plural and Possessive contexts, the /___[−voice]/ stem elsewhere. But there is no way within the Hudson–Hooper framework to stop this distribution statement from applying also to *wife*, wrongly predicting a Singular Possessive form **wive's*. In other words, where two or more items have parallel stem allomorphy, the suppletion approach predicts that the alternants should always be distributed in parallel fashion throughout their inflectional paradigms, so that a language such as E2 should not exist; on the other hand, the MP-rule approach entails no such claim. Testing this implication of the suppletion approach is therefore another line of enquiry generated by NGP.[4]

This consequence of Hooper's NGP is reminiscent of, though not equivalent to, Lieber's claim that affixal inflection correlates with morpholexical alternation, so that lexical diacritics like [1 Dec] or [2Conj] are unnecessary (see section 2.6 above). Indeed, Lieber's analysis of German nouns, whereby the *-en* of *Staaten* 'states (Plural)' and *Bären* 'bears (Plural)' is part of the stem rather than an inflectional suffix, is at first sight incompatible with the Hudson–Hooper suppletion approach, because the forms *Staaten* and *Bären* are not distributed in parallel fashion throughout their paradigms; *Staaten* occurs only in the Plural whereas *Bären* occurs everywhere except in the Nominative Singular. But Lieber's analysis of German nouns is controversial, and other analyses may well be consistent with the Hudson–Hooper model.

The practitioners of NGP have in the main turned their attention more recently to other matters. But, in the case of Hooper, exploring phonological abstractness has led to an interest in morphology for its own sake, as we will see in chapters 6 and 8, and the issues concerning morphological change and stem allomorphy which NGP practitioners raised, consciously or unconsciously, are still by no means resolved.[5]

At the beginning of this section we mentioned Kiparsky's article 'How abstract is phonology?', but we have not yet discussed his own answer to his question. The views of Kiparsky and his colleagues have changed considerably over the years, and his most recent work will be discussed in section 3.1.4; but the answer that Kiparsky proposed in 1968 is still of interest because of its subsequent influence. Whereas the NGP reaction to *SPE* was to insist that phonological rules should be in certain respects phonetically 'natural', Kiparsky's first reaction was to constrain the way in which a rule could apply to a given morpheme in different contexts. This was achieved by means of an **Alternation**

Condition, stating that obligatory neutralisation rules cannot apply to all occurrences of a morpheme (1982c: 148). We will use English, German and Hungarian examples to illustrate what kinds of analysis this Condition does and does not permit.

A plausible example of a rule which applies to all occurrences of a morpheme is the rule whereby, in English, voiceless plosives are aspirated at the beginning of stressed syllables, so that, for example, *team* is pronounced [tʰim], with aspirated [tʰ], in contrast to *steam* [stim]. This looks like an innocuous rule of low-level allophony, permitting an analysis of *team* as underlyingly /tim/, which our phonological theory should surely allow. And the Alternation Condition does indeed allow it; because [tʰ] has no source apart from the aspiration rule, the application of the rule never neutralises an underlying contrast between /t/ and some other segment, so the rule is not an obligatory neutralisation rule. By contrast, the rule which obligatorily devoices syllable-final obstruents in German is a neutralisation rule, because it causes the final /d/ that we may plausibly posit in the the underlying representation of, for example, *Bund* 'league' to emerge as phonetically identical with the underlying final /t/ of *bunt* 'many-coloured'; *bunt* and *Bund* thus become homophonous. But the obstruent-devoicing rule does not apply to the morpheme *Bund* in all contexts; for example, it does not apply in the genitive or compounding form *Bundes* [bundəs] (as in *Bundespost* 'federal postal service'). Consequently, the Alternation Condition does not prevent us setting up /bund/ as the underlying representation of *Bund*.

Hungarian supplies an example of a plausible analysis involving a phonological rule which both applies to some morphemes in all contexts and is neutralising in its effect. In Hungarian, most suffixes are subject to vowel harmony, having a back-vowel variant (*a* or *o*) after back-vowel stems and a front-vowel variant (*e* or *ö*) after front-vowel stems. Thus, the suffix *-om/-am/-em/-öm* meaning 'my' appears as *-am* after *ház* 'house' (*hazam* 'my house') and as *-em* after *kéz* 'hand' (*kézem* 'my hand'). But there are some words which are harmonically anomalous, having front-vowel stems but back-vowel suffixes, such as *híd* 'bridge' and *héj* 'rind', which form *hídam* 'my bridge' and *héjam* 'my rind'. With the resources of *SPE* phonology, it seems convenient to analyse these words as having underlying back vowels, distinct from *u* and *o* in being unrounded; the apparent exceptions to vowel harmony then disappear, because the back-vowel alternant *-am* is what will automatically appear after the back vowel in the stem. Then, to cope with the fact that *híd* and *héj* emerge phonetically with front rather than back vowels, all that is needed is a late phonological rule which makes all unrounded vowels [−back]. However, this analysis is abstract in the sense that it attributes to the segmental inventory of Hungarian a couple of vowels of a kind which never show up phonetically and whose sole motivation is the desire to render vowel harmony exceptionless. Moreover, as Kiparsky points out, the positing of underlying segments on this basis arouses expectations about possible phonological changes of a kind which never take place; in particular, segments like the Hungarian unrounded back vowels never 'resurface' phonetically, as the *SPE* framework would allow them to do. But how can the framework be amended so as to exclude such segments?

Here the Alternation Condition comes into play. The rule which fronts unrounded back vowels is a neutralisation rule, because it renders these vowels homophonous with the corresponding un-rounded front vowels /i/ and /e/, which exist independently in Hungarian. Moreover, it is a rule which must apply to morphemes such as *híd* and *héj* in all their occurrences, because in no contexts are these words left with unrounded back vowels. Consequently, by the Alternation Condition, the rule cannot apply to *híd* and *héj* at all. But this has the effect of blocking the analysis of *híd* and *héj* as containing unrounded back vowels; we have no choice but to analyse them as containing front vowels underlyingly as well as on the surface, and to treat them as genuine, not merely apparent, exceptions to vowel harmony.

The Alternation Condition itself poses problems, however. In effect, it requires that no final decision can be made about the underlying phonological representation of any morpheme until we can be sure that, for every neutralising phonological rule that the morpheme provisionally undergoes, there is at least one context in which the morpheme can appear without the rule applying to it. Reaching that state of certainty could involve a formidable amount of computation, and might require evidence of a kind not readily available to a child learning its first language. In any case, Kiparsky later abandoned the Alternation Condition in the version discussed here, as we shall see. But the Condition is still significant as representing the first attempt within the generative tradition to take seriously, in relation to morphological alternation, the paradigmatic dimension of linguistic structure. Kiparsky experimented in the early 1970s with a principle of 'paradigm coherence' as one of a variety of 'functional' (as opposed to 'formal') factors which might inhibit or encourage the operation of phonological rules (Kiparsky 1972).[6] But this principle was never made precise, and in his subsequent work Kiparsky has reverted to explanations based on the formal characteristics of phonological representations, looking at the syntagmatic dimension alone. This change of direction has yielded interesting results; nevertheless, it helped to delay the already overdue revival of interest in the paradigm among generative morphologists.

3.1.2 Boundaries and the Cycle

The *SPE* framework shares with earlier American phonology (the 'classical' phonemic model) the characteristic that a phonological representation is seen as a single linear sequence of elements. These elements include not only segments but also boundaries between words and morphemes. The acceptance of boundaries as phonologically relevant was not new, since many American and European phonologists had more or less willingly recognised 'junctures' as phonological entities whose phonetic manifestation was indirect, through their effect on neighbouring phonemes, rather than direct. For Chomsky and Halle, however, the recognition of junctures was less problematic methodologically than for most of their American predecessors because they happily allowed information about morphological and syntactic structure to be available to the phonological component. So, given the well-established status of the notions 'morpheme' and 'word' in grammatical analysis, it is not surprising that two of the boundaries that Chomsky and Halle recognised as phonologically relevant should be the **morpheme boundary** or **formative boundary** (symbolised +) and the **word boundary** (symbolised #). In *SPE*, however, the distinction between the two kinds of boundary relies on phonological rather than morphological evidence; one set of affixes has one set of phonological effects while another set has different effects. An obvious question therefore arises: to what extent do these phonologically motivated boundaries correspond with ones motivated on nonphonological (particularly morphological) grounds? Much of the work of Siegel, Allen and the 'Lexical Phonologists' described below can be seen as an attempt to answer that question.[7]

Given that the criteria for the distinction between the two kinds of boundary are phonological, the terms 'morpheme boundary' and 'word boundary' may seem to beg questions about their morphological relevance. In her *Topics in English Morphology* (1979) (originally completed as a thesis in 1974), Siegel avoids this danger by referring to **Class I affixes** (those attached to their stems with a + boundary, in *SPE* terms) and **Class II affixes** (those attached with a # boundary). An example of a Class I suffix is the noun-forming -*y*, found in *democracy* and *telegraph*; this can both spirantise a stem-final coronal segment and affect stress (contrast *democrat* and *telegraph*). The adjective-forming -*y*, on the other hand, is a Class II affix, because it does neither of these things (compare *chocolaty, matey*). In fact, the characteristic of being 'stress-neutral' is the main criterion distinguishing Class II affixes from Class I. This contrast shows up clearly in the behaviour of two suffixes which both form nouns from adjectives: Class I -*ity* (as in *sensitivity, opacity*) and -*ness* (as in *sensitiveness, opaqueness*). Prefixes are harder to classify unequivocally; nevertheless, Siegel assigns to Class I, for example, the stressless *re-* of *restore, refer, remit*, and to Class II the stressable *re-* of *re-store* ('store again'), *rewrite, re-restore* ('restore again').

How are Class I and Class II affixes distributed within words? In answering this, Siegel makes a distinction between two kinds of base to which affixes may be attached: words, which are free forms (whether derived or underived), and 'stems', which are bound monomorphemic elements such as -*clude*, -*duce*, -*mit*. She observes that, since there are two classes of prefix, two classes of suffix and two kinds of base (stems and words), the total number of possible kinds of base-affix combination is eight, as shown in (3):

(3) a. Class I prefix plus stem: *deduce, refract, concede*
     b. Class II prefix plus stem: unattested
     c. Stem plus Class I suffix: *vacate, legible, modify*
     d. Stem plus Class II suffix: *gruesome, hapless, feckless*
     e. Class I prefix plus word: *insobriety, degenerate, compassion*
     f. Class II prefix plus word: *re-wash, extrasensory, autoimmune*
     g. Word plus Class I suffix: *profanity, Icelandic, solidify*
     h. Word plus Class II suffix: *kindness, inducement, useless*

However, of these possible combinations, (3b) never occurs and (3d) is rare. What these two combinations have in common is that they involve a Class II (stress-neutral) affix and a stem. Is there any principle of grammatical organisation which would predict these observational gaps? According to Siegel, the answer is yes. If we assume that at least some stress assignment (call it 'cyclic') takes place on words (whether derived or underived) before Class II affixes are added, then the absence or near-absence of words of the (3b) and (3d) kinds is explained; in their derivation, the relevant stress assignment could take place neither before the affix is added (because the base is a stem rather than a word), nor after the affix is added (because the affix concerned is of the stress-neutral kind). Siegel sums up her view of the relationship between the various processes concerned in a diagram which is reproduced in simplified form in (4):

(4)

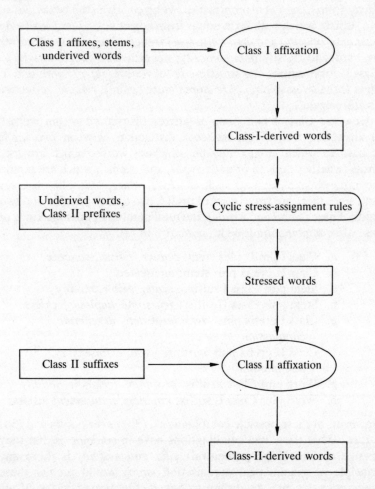

This framework, if it is broadly correct, suggests a motivation for the *SPE* terminology of 'formative boundary' and 'word boundary'; for it seems evident now that Class II affixes attach only (or almost excusively) to words, while Class I affixes can attach to bound stems as well as to words. We thus seem to have found some degree of justification for equating phonologically motivated boundaries with morphologically motivated ones. More importantly, Siegel's diagram entails a claim about the order in which affixes can appear in multiply affixed words. Since Class II affixation takes place after Class I affixation, there is no way in which a Class I suffix can ever follow a Class II suffix. The framework therefore predicts that we may find in succession two Class I suffixes (e.g. *histor-ic-ity*), two Class II suffixes (e.g. *cheer-ful-ness*), a Class I and a Class II suffix (e.g. *histor-ic-ness*) but never a Class II and a Class I suffix (e.g. **late-ness-ic, *cheer-ful-ify*).

The correctness of this prediction has been a matter for considerable debate. If, for example, the suffixes *-ise* and *-able* belong to Class II, as is suggested by their stress-neutrality in words like *compartmentalise* and *retrainable*, then Siegel's prediction encounters difficulty with *compartmentalisation* and *retrainability*, where a Class I suffix is added. Some researchers have accordingly suggested that the same affix may belong sometimes to Class I and sometimes to Class II, or that there may be distinct but homophonous affixes in the two classes. But what is most important here is not the correctness of Siegel's classification of affixes but its influence on subsequent work. The diagram at (4) illustrates a model of word formation in which affixes are not merely classified according to their phonological properties but also in some sense layered or stratified. This aspect of the model is emphasised by Allen (1979), who introduces the term **level-ordering**. According to her, English word formation involves three distinct levels, with Levels I and II corresponding essentially to Siegel's Classes I and II, and Level III embracing compounding. A more far-reaching development of the level-ordered model came with Kiparsky's Lexical Phonology, discussed in section 3.1.4. But first we must examine the development of the notion of the phonological cycle.

In *SPE*, the linear strings of segments and boundaries which constitute phonological representations have a constituent structure, or labelled bracketing, just as the strings of words which constitute sentences do. Above the level of the word, this phonological bracketing is in most respects identical with the syntactic structure (although readjustment rules may alter the bracketing to explain, for example, the peculiar stress pattern of right-branching sentences like *This is the cat that chased the rat that ate the malt that lay in the house that Jack built*). Below the level of the word, phonological bracketing is held to reflect morphological structure. This claim is based mainly on evidence drawn from English stress. In a famous discussion,

Chomsky and Halle compare the stress patterns of the words *theatre,* *theatrical* and *theatricality*, and demonstrate that, given an appropriate formulation of the stress rule, the stress pattern of *theatricality* can be accounted for by bracketing it [[[*theatr*]*ical*]*ity*] and applying the same rule twice, first on the constituent [[*theatr*]*ical*] and then on the whole word. But this bracketing is not morphologically random, since *theatre* is a noun, *theatrical* an adjective and *theatricality* another noun. We can therefore assign morphological labels to the brackets that are needed for the purpose of the stress cycle in phonology: [[[*theatr*]$_N$*ical*]$_A$*ity*]$_N$. And this convergence of phonological and morphological structure is highly desirable, if it can be sustained as a principle of Universal Grammar.

If phonological rules (or a subset of them) apply cyclically, an apparently trivial consequence follows: if a cyclic rule can apply to B in the string ABC, then in the string $[_n[_m ABC]_m D]_n$ it will apply on the cycle labelled *m* rather than that labelled *n*. Less formally, if a rule has a chance to apply to a given segment on an earlier cycle rather than on a later cycle, it will always apply on the earlier cycle. But this apparently trivial consequence has major implications, in that it helps the formulation of a substitute for Kiparsky's Alternation Condition.

The Alternation Condition, as we saw in the previous section, stated that an obligatory neutralisation rule cannot apply to all occurrences of a morpheme. But a rule which does not apply to all occurrences of a morpheme must be a rule which makes crucial reference either to material in the phonological string outside that morpheme, or else to material within the morpheme which has been changed by some prior phonological rule. Kiparsky gives the title '**derived environment**' to environments of the two kinds just mentioned – involving either 'new' morphological material or else the prior application of a rule – and formulates the **Revised Alternation Condition** (RAC) as follows: obligatory neutralisation rules apply only in derived environments (1982c: 152). It is a straightforward matter to check that, for the Hungarian examples discussed in the previous section, the RAC has the same consequences as the earlier Alternation Condition. If we postulate underlying representations for *híd, héj, hídam* and *héjam* with unrounded back vowels in the stem, the rule which fronts these vowels applies in an environment which is underived (in Kiparsky's sense), since the vowels concerned are not created by any prior rule and there is no crucial reference to anything outside the stem. So, since the rule is a neutralisation rule, it cannot apply here at all, and the analysis of these forms as containing an underlying unrounded back vowel is effectively barred.

But does the RAC need to be stipulated within phonological theory, independently of the principle that (some) phonological rules apply cyclically? Clearly it would be desirable if something like the RAC could be shown to be a consequence of the cycle. And what we have seen so far of the relationship between the cycle and morphological structure suggests that this may indeed be so. In our discussion of *theatricality*, we observed that a bracketing [[[*theatr*]*ical*]*ity*] seemed not only to be motivated phonologically (by the stress pattern) but also to reflect morphological structure. Let us now assume that this correlation holds invariably, so that morphological bracketing always yields a constituent structure which is phonologically relevant also. This implies that *hídam* will be bracketed $[[híd]_m am]_n$ for phonological purposes. But it is evident now that, if the rule which fronts unrounded back vowels is cyclic, there will never be an unrounded back vowel in the stem at the stage in the derivation when vowel-harmony rules apply; for vowel harmony cannot apply until the outer cycle (labelled *n*), whereas unrounded vowel fronting (at least in its most obvious formulation, as a rule applying without any contextual restriction) will have taken place on the inner cycle (labelled *m*). Consequently, once again, the analysis of *híd* as containing an unrounded back vowel does not achieve the purpose for which it was devised, and the constraint on abstractness which followed from the RAC can be derived in substance from the principle that certain rules should be applied in a strictly cyclic fashion. Various versions of a **Strict Cyclicity Principle** for rule application have been proposed, of which (5) (due to Halle 1979) is one of the most straightforward:

(5)   A cyclic rule R applies properly on cycle j if and only if there is an immediately preceding cycle j−1 such that R must make specific use of information not present in the string at the end of that cycle.

In relation to our *hídam* example, (5) precludes any conceivable analysis involving back unrounded vowels. For the vowel-harmony rule to achieve the desired effect, the fronting rule would have to follow it on cycle *n*; but then the fronting rule would not make any specific use of the information not present in the string at the end of the immediately preceding cycle *m*, namely the suffix *-am*. And even if one were to contrive a version of the fronting rule which artificially referred to the presence of the suffix, so as to legitimise its application on cycle *n*, there is no version of the rule which could ever apply to the unsuffixed form *híd* on cycle *m*; for cycle *m* has no immediately preceding cycle.

For the phonologist, the Strict Cyclicity Principle raises a variety of questions. Other versions of the Principle have been proposed, with somewhat different empirical consequences. If possible, criteria for distinguishing between cyclic and noncyclic rules need to be established independently of whether the rules obey the Principle, in order to reduce the element of circularity that will otherwise weaken it. An obvious suggestion is that the cyclic rules may be precisely the obligatory neutralisation rules which the Revised Alternation Condition refers to; but some phonologists have challenged this straightforward identification.[8] What matters for the morphologist, however, is what this view of phonology implies for the extent and nature of allomorphy and for the morphological segmentation of words.

The constraints that the Strict Cyclicity Condition imposes on abstractness reduce the scope for accounting for allomorphy by means of 'phonological' rules, and so may in principle increase the number of phonologically distinct alternants which need to be posited for some morphemes. Somewhat less obvious are the morphological implications of the assumption that it is morphological structure which yields the bracketing needed for the proper operation of phonological rules. This assumption can be used to argue backwards, as it were – to motivate morphological structure on the basis of what is needed to make the phonology work. As an example of this, consider Kiparsky's discussion (1982c: 145) of the Spanish verb-form *desdeñes* 'you disdain (2nd person singular subjunctive)'.[9] On the surface, at least, this seems to contain three elements: a stem *desdeñ-*, terminating in a palatal nasal, a subjunctive marker *-e-* (contrast *desdeñas* 'you disdain (Indicative)') and a person-number marker *-s*. But if (as Kiparsky assumes) Spanish has a cyclic rule which depalatalises nasals in the syllabic coda (compare the noun *desden* 'scorn', with dental *-n*), then a bracketing such as [[*desdeñ*]*e*+*s*] or [[[*desdeñ*]*e*]*s*] for the subjunctive verb-form risks yielding [[*desden*]. . .] through the operation of depalatalisation on the first cycle, and ultimately **desdenes*. (Depalatalisation is allowed to apply on the first cycle, in apparent violation of the Strict Cyclicity Principle, because it is fed by syllable-structure formation, which, being a 'structure-building' rather than a 'structure-changing' rule, is exempt from the Principle (1982c: 160–1); we return to this in section 3.1.4.) But Kiparsky avoids this unwanted result by positing an underlying morphological structure [[*desdeñ*+*a*]*e*+*s*], containing a 'theme vowel' *a*, allegedly the same morphological item as the *-a-* of the Indicative. This theme vowel must be deleted by a vowel-truncation rule on the second cycle;

but, crucially, its presence on the first cycle causes the preceding palatal nasal to be assigned to a syllabic onset rather than a coda, so the condition for depalatalisation is not met. The plausibility of this analysis depends heavily on whether there is independent evidence in Spanish for vowel truncation. But, whether plausible or not, it serves well to illustrate how the assumptions of cyclic phonology can have morphological consequences.[10]

Mention of syllable structure reminds us that recent proposals about phonological constituency invoke elements such as the syllable, the foot, the colon and the phonological word, which in many languages at least do not correlate with any plausible morphological constituents. Indeed, one way to see the shift in emphasis from cycles to 'levels' in Lexical Phonology (discussed below) is as a reaction against the evident drawbacks of equating morphological and phonological structure too closely. There still remains a worthwhile domain of enquiry here, however. It has often been noted that, in many of the better-known 'agglutinating' languages (such as Turkish, Japanese and Hungarian), morphological structure tends to correlate with phonological structure at least to the extent that suffixes and prefixes constitute well-formed syllables or combinations of syllables, whereas this is less generally so in 'fusional' languages.[11] So there are questions about the relationship between phonological and morphological structure which the principle of cyclicity usefully provokes, even if it does not go far towards answering them.

3.1.3 Adjacency and Bracketing Erasure

The Strict Cyclicity Condition claims that, roughly speaking, rules of a certain kind, in order to apply legally, must 'notice' a minimum of one layer of morphological embedding. Is there any maximum number of layers of embedding that the relevant rules can 'notice'? Clearly it will be satisfying if the maximum turns out to be one, just like the minimum. If that is correct, then it will be possible for one of these rules to be constrained so as to apply only to nouns, for example, since this will involve simply noticing the category label on one bracket (. . .$_N$[. . . or . . .]$_N$. . .); but it will not be possible for it to be constrained so as to apply only to deverbal nouns, since this will involve noticing the category of a constituent at a second layer of embedding (. . .$_N$[. . .$_V$[. . . or . . .]$_N$. . .]$_V$. . .). Siegel (1978) and Allen (1979) independently proposed a condition with precisely this kind of effect, which they call the **Adjacency Condition**. Allen's version at (6) is formulated as a constraint on morphological rules:

(6)   No WFR [word-formation rule] can involve X and Y, unless
       Y is uniquely contained in the cycle adjacent to X.

A WFR applying specifically to deverbal nouns will violate this
condition; in adding some affix X it 'involves' X, yet the bracket
labelled V is not 'uniquely contained in the cycle adjacent to X', which
is the cycle represented by the bracket labelled N. Siegel illustrates
the effect of the condition by reference to the adjectival prefix *un-*.
This does not attach to adjectives with a 'negative' or pejorative
sense:*unbad*, *unugly*, *unjealous*, *unhorrible*. Yet some such forms
are acceptable, despite the 'negativity' of their bases: *unhorrified*,
unenvious, *unspiteful*, *unblemished*. Siegel's explanation (assuming
one shares her acceptability judgements) involves bracketing. In
all the unacceptable forms, there is only one bracket separating
un- from the 'negative' element (*[un[bad]], *[un[jealous]]), whereas
in the unexpectedly acceptable forms, there is more than one
bracket ([un[[[horri]fi]ed]], [un[[envi]ous]]). Unfortunately, judgements about *un-* words are not always clearcut, and some which the
Adjacency Condition ought to 'save', according to Siegel, nevertheless
seem unacceptable (e.g.*[un[[dis[illusion]]ed]], *[un[[danger]ous]]).
Still, Siegel's argument clearly illustrates what the Condition is meant
to do.
   One way of ensuring that embedded brackets shall not be 'noticeable' by a cyclic phonological rule is to ensure that the brackets are
not there at the point when the rule applies. This can be achieved by
specifying that at the end of a cycle (that is, when all the relevant rules
have been run through), all internal brackets are erased. A **Bracketing
Erasure Convention** with something like this effect was originally
proposed in *SPE*. Here is a more formal statement of it drawn from
the often-cited but never-published paper 'Russian morphology and
lexical theory' by Pesetsky (1979):

(7)   Given the nested constituents
       $[_n \cdots [_{n-1} \cdots _{n-1}] \cdots]$
       the last rule of cycle n is: Erase brackets n−1.

If they can be sustained, the Adjacency Condition and the Bracketing
Erasure Convention certainly impose desirable restrictions on the
operation of morphological rules, and it is reasonably clear what
potential counterevidence will look like.[12] Unfortunately, such counterevidence is also fairly easy to find (quite apart from the difficulties
with Siegel's *un-* example). Consider a Latin verb-form *utebantur* 'they
were using' from the verb *utor* 'use'. *Utor* belongs to the class of

verbs traditionally labelled 'deponent', that is 'passive in form but active in meaning'; if *utor* were an ordinary nondeponent verb, the form for 'they were using' would be not *utebantur* but **utebant* (cf. *amabantur* 'they were loved' versus *amabant* 'they loved'). A plausible morphological bracketing for *utebantur* is [[[[u:t]-e:ba]nt]ur], glossable as '[[[[use] imperfective-past] 3rd-plural] passive]'.[13] The problem for the Adjacency Condition arises from the suffix *-ur*, glossed as 'passive'. Recall that this verb-form is not syntactically passive; the suffix *-ur* is required only because the root *ut-* is lexically marked as deponent. But then the rule which suffixes *-ur* to *utebant* 'involves', or makes reference to, a feature of the root, which is certainly not 'uniquely contained in the cycle adjacent to' *-ur*, since the cycle adjacent to *-ur* contains only the suffix *-nt*. The Adjacency Condition as formulated at (6) is therefore violated, seemingly.

One way out of this difficulty may be to invoke Lieber's feature-percolation conventions, summarised in chapter 2. The affixes *-eba-* and *-nt* are both found on ordinary as well as deponent verbs, so will be unmarked for deponency. The lexical feature [+deponent] borne by the root *ut-* will therefore be free to percolate outwards to the brackets enclosing *-eba-* and *-nt*, and so will reach the outermost brackets enclosing [*utebant*]. This means that [+deponent] will after all be 'contained in the cycle adjacent to' *-ur* when the morphological rule adding *-ur* applies. Equally, in terms of the Bracketing Erasure Convention, [+deponent] will be present on the one pair of brackets which remains at the end of the *-nt* cycle. This appeal to feature percolation may, however, be all too effective. It waters down the empirical effect of the Adjacency Condition and the Bracketing Erasure Convention to such an extent that it allows any morphological rule to 'see' any feature of the root which is not contradicted (as it were) by some feature of an intervening affix.

The Latin example shows how, with feature percolation, the Adjacency Condition and the Bracketing Erasure Convention may be too weak. But there is also evidence from Zulu which suggests that the Condition (although not the Convention) may in some respects be too strong, even with feature percolation. In Zulu, a characteristic phonological or morphophonological dissimilation affects the stems of verbs ending in labial consonants when the stem is followed by the Passive suffix *-wa*, as shown in (8) (where prefixes are omitted as irrelevant):

(8) Active   Passive
     -bamb-a 'catch'   *-banj*-wa 'be caught'

-*boph-a* 'tie'   -*bo*sh-wa 'be tied'

This reflects a general characteristic of Zulu phonotactics; [w] never follows a labial consonant. Yet we call the dissimilation morphophonological rather than phonological, because it even operates, rather surprisingly, when the verb stems are separated from the Passive -*wa* by an intervening suffix, such as Causative -*is*- (Doke 1961: 21, 136–7):

(9)   Active   -*bamb-is-a*   'cause to catch'
                  -*boph-is-a*   'cause to tie'
      Passive   -*banj-is-wa*   'be caused to catch'
                  -*bosh-is-wa*   'be caused to tie'

A form such as -*banj-is-wa*, if it is bracketed [[[banj]is]wa], violates the Adjacency Condition because the dissimilation 'involves' -*banj-* and -*wa-*, two cycles apart; and, by contrast with Latin *utebantur*, there is no independent ground for assigning to -*banj-* a feature such as [+passive] which might percolate out to the brackets surrounding [banjis]. On the other hand, -*banj-is-wa* may not violate the Bracketing Erasure Convention, because the dissimilation could be argued to depend on only phonological characteristics, not the internal constituency or labelling, of the string [banjis]. But whether all counterexamples to the Adjacency Condition can be reconciled with the Bracketing Erasure Convention in this way remains unclear.

3.1.4 Lexical Phonology and morphology

Until the early 1980s, the implications of level-ordering (as proposed by Siegel and Allen) and of the cycle were explored largely independently. Kiparsky (1982b; 1982c) and Mohanan (1986) then pioneered a model known as **Lexical Phonology** in which features of both approaches were combined.[14] This model's most striking departure from the *SPE* framework is that lexical representations – that is, the phonological portions of lexical entries – are no longer the raw material on which the phonological component operates, but rather the outcome of a substantial amount of phonological manipulation through phonological rules which, like Jackendoff's redundancy rules and Lieber's morpholexical rules, operate 'inside' the lexicon. Furthermore, complex words are not fully constructed morphologically before any phonological rules apply to them; rather, phonological rules apply on each level (or **stratum**, in Mohanan's terminology) before the morphological rules of the next stratum add further affixes or alter the phonological string in some other way. In Kiparsky's version of the model, the Bracketing Erasure Convention is held to apply at the end of every level rather than every cycle – a weakening designed partly to enable the model to accommodate morphological behaviour in breach of the Convention or the Adjacency Condition, such as the Latin and Zulu behaviour discussed in section 3.1.3.

This framework is illustrated for English in the chart in (10) (based on Kiparsky 1982c and Kaisse and Shaw 1985):

(10)

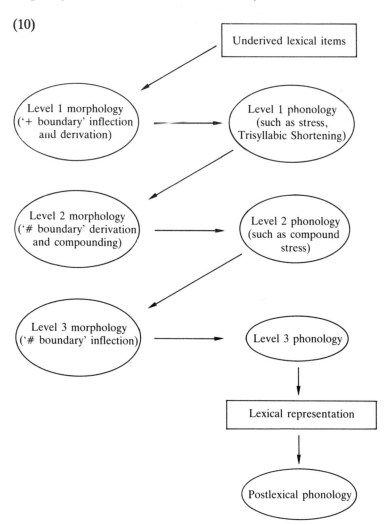

The rule of 'Trisyllabic Shortening' mentioned at Level 1 is what is said to produce the lax vowel in the first syllable of *sanity* and *ominous* from an underlying representation containing a tense vowel (cf. *sane*, *omen*). But what matters for immediate purposes are not the details of which phenomena are assigned to which level or even how many levels there are (on both of these questions there is disagreement), but rather the general shape of Lexical Phonology model and the morphological consequences which follow from it.

Lexical Phonology has been developed mainly in application to two languages in which the vocabulary is divisible into more than one 'level' in a historical sense also, namely English, with its distinct Germanic and Latin-derived wordstores, and Malayalam, which has both native Dravidian and borrowed Sanskrit vocabulary. Lexical Phonologists would nevertheless reject any suggestion that their model is unduly influenced by the cultural history of these languages. The model incorporates the level-ordered characteristic of Siegel's and Allen's models, in that Level 3 morphological processes follow Level 2 processes, which in turn follow Level 1. Lexical Phonologists therefore make predictions similar to Siegel's and Allen's about the order in which affixes can appear within a word, and so encounter similar difficulties with apparent counterexamples such as *compartmentalisation*.[15] What is new is their emphasis on how level-ordering allows some phonological rules to precede some morphological ones, as the arrows in (10) imply. This has implications for those morphological processes which are sensitive to phonological characteristics of the stems on which they operate. The model will be supported if we can find clear examples of such processes applying to stems on which phonological rules have already operated. One such example may be the affixation of noun-forming *-al*, which applies only to stems with stress on the final syllable, as in *refusal*, *arrival*, *committal* versus **abandonal*, **developal* (Ross 1972, quoted by Siegel 1979). Another may be the deadjectival verb-forming suffix *-en*, which attaches to adjectives ending in a single obstruent but apparently not those ending in an obstruent cluster (*tighten*, *stiffen* versus **crispen*, **laxen*); if the verbs *soften*, *fasten* have underlying representations containing the clusters /ft/, /st/, then whatever rule deletes the /t/ so as to reduce the cluster to a single obstruent must apply before the suffixation rule (Halle 1973). But, so far as the morphologist is concerned, one of the most interesting aspects of the model is that it may enable us to derive the main consequences of the Strict Cyclicity Principle (including the constraints it imposes on abstractness) from what Kiparsky calls the **Elsewhere Condition**, and so render the Strict Cyclicity Principle redundant.

The Elsewhere Condition was first developed as a general principle to predict the order in which certain rules would apply in phonology; essentially, when two such rules can apply to the same form, the one whose environment is more precisely specified takes precedence over the one whose environment is less precisely specified (Kiparsky 1973; compare the Proper Inclusion Precedence Principle of Koutsoudas, Sanders and Noll 1974). The version given by Kiparsky in his exposition of Lexical Phonology (1982c: 136) is as in (11):

(11) Rules A, B in the same component apply disjunctively to a form f if and only if
   (a)   the structural description of A (the special rule) properly includes the structural description of B (the general rule);
   (b)   the result of applying A to f is distinct from the result of applying B to f.

In that case, A is applied first, and if it takes effect, then B is not applied.

A few comments on this definition are called for. The last sentence in effect defines disjunctive ordering, and so recapitulates the opening. To say that the structural description of A properly includes that of B is to say that it contains everything (features, segments, brackets, boundaries and so on) which is in the structural description of B, but with some extra material added; thus, for example, a structural description of the form CDEFG properly includes one of the form DEF. A moment's reflection will confirm that, if rules A and B are related in this way, B is more general in that it applies to a larger class of potential input strings than A does: not only to CDEFG (to which A can apply too) but also to HDEF, DEFK, HDEFK and so on (to which A cannot apply). Finally, the label 'Elsewhere Condition' recalls the fact that the most general of a set of competing rules is the one which can most conveniently be stated as applying 'elsewhere', after all the special cases have been taken care of.

Kiparsky invokes the Elsewhere Condition to explain two kinds of morphological phenomenon, which can be exemplified by the non-English plural forms *cattles* and *oxens*. *Cattle* is syntactically plural (*the cattle were grazing*, not **the cattle was grazing*), so its lexical entry must be marked [+Noun, +Plural]. Let us suppose now that we construe each lexical entry as a rule (a **lexical identity rule**), whose structural description and structural change are identical. The lexical identity rule for *cattle* (or rather the relevant portion of the rule) is shown in (12):

(12) $cattle]_{Noun, +Plural} \rightarrow cattle]_{Noun, +Plural}$

The regular, or general, plural rule will be as in (13) (where X is an unspecified or 'empty' phonological representation):

(13) $\emptyset \rightarrow /z/$ in environment X____$]_{Noun, +Plural}$

Rule (13) is exactly equivalent to (14), which is arranged so that the whole structural description is to the left of the arrow:

(14) $X]_{Noun, +Plural} \rightarrow X/z/]_{Noun, +Plural}$

Comparing (12) and (14), we see that (12) is much more precise. In particular, the structural description of (12), which contains the phonological specification *cattle* or /kætl/, properly includes that of (14), since (14) contains no phonological specification at all. Moreover, the effects of applying (12) and (14) to *cattle* are distinct: *cattle* and *cattles*. The Elsewhere Condition therefore comes into play, requiring us to apply (12) to *cattle* in preference to (14). The Condition thus has the desired effect of blocking the 'regular' plural **cattles* for *cattle*.

For *oxen*, the relevant Plural rule is (15) (where, as in (14), we use for clarity the format which places the entire structural description on the left):

(15) $ox]_{Noun, +Plural} \rightarrow oxen]_{Noun, +Plural}$

At first sight, when we compare (15) and the 'elsewhere' rule at (14), we may be inclined to account for the nonexistence of **oxes* by reference to the Elsewhere Condition; the structural description of (15) properly includes that of (14), so the Condition requires us to give preference to (15). In fact, the order of the levels to which irregular and regular plural formations belong makes appeal to the Condition unnecessary; in Kiparsky's version of lexical phonology, irregular plurals such as *teeth* and *oxen* are formed on Level 1 whereas regular plural formation is not until Level 3, so the plural of *ox* will always receive the suffix *-en* before the suffix *-es* gets a chance. But level-ordering by itself does not explain why we do not encounter a doubly marked plural form **oxens*, with plural rules applying at both Level 1 and Level 3. Kiparsky explains the absence of **oxens* by saying that the set of lexical entries includes not only underived items like *cattle* and *ox* but also the output of each word-forming process and, *a fortiori*, the output of each lexical level. If so, then *oxen*, which is among the output of Level 1, is a lexical entry. But, in Kiparsky's framework, this is tantamount to saying that there is a lexical identity rule (16):

(16) $oxen]_{\text{Noun, +Plural}} \rightarrow oxen]_{\text{Noun, +Plural}}$

We must think of *oxen* as 'undergoing' this identity rule as it passes from Level 1 to Level 2 and again as it passes unchanged from Level 2 to Level 3. And if we now compare (16) with the general Level-3 plural rule (14), we see that the two come within scope of the Elsewhere Condition and that (16) is required to apply in preference to (14). The Elsewhere Condition thus has the effect of ensuring that any word-form which has already received inflectional marking for some morphosyntactic property cannot be re-marked for the same property.

The Elsewhere Condition has here been justified so far on morphological grounds. But, according to Kiparsky, the Condition has desirable phonological consequences too. Recall that for the Hungarian form $[[híd]_m am]_n$ 'my bridge', with its anomalous vowel harmony, the Strict Cyclicity Principle prevents any analysis involving an 'abstract' unrounded back vowel. But the Elsewhere Condition has the same effect, when combined with the lexical identity rule for the lexical entry of *híd*. Let us suppose that *híd* has the abstract vowel underlyingly, and that we try to apply the vowel-fronting rule on cycle *n*, after vowel harmony has assigned the correct vowel to the suffix. There will then be two rules potentially applicable to the vowel of *híd* on cycle *n*: (a) the fronting rule and (b) the lexical identity rule for *híd* as it passes from cycle *m* to cycle *n*. But the structural description for the fronting rule will specify an 'empty' environment, since the rule must apply to the unrounded back vowel in all contexts; consequently, this structural description will be properly included in the structural description of the lexical identity rule, and the lexical identity rule will take precedence. Similar considerations will apply at whatever cycle we try to apply the fronting rule. There is therefore no stage in the derivation where the Elsewhere Condition will allow us to apply the fronting rule, and so no alternative to analysing *híd* as containing a front vowel underlyingly.

The Elsewhere Condition seems thus to be as effective in constraining abstractness as the Strict Cyclicity Principle. It has an added advantage, according to Kiparsky, in respect of underived stems. Some phonological rules do apply to underived stems, in apparent violation of the Strict Cyclicity Principle. Stress rules in English must presumably be allowed to apply to underived, or monomorphemic, items just as much as to derived ones; and our discussion in section 3.1.2 of the Spanish noun *desden* 'scorn' and verb form *desdeñes* presupposed that the syllabification rules for Spanish should be allowed to apply to the stem [*desdeñ*], even though it is underived. What is it about stress and syllabification which exempts them from strict cyclicity? One difference between these processes and vowel-fronting rules of the sort involved in the abstract analysis of *híd* is that the former 'build' phonological structure (by creating metrical or syllabic constituents) while the latter 'change' it (by substituting one segment for another). We could simply stipulate that the Strict Cyclicity Principle applies only to structure-changing and not to structure-building processes; but we would naturally prefer this contrast to follow directly from our phonological-morphological framework. And it does indeed follow directly when we consider the implications of the term 'distinct' in part (b) of the Elsewhere Condition at (11). The effects of applying the vowel-fronting rule and the lexical identity rule to *híd*, assuming an underlying back vowel, are distinct, in the sense that the vowel emerges with mutually incompatible values for backness ([−back] from the first, [+back] from the second). On the other hand, the effects of applying syllabification rules and the lexical identity rule to [*desdeñ*] are not distinct, in the relevant sense; the identity rule says nothing about syllable structure at all, so it says nothing to contradict the outcome of syllabification. The Elsewhere Condition therefore requires that the lexical identity and vowel-fronting rules should apply disjunctively in the derivation of *híd*; and, since the structural description of the lexical identity rule properly includes that of the vowel-fronting rule, lexical identity applies first, blocking vowel fronting. On the other hand, the Elsewhere Condition imposes no disjunctivity on the lexical identity and syllabification rules in the derivation of *desden*, so both can apply. The Condition thus mimics the effect of the Strict Cyclicity Principle in just the right places, with no need for any stipulation to stop it applying in the wrong places. The Elsewhere Condition is therefore superior to the Strict Cyclicity Principle in an important respect (according to Kiparsky) and should replace it entirely.

Kiparsky's search for constraints on abstractness has led to a novel outcome. In both *SPE* phonology and NGP, the extent to which morphological alternation is accounted for phonologically depends on the power of the phonological component. In Kiparsky's version of Lexical Phonology, by contrast, a principle motivated currently on mainly morphological grounds (the Elsewhere Condition) is used to constrain phonological rules. This is what makes Kiparsky's Lexical Phonology especially interesting to the morphologist – more interesting than the versions of Lexical Phonology proposed by Mohanan (1986) and Halle and Mohanan (1985), in which a more purely phonological principle of cylicity retains a central role. It is therefore vital to consider how strong the morphological evidence for the Elsewhere Condition is, and, in general, how effectively Lexical Phonology constrains what can happen in morphology.

Superficially at least, it is easy to find counterexamples to the Elsewhere Condition without looking beyond English. The verb *drive* has a past participle *driven* with a stem [drɪv] which is peculiar to this form of the verb; the stem [naiv] of the noun *knife* is peculiar to the plural; and the stem [wen] of the verb *go* is peculiar to the past. If these stems constitute appropriately formulated lexical identity rules analogous to (12) or (16), then the Elsewhere Condition ought seemingly to block the subsequent suffixation of *-en*, *-s* and *-t* respectively (assuming that this *-t* is the past suffix which occurs also in *bent*, *knelt*, etc.). To avoid this consequence, these stem-forms cannot be analysed as lexical entries in the sense in which *cattle* and *oxen* are; instead, they must come into existence only 'after' *-en*, *-s* and *-t* have been suffixed to them. But this in turn entails that not only the /draiv/~/drɪv/ and /naif/~/naiv/ alternations but also the /gou/~/wen/ alternation must be handled (at whatever level) by rules which alter phonological shape on the basis of morphological context in the course of a derivation. Clearly, to cope with /gou/~/wen/, these rules (whether we call them 'phonological' or not) must have considerable power. But, if we balk at a rule for /gou/~/wen/, then the Elsewhere Condition requires us to analyse *went* as a simple unsuffixed form ([went]$_{\text{Verb, +Past}}$), whose similarity in its final consonant to suffixed past-tense forms such as *bent* and *knelt* is merely accidental. This kind of analytical dilemma is a direct consequence of the Elsewhere Condition, and is therefore quite embarrassing in view of the central role that Kiparsky attributes to the Condition in phonology as well as morphology.[16]

Apart from the Elsewhere Condition, does Lexical Phonology make interesting predictions about what can and cannot happen in morphology? Kiparsky cites a number of intriguing facts which the level-ordering that he assumes for English can explain, such as the acceptability of verbs 'zero-derived' from nouns with Level 1 suffixes (*to pressure, to commission, to reverence*) but not of ones from nouns with Level 2 suffixes (*to beating*, *to freedom*, *to sisterhood*) (1982c: 141). If it is stipulated for English (a) that noun-to-verb zero derivation takes place on level 2 and (b) that zero derivation cannot apply to suffixed forms, then the absence of *to freedom* etc. follows directly; on the other hand, since the framework incorporates a version of the Bracketing Erasure Convention, whereby internal brackets are erased at the end of every level, the suffixed status of *commission* etc. on Level 1 is 'invisible' on Level 2, so stipulation (b) cannot prevent zero derivation from applying to these nouns. But this explanation relies on two stipulations about English ((a) and (b) above) which are not consequences of the Lexical Phonology framework. The framework could accommodate without trouble a pseudo-English in which, instead of (b), it is stipulated that noun-to-verb zero derivation applies *only* to suffixed forms; in this pseudo-English, acceptability judgements about zero-derived verbs will be exactly reversed.[17]

Are there, then, any versions of pseudo-English which Lexical Phonology excludes in principle, as contravening general constraints on how morphology works? Acknowledging the importance of this question, Kiparsky suggests that the answer is yes. Analysing examples such as *oxen*, *inhabitant* versus *oxes*, *inhabiter*, he assigns the relatively unproductive suffixes *-en*, *-ant* to Level 1, so they get a chance to apply before the more productive affixes *-er* at Level 2 and *-(e)s* at Level 3 (1982c: 134–6). He goes on: 'An adequate theory of morphology must exclude in principle, for example, a language in which the English facts are reversed and it is the Level 3 inflections which occur only with specially designated words. Given the [level-ordered] format for morphology, this simply follows from the ordering of levels' (1982c: 136). The sort of behaviour that Kiparsky apparently wishes to exclude is a pattern of plural inflection, for example, whereby all simple nouns have a single 'regular' plural marker while derived nouns display a variety of different markers. But there are two conceivable versions of that pattern: (a) each derivational suffix is associated consistently with one plural marker, or (b) each derivational suffix can occur with a variety of plural makers, the choice being determined by the word as a whole rather than the outermost suffix. Version (b) certainly appears quite implausible, and should probably be excluded in principle. But it is in any case excluded, without recourse to level-ordering, if each noun-forming suffix must consistently 'choose' one and only one of the rival plural markers – a natural extension of Pinker's Unique Entry Condition (1984) or Carstairs's Inflectional Parsimony Hypothesis (1987a), forbidding the coexistence in one linguistic variety of two or more inflected forms which are exactly synonymous in all respects, stylistically as well as cognitively. Version (a) would apply to a situation where, for example, the agentive suffix *-er* consistently takes one plural marker while *ist* consistently takes another and so on. But this is precisely what happens with the suffixes *-er* and *-ist* in German (e.g. *Führ-er* 'leader', Plural *Führ-er-Ø*; *Kompon-ist* 'composer', Plural *Kompon-ist-en*). Granted, underived nouns too exhibit a variety of plural markers in German; but it is not obvious that a pseudo-German with a uniform plural suffix for all underived nouns should be regarded as an impossible language. So, as an illustration of morphological behaviour which Lexical Phonology is supposedly right to exclude, Kiparsky's pseudo-English example is not altogether persuasive.

The framework of Lexical Phonology provokes a number of obvious questions. Are there any restrictions on the number of levels? What independent criteria determine whether a rule is lexical or postlexical? Are there any restrictions of either a formal or a substantive kind on the phenomena which can be handled at each level? Unfortunately, the tendency since 1982 has been towards less restrictive rather than more restrictive answers to these questions, so an already powerful mechanism is tending to become even more powerful. Halle and Mohanan (1985) and Mohanan (1986) retain a version of the Strict Cyclicity Principle but allow lexical levels to be either cyclic or noncyclic, and the principle of level-ordering is compromised by a 'loop' option, whereby the output of one level can feed back to the immediately preceding level. In Kiparsky's own more recent work (1985), the last level is permitted to be noncyclic (or escape the Elsewhere Condition), so that, for example, words like *damn* and *hymn* may be analysed as containing an underlying final /n/ (cf. *damnation*, *hymnal*) which can be deleted even in a nonderived environment. Some of this excessive power seems to be due to reluctance to question the assumption, inherited from *SPE*, that the stems of pairs of related words like *hymn* and *hymnal* should always be derived from a single phonological source. Whereas NGP is perhaps over-ready to see morphological alternations as suppletive, Lexical Phonology is still determined to handle as many as possible phonologically. Yet abandoning this phonological bias would undermine Lexical Phonology's *raison d'être*. The challenge remains: to devise a model of morphophonology which is restrictive enough to make interesting, testable claims but not so restrictive that all partial regularities are swallowed up in the maw of suppletion.[18]

3.2 AUTOSEGMENTAL PHONOLOGY AND NONCONCATENATIVE MORPHOLOGY

Since the mid-1970s, phonological theory has moved away from the *SPE* preoccupation with morphological alternations. Morphological issues have therefore largely disappeared from phonological debates, except within Lexical Phonology. The exception to this general picture has been the development of methods of handling certain **nonconcatenative** or nonaffixal morphological processes through the mechanisms of **autosegmental phonology**. We will summarise first the aspects of autosegmental phonology which are most relevant to its morphological applications.[19]

In *SPE* phonology, a phonological representation consists of a single string of segments and nonsegments (boundaries), hierarchically organised through labelled bracketing. A segment is a matrix of universally defined phonological features (syllabic, consonantal, anterior, high, etc.), each with a value (plus or minus). The fundamental innovation of autosegmental phonology – an innovation within the generative tradition, but not within twentieth-century phonology as a whole – was the splitting up of the single string into several strings, or **tiers**, in parallel. Each tier is a string of segments which are to some degree autonomous (hence the term **autosegment**); they are autonomous in the sense that there is not necessarily a one-to-one correspondence between the segments on one tier and the segments on another. However, every tier in a phonological representation is **associated** with at least one other tier, and a large part of autosegmental theory is devoted to distinguishing the universal from the language-particular aspects of this association.

The original motivation for autosegmental analyses was the behaviour of tone in a variety of languages, particularly African and American. Superficially, a language may have, say, a high tone, a low tone, a rising tone and a falling tone; but we may find that the rising tone occurs only in contexts where there are independent grounds to analyse it as a succession of a low and a high tone, and the falling tone may similarly be best analysed as a succession of a high tone and a low tone. In addition, one may find that a particular stem or affix is always associated with some tone, but that this tone is displaced, manifesting itself phonetically elsewhere (usually later) in the word. Phenomena of this kind suggested that in many languages a tonal tier, containing segments such as H (High) and L (Low), needed to be distinguished from a (confusingly named)

melody tier on which 'ordinary' segments were located. Later, other phonological phenomena, such as vowel harmony and prenasalisation of consonants, came to be handled by hiving off appropriate features (e.g. [±back] or [±nasal]) from the melody tier and locating them on tiers of their own. This kind of analysis could ultimately denude the melody tier of virtually all its substantive content, leaving it as a **skeletal tier** of segments identified at most as C (consonant) or V (vowel); these segments act like a string of vertebrae to which the phonological flesh of the other tiers is attached according to the principles of association.

In a language where words or stems must conform to one of a small repertoire of permissible shapes or **CV-templates**, the skeletal tier provides a convenient way of representing the template to which a given word conforms. This usefulness is reinforced if some lexical items conform to different CV-templates according to context. In New Zealand Maori, as (17) illustrates, there are a few nouns which express plural by lengthening the vowel of the first syllable:

(17) Singular   *tangata*   'person'
                    wahine   'woman'
                    matua   'parent'
     Plural   *taangata*   'people'
                    waahine   'women'
                    maatua   'parents'

In an autosegmental framework, one might represent this difference by assigning to the singular and plural forms phonological representations which are identical except in the skeletal tier. For example, *wahine* and *waahine* might be differentiated as in (18):

(18)

The length of the first vowel in *waahine* is represented in (18b) by the association of *a* with not one but two V slots on the skeletal tier. The orthographic symbols should be read as abbreviations for bundles of features excluding [±syllabic]. Whether or not all these features would be assigned to a single tier in a full autosegmental analysis of Maori is irrelevant for present purposes. What is important is that the contrast between the two CV-templates on the skeletal tier in (18a) and (18b) is not merely phonological but morphosyntactic. In a word-form such as English *cats*, there is no obvious reason to assign the affixal (or concatenative) representation of plural, the suffix /s/, to a different tier from the representation of the lexical item /kæt/. By contrast, in the Maori word-form *waahine*, the nonaffixal (nonconcatenative) representation of plural can plausibly be assigned to a different tier from the lexical content. So, although the autosegmental framework was originally proposed for reasons substantially independent of morphology, it seems to lead us in this simple Maori example towards an analysis where different 'morphemes' (meaning 'woman' and 'plural') are represented on different autosegmental tiers. Is this true of all nonconcatenative morphology? And, if it is, to what extent is nonconcatenative morphology constrained in interesting ways by the autosegmental framework?

To these two questions, the most positive answers one could give are 'yes' and 'to a considerable extent'. Such are the answers which emerge from the work of John J. McCarthy (1981; 1982), the pioneer of autosegmental morphology. The focus of the discussion here will be on how far such positive answers are justified.

The first nonconcatenative morphological material to be analysed autosegmentally was in Classical Arabic (McCarthy 1981), where, as is well known, the lexical content of most words is contained in a three-consonant or four-consonant 'root', while the vowels, along with various affixes and infixes, yield derivatives and inflected word-forms. To be more precise, the various forms related to a given verbal root are grouped into up to fifteen so-called 'conjugations' (or, in Hebrew, 'binyanim'), each associated with a given CV-template and possibly an affix or infix, while the vowels which occupy the V-positions signal distinctions of a mainly 'inflectional' kind, such as aspect and voice. The first three conjugations differ just in their CV-templates, which we illustrate in (19) in conjunction with the triconsonantal root *ktb* 'write' and the vowel melody *-a-a-*, which may be glossed 'Perfective Active':

(19)	Conjugation	*Ktb* form	Template
	I	katab	CVCVC
	II (Causative)	kattab	CVCCVC
	III (Reciprocal)	kaatab	CVVCVC

One can think of each of these forms as combining three 'morphemes': the lexical root, the conjugation and the Aspect-Voice inflection. McCarthy proposes that we should assign each morpheme to a distinct tier, as in (20):

(20)

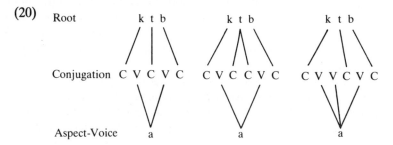

Just as in (18), the multiple association lines linking the skeletal tier with *t* in Conjugation II and with *a* in all three conjugations illustrate the autonomy of the tiers – a central feature of the autosegmental framework in both phonological and morphological applications. But are there any kinds of association which the framework excludes in principle? If there are, then the framework can be used not merely to describe these Arabic forms but to explain them, in the sense that it will incorporate claims about conceivable relationships between CV-templates and the other tiers which can never occur. The nonexistence of certain conceivable conjugations will therefore be a universally motivated, not a language-particular matter.

Attempts to establish universal well-formedness conditions for tier association have not been as successful as the earliest workers in autosegmental phonology had hoped. One requirement that has been consistently maintained, however, is that association lines must not cross. Applied to the Arabic material, this requirement predicts that there cannot be hypothetical conjugations yielding forms such as **kabat* or **batak*; for the association between the CV-template and the root tier would involve crossed lines, as in (21):

(21)

And this prediction seems correct; for, in all the Arabic conjugations, the relative order of the consonants in a given root remains the same.

McCarthy is not claiming here that metathesis of root segments can never occur as a synchronic phenomenon (such a claim would certainly be too strong), but only that a consistent pattern of reordering of root segments, irrespective of their phonetic content, cannot be the morphological expression of any derivational or inflectional relationship (or of any 'morpheme').[20] If corresponding predictions turn out to be correct in all languages, then the autosegmental framework has contributed valuably to our understanding of morphology.

Unfortunately, this prediction is not as strong as it seems at first. This is because of the mechanism which the autosegmental framework provides to handle reduplication.[21] In Classical Arabic, the (relatively rare) biconsonantal roots are reduplicated in the Perfective Active, so to the root *zl* 'shake' there corresponds a form *zalzal* 'shook'. McCarthy (1982: 193) handles this by simply reduplicating the 'morphemic template' or root tier:

(22)

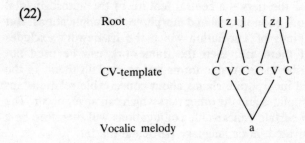

Here there is enough room in the CV-template to accommodate all the consonants of the reduplicated root. Sometimes, however, this is not so. The language Temiar, spoken on the Malay Peninsula, has a 'Continuative Active' template with four consonantal positions: CCCVC. Some Temiar verb roots (e.g. *kow* 'call') have only two consonants in the root, and fitting these to the Continuative Active template, with reduplication, is straightforward (McCarthy 1982: 211):[22]

(23)

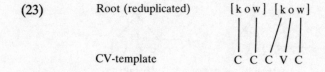

The first *o* automatically fails to get associated to the CV-template because there is no V position for it, so that the Continuative Active form of *kow* emerges from tier association as *kwkow*. (Initial consonantal clusters are broken up by epenthesis processes which need not concern us here.) But what happens with a three-consonant root like *slog* 'lie down'? Its Continuative Active form is *sglog*. This is handled by McCarthy as in (24):

(24)

Root (reduplicated)

CV-template

The detailed rationale for all the associations in (24) does not matter here. What matters is that the associations are not all derivable from universal principles. In particular, the association between the second C-position of the template and the last consonant of the first copy of the root must be stipulated for Temiar. Unfortunately, however, with language-particular stipulation of this kind, it is possible to construct CV-templates for Arabic which would yield hypothetical 'conjugations' like **kabat* and **batak* – just what the ban on crossing association lines was claimed to prevent. Example (25) illustrates how this would work:

(25)

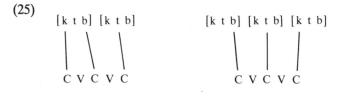

Since the framework allows us both to copy morphemes on the root tier and stipulate which segments on that tier are associated with which C-positions on the CV-tier, the effect of the ban on line-crossing is subverted, and the framework's purported explanation for the nonexistence of conjugations of the **kabat* and **batak* types vanishes. McCarthy might argue that the amount of language-particular stipulation needed in the representations at (25) will render them excessively 'costly' and therefore unlikely to occur in actual languages; but, until such an argument is presented, the predictive force for morphology of the framework's constraints on association remains weak.

A second weakness in autosegmental morphology follows from McCarthy's answer to the question of how we decide how many morphological tiers there should be and what material belongs on each. In (22), (23) and (24) we placed the two copies of the root morpheme on the same tier, one after the other. That fits the way in which phonological features are generally handled in autosegmental phonology; each feature generally appears consistently on just one tier. (After all, we would not expect a high-tone feature H, for example, to appear sometimes on the tonal tier and sometimes on the segmental melody tier or the skeletal tier.) By analogy, one might expect all morphemes with substantive consonantal content (i.e. not just C or [−syllabic]) to share the root tier in Arabic. But infixation will then pose a problem. Conjugation VIII of the Classical Arabic verb has a four-consonant template CCVCVC, but the second C-position is always occupied by *t*: *ktatab*. (This *t* is constant, whatever the root, so has nothing to do with the second root consonant in *ktb*.) Yet, if we place this *t* on the root tier, we are faced with two unattractive alternatives. The *t* may interrupt the root on the root tier itself, 'before' as well as 'after' association with the CV-template for Conjugation VIII; but that interruption would seemingly require a kind of root-tier metathesis (*t+ktb→kttb*) which could also legitimise hypothetical conjugations like **kbt* and **btk*, discussed above. Alternatively, we may prefix *t* to *ktb* on the root tier, but associate the tiers as in (26):

(26)

$$[t]\ [k\ t\ b]$$

C C VCCC

But that of course involves line-crossing, the worst autosegmental offence. McCarthy's solution is to place the infixed *t* on a tier of its own; it can then associate with the second C-position in the template without crossing any of the lines from the root tier, because its association line and the root-tier lines will be on different planes, so to speak. Representing this requires a three-dimensional model, not a two-dimensional diagram, so (27) should be visualised as a picture of such a model:

(27)

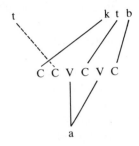

Positing this extra tier may seem like an awkward necessity to deal with an uncomfortable predicament. But McCarthy makes a virtue out of the necessity; the need to provide a separate tier for the infixed *t* is seen as vindicating a framework in which morphemes may occupy separate tiers. Indeed, the label **Morphemic Tier Hypothesis** has come to be applied to the claim that, in nonconcatenative morphology, distinct morphemes not merely may but must occupy separate tiers (Pulleyblank 1988: 353–4; Goldsmith 1990: 102, 313–18). So, if we assume that the infixed *t* of the Conjugation VIII form *ktatab* is a morpheme (whether or not this is a straightforward assumption depends on how 'morpheme' is defined), then the analysis in (27) is the only one possible within the autosegmental framework. This looks like a desirable narrowing of the analytic options, which should have positive empirical implications; and McCarthy (1981: 405–7) is indeed keen to emphasise that his formalism has a lower 'generative capacity' than that of *SPE*.

Appearances are deceptive, however, because any multi-tier frame-work of morphological description is intrinsically more powerful in some respects, and thereby empirically less restrictive, than a single-tier framework, and the Morphemic Tier Hypothesis exacerbates this drawback. To see this, consider the formation of English compounds such as *lapdog, pop-song, mailbox*. At first sight, there is little to say about how these compounds are formed; the words concerned are simply concatenated and a particular stress pattern is superimposed. But, with the Morphemic Tier Hypothesis, this is by no means the only option available for compound formation. Let us imagine a pseudo-English in which the two elements of a compound are hooked together, so to speak, by placing the last consonant of the first element after the first consonant or consonant-cluster of the second. Compounding *lap* and *dog* on pseudo-English will yield not *lapdog* but *ladpog*; *pop* and *song* will yield *pospong*; and *mail* and *box* will yield *maiblox*. Most linguists would probably agree that this sort of compound formation is bizarrely unnatural and that morphological theory should exclude it. Yet, if our morphological theory incorporates the Morphemic Tier Hypothesis, this bizarre type of compounding is easy to accommodate. All we need do is assign the two elements of each compound to separate tiers, and link both to a CV-template by rules which include the stipulation that the last consonant of the first element of a compound must be associated with a C-position which immediately precedes a V-position. The compound formed from *lap* and *dog* will then be represented as in (28):

(28)

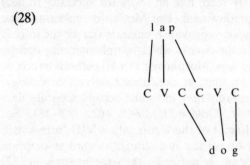

The Morphemic Tier Hypothesis originated from the need to allow the intercalation of consonantal as well as vocalic material among the root segments in some Arabic verb conjugations. But, as currently formulated, it permits much more than that – unfortunately, too much.

Although our discussion of autosegmental morphology has been critical, we must acknowledge its great merit in bringing relatively neglected nonaffixal morphological behaviour into the mainstream of theoretical debate. The fact that major questions remain after only ten years' work by a small group of scholars is hardly surprising. Besides, neither of the main weaknesses that we have focused on is necessarily fatal. We have already hinted at ways of more effectively discouraging evasions of the line-crossing ban, as in (25). And one obstacle to bizarre compounding mechanisms such as in (28) might be a better criterion for distinguishing concatenative from nonconcatenative morphological behaviour. One might perhaps argue that, because English compounds do not crucially observe any constraints on CV structure, there is no morphological ground for linking the elements of compounds to a CV-template and so no scope for using the template to hook the elements together in the fashion that we envisaged. (This argument would still leave 'hooked' compounds as an unwelcome theoretical possibility in any language where CV-structure constraints on compounds did exist.) Alternatively, one might modify the Morphemic Tier Hypothesis so as to assign to separate tiers not all distinct morphemes but only morphemes of different 'types', in some sense – perhaps lexical and nonlexical, or inflectional and noninflectional. McCarthy himself hints at this possibility (1981: 383): 'each language has the option of restricting every tier to autosegments which are members of a particular morpheme *or morpheme class*' (my emphasis). Under the Hypothesis, so modified, the infixed *t* of *ktatab* would belong on a different tier from the root *ktb* in Arabic, but the two lexical words *lap* and *dog* would necessarily belong to the same tier, so that a hypothetical compound **ladpog* would be blocked straightforwardly by the ban on line-crossing. There are evidently various avenues to explore here.

4 Morphology and syntax

4.1 INTRODUCTION

In chapter 2 we looked at the generative semantic view of the relationship between syntax and the lexicon, according to which lexical items were derived by syntactic transformations operating on phrase markers some or all of whose terminal elements could be semantic features or components. But Chomsky's (1970) criticism of this approach to derived nominals such as *arrival* and *destruction* was so influential that the possibility of any syntactic role in the formation of most complex words was discounted by 'mainstream' generative morphologists for around fifteen years. During that time, all derivational morphology, and generally also inflectional morphology and compounding, were seen as being 'in the lexicon', insulated from direct syntactic interference. This view is encapsulated in a hypothesis which has acquired various titles (Generalised Lexical Hypothesis, Strong Lexicalist Hypothesis or **Lexical Integrity Hypothesis**) and been formulated in various versions over the years; but the essence of all versions is that syntax is blind to the internal structure and composition of words and cannot affect it (except in the sense in which syntax necessarily affects inflectional morphology).[1]

The Lexical Integrity Hypothesis is born of a concern with two questions which are in principle distinct: (a) what is the relationship between morphology (or word-structure) and syntax? and (b) what is the relationship between morphology and the lexicon? The Hypothesis in its strictest form (perhaps never seriously entertained by anyone) answers these two questions like this: (a) despite a partially shared vocabulary (terms such as 'noun' and 'verb'), morphology and syntax obey quite different principles; (b) morphology is handled entirely within the lexicon (by means of Aronovian word-formation rules, Jackendovian redundancy rules, Lieberian tree structures, or whatever). But there is no necessary connection between these two answers. As we saw in chapter 2, scholars in the lexicalist tradition came to recognise not only lexically listed items which are not words (morphemes as well as some phrases and clauses, according to Di Sciullo and Williams) but also words which are not lexically listed (such as words formed by fully productive WFRs, according to Aronoff). If we analyse expressions such as *law degree* and *language requirement* as compound words, then the extreme productivity of at any rate this area of word formation in English compels us to recognise the existence of an indefinite number of words which are not lexically listed, simply because, so far as competence is concerned, there appears to be no upper limit on the length of an English word (*law degree language requirement; law degree language requirement change; law degree language requirement change decision*; and so on). These considerations make for rejection of the strong lexicalist answer to question (b). This by itself entails no radical departure from Chomsky's position in *Aspects* or 'Remarks on nominalization'. As we saw in chapter 2, Chomsky acknowleged that the spheres of morphology and the lexicon were not coterminous, because of the existence of nonword lexical items such as phrasal verbs (*give up, take off*) and idioms. But generative morphologists have also tended increasingly to reject the strong lexicalist answer to question (a) also; that is they have increasingly come to regard the domains of morphology and syntax as overlapping, perhaps even indistinguishable. This may sound like a reversion to the generative semantic approach to word formation; but the fundamental changes in mainstream generative syntax since the late 1960s ensure that is far from the case.

We will list the factors which have led to the new morphosyntactic reconvergence before examining some of them more closely in the following sections:

(1) The existence of extremely productive phenomena traditionally regarded as on the borderline between syntax and morphology, especially secondary, verbal-nexus or **synthetic compounds** in which the first (nominal) component is in a quasi-syntactic relationship (usually that of direct object) to a verbal element in the second component (e.g. *meat eating, road sweeper, slum clearance*).

(2) The problem of **clitics** – bound forms which are phonologically part of an adjoining word but which behave grammatically more like independent words than like affixes, such as *-'s* in *the man next door's car* and *-'ll* in *We'll go*.

(3) Mismatches between between semantic and phonological-

morphological structure of the kind which have come to be called **bracketing paradoxes** (e.g. *nuclear physicist*, whose meaning suggests a bracketing [[nuclear physic]ist] but whose grammatical structure implies [nuclear [physic-ist]]).

(4) Parallels between the order of affixes corresponding to syntactic phenomena such as causative, reflexive and passive, on the one hand, and the 'order', or nesting, of the syntactic processes themselves: Baker's (1985) **Mirror Principle**.

(5) Increased interest on the part of linguistic theorists in polysynthetic or incorporating languages such as Eskimo.

(6) Radical changes in Chomskyan syntactic theory since 1970, with a new framework (Government-Binding or Principles-and-Parameters) incorporating new levels of representation (D-structure, S-structure, Phonological Form and Logical Form) and new ways of relating these levels, the role of syntactic transformations being sharply reduced in favour of a variety of interacting subtheories and principles.

Of these factors, the one whose relevance to the syntax-morphology issue is perhaps least obvious at first sight is (3) – the bracketing paradox. At the same time, it is the one which seems to point towards the most radical reassessment of the relationship between morphology, syntax and semantics. We will therefore devote a section to it first.

4.2 BRACKETING PARADOXES AND THEIR IMPLICATIONS

In chapter 2, we encountered a variety of attitudes to the relationship between the meaning of a complex (derived or compound) word and its composition, from the point of view of lexical listing. Despite their differences, these attitudes share the presupposition that at least for some complex words one can identify an 'expected' meaning, derivable from its composition, from which the actual meaning may or may not deviate. When a complex word has only two components, any such deviation from the expected meaning must be independent of structure, because there is only one way to bracket a string of two items. But where a complex word or phrase has more than two ultimate components, the possibility exists that the difference between expected and actual meanings may involve structure; that is, the bracketing suggested by the meaning of the whole complex differs from the bracketing suggested by its grammatical structure (where 'grammatical' means 'phonological, morphological, syntactic or some combination of these').

Perhaps the first linguist in the Chomskyan tradition to notice conflicts between semantic and grammatical criteria in the determination of word-internal structure was Pesetsky, in 'Russian morphology and lexical theory' (1979). For reasons to do with certain high vowels (traditionally known as 'yers') posited in underlying phonological representations for Russian verb-forms, certain cyclic phonological rules must apply to the complex consisting of the stem plus the inflectional suffix(es) before the prefix (if any) comes into consideration. This implies a bracketing [prefix [stem suffix]]. On the other hand, the prefix's contribution to the meaning is often semantically unpredictable, suggesting that the complex consisting of the prefix plus the stem should be considered a distinct lexical item. This in turn suggests a bracketing [[prefix stem] suffix]. A comparable situation exists in English adjectives. The comparative suffix *-er* is, broadly speaking, restricted to bases which are monosyllabic or disyllabic with an unstressed second syllable (*riper, kinder, happier,* ?*pleasanter*; **immenser,* **repulsiver,* *frolickier). On the other hand, if an adjective has a suffixal comparative form, then any corresponding derived adjective with the prefix *un-* also has a suffixal comparative form, even though this derived adjective may be trisyllabic or end-stressed (*unriper, unkinder, unhappier*). The phonological constraint on the suffixation of comparative *-er* suggests that the suffix is added 'before' the prefix is, implying bracketings such as [un[kind-er]], [un[happi-er]]; on the other hand, since *unkinder* means 'more unkind' rather than 'not more kind', the bracketing which makes sense semantically is [[un-kind]er], [[un-happi]er]. A quite similar dilemma affects the analysis of phrasal collocations such as *nuclear physicist* and *transformational grammarian*; a *nuclear physicist* is someone who does nuclear physics, not a physicist who is nuclear.

The earliest reactions to these paradoxes fell into two categories: those which treat the grammatically motivated bracketing as definitive, and those which attempt to bring the *prima facie* grammatical bracketing into line with the semantic. In the first category belong Lieber (1981b) and Selkirk (1982), who argue that the paradoxes can be ignored for morphological purposes; the discrepancy between morphological structure and meaning will be taken care of elsewhere, by whatever component deals with lexical semantics. Williams (1981a) elaborates on this position by defining a new term 'lexically related' such that *nuclear physics* and *nuclear physicist* can be said to be lexically related even though the former is not a constituent of the latter in grammatical structure (see section 4.3.2 below). In the second category belong the 'Lexical Morphologists' Strauss (1982a; 1982b) and Kiparsky (1983). For them, the semantic bracketing of a word such as *ungrammaticality* or *vice-presidential* is anomalous from the level-ordering point of view; *un-* and *vice-* are Level 2 (stress-neutral) prefixes, so they should be able to appear only 'outside', not 'inside', Level 1 suffixes such as *-ity* and *-(i)al*. Strauss's solution is to relax the requirements of level-ordering so as to apply only to the ordering of affixes on the same side of the stem; the bracketing [[un+grammatical]ity], with *un-* 'inside' *-ity*, is thereby grammatically permissible as well as semantically appropriate. Kiparsky's solution involves reanalysis: $[[grammatical]_A ity]_N$ is produced on Level 1, and *un-* is prefixed to it on Level 2; but since the negative *un-* can attach (productively, at least) only to adjectives and not to nouns, $[un[[grammatical]_A ity]_N]$ has to be reanalysed (rebracketed) as $[[un[grammatical]_A]_A ity]_N$. However, this requires that on Level 2 we should be able to 'see' not only the noun-labelled brackets around *grammaticality* but also the adjective-labelled brackets around *grammatical*, in violation of the Bracketing Erasure Convention described in chapter 3. Kiparsky is therefore forced to concede the possibility that a word may be lexically marked as an exception to bracketing erasure – an otherwise unmotivated weakening of his theory.

Neither Strauss's proposal nor Kiparsky's involves any appeal to syntactic principles or movement rules, nor any radically new view of the relationship between syntactic and phonetic representations. These are the directions in which more recent proposals have gone. But, before considering them later in this chapter, we will examine a claim by Spencer (1988a) that a proper understanding of some bracketing paradoxes, at least, involves lexical semantics.[2] This claim, if correct, has far-reaching consequences. If a bracketing paradox is not to be resolved through manipulating its structure (whether syntactic, morphological, phonological or logical) or through relating representations at these various levels, then it cannot constitute evidence that grammatical theory needs to allow that kind of manipulation or interlevel relationship. So, given that (as we will see later in this chapter) bracketing paradoxes have indeed been cited in this way as evidence for quite far-reaching theoretical conclusions, Spencer's claim requires us to treat these conclusions with extreme caution.

Spencer concentrates on personal nominal expressions such as those listed on the right in (7), all bearing a consistent semantic relationship to the noun or phrase on the left: 'someone studying or expert in . . .' for (7a), and 'someone who comes from . . . .' for (7b):

(7) a. generative grammar   generative grammarian
         ancient history   ancient historian
         moral philosophy   moral philosopher
         chemical engineering   chemical engineer
         theoretical linguistics   theoretical linguist
         modern languages   modern linguist
         medieval China   medieval sinologist
         modern Spain   modern hispanist
         baroque flute   baroque flautist
         aerobic gymnastics   aerobic gymnast
     b. East Germany   East German
         the South Island   South Islander
         southern Denmark   southern Dane
         central London   central Londoner

These all involve meaning paradoxes of the by now familiar kind; clearly, for example, a moral philosopher is not a philosopher who is virtuous, but rather one who specialises in moral philosophy. A few of the examples might be accounted for by an analysis according to which the same morphological material is organised in different fashion at different levels of representation (whether Phonetic Form, Logical Form, D-structure or S-structure); thus, [[generative] [grammarian]] and [[generative grammar][ian]], or [[South] [Islander]] and [[South Island][er]]. But most cannot be so analysed without invoking radical and otherwise unmotivated allomorphy. For example, if we are to account for the meaning of *theoretical linguist* on the model of the analysis of *generative grammarian* just outlined, we must posit a representation at one level something like [[theoretical linguist+ics][ian]] and at another level [[theoretical linguist][ics+ian]], with a 'truncation rule' deleting [ics+ian]. Similarly, to account for the relationship between *moral philosophy* and *moral philosopher* on these lines involves an otherwise unmotivated rule converting [y+er] into *-er*.

Spencer argues that the way out of the problem involves lexical semantics, not structural manoeuvres. All the examples of (7a) involve a subject-matter or specialism; and the terms in the right-hand column, in satisfying the semantic pressure to provide a term for a person concerned with that specialism, do so regardless of their morphological or syntactic constituency. In (7b), similarly, there is a semantic pressure to provide a term for someone who lives in or comes from a certain place. Spencer further claims (1988a: 675) that 'paradoxes can only be formed from members of the permanent lexicon, where this includes lexicalised phrases'. This is why a theoretical linguist is concerned with linguistics whereas a modern linguist is concerned with languages; *linguist* is the personal noun corresponding to both *linguistics* and *language(s)* but only *theoretical linguistics* and *modern languages*, not *theoretical languages* or *modern linguistics*, are lexicalised or institutionalised phrases.

Spencer does not account for any bracketing paradoxes apart from personal terms; for example, he does not explain the unacceptability of forms such as **sheet metallic*, **symphony orchestrate*, **freak accidental*, which Kiparsky (1983) attributes to level-ordering. Furthermore, it is not clear that all the bracketing paradoxes in (7) are formed from lexicalised phrases, since it seems odd to claim that, for example, *medieval China* and *southern Denmark* are lexicalised. What Spencer does show, however, is the relevance of lexical semantic pressure in accounting for what some complex words or phrases, however formed, will mean.

Is such pressure relevant only to complex words, not simple (or monomorphemic) ones? It would be surprising if this were so, if (as Spencer suggests) it operates without regard to morphological structure. And, in fact, examples of precisely this kind of pressure affecting monomorphemic words can be seen in the set of terms for domestic animals which were discussed in section 2.7 and which are repeated here:

(8)	SPECIES		horse	pig	cow	sheep	dog
	ADULT:	MALE	stallion	hog	bull	ram	dog
		FEMALE	mare	sow	cow	ewe	bitch
	YOUNG		foal	shoat	calf	lamb	pup

Spencer's examples and the domestic-animal terms illustrate semantic matrices involving nouns (or nominal expressions). But other kinds of matrices are easy enough to construct. In English, there appears to be a quite strong semantic pressure to supply an adjective corresponding to the term for a public official, as *ministerial* corresponds to *minister*. This is the adjective which can replace the blank in a context such as 'The _____ limousine arrived promptly at noon.' A set of such terms is given below:

(9)	minister	ministerial
	prime minister	prime-ministerial
	president	presidential
	ambassador	ambassadorial

emperor	imperial
governor	gubernatorial
bishop	episcopal
king	royal
queen	royal
prince	royal
princess	royal
viceroy	vice-regal
governor-general	vice-regal

Although a nearly synonymous alternative expression with a possessive suffix is always available (*the minister's limousine* etc.), what is important to note is that, if an adjective is to be used in this context, these are the only adjectives available. *Royal* serves as the corresponding adjective for any royal personage; *regal*, *kingly*, *queenly* and *princely* are not appropriate in this context, since in a down-at-heel kingdom the royal limousines may be by no means regal or even princely. Most significantly, *vice-regal* doubles as the adjective for not only *viceroy* but also (in New Zealand and Australia) *governor-general*. In its latter capacity especially, *vice-regal* manifestly derives its meaning from its position in the matrix, not from its morphological make-up. It is beside the point, therefore, to worry about whether, and at which level, its structure is better represented as [[vice-reg][al]] than as [[vice-][regal]]. Alleging a mismatch between structure and meaning in examples such as (7) or in *vice-regal* involves fundamentally misunderstanding how the meaning of at least some complex words and phrases is determined.

It is not clear how many other types of bracketing paradox will respond to the same treatment or how many other superficially morphological problems may turn out to involve lexical semantics. But it is important to bear in mind, when evaluating claims emanating from syntactically oriented work on morphology, that this work has so far almost completely ignored the lexical-semantic dimension of linguistic organisation.

4.3 X-BAR SYNTAX IN MORPHOLOGY

4.3.1 Categories and projections

Chomsky's 'Remarks' emphasised the respects in which the structure of words and that of phrases and clauses differ from one another. Selkirk, in *The Syntax of Words* (1982), encouraged a new focus of attention on the respects in which they resemble one another. On the degree of resemblance, she is cautious, and she explicitly retains a distinction between morphology (or **W-syntax**) and syntax proper (or **S-syntax**): 'the category Word lies at the interface . . . of two varieties of structure, which must be defined by two discrete sets of principles in the grammar' (1982: 2). She also maintains a version of the Lexical Integrity Hypothesis: 'no deletion or movement transformation may involve categories of both W-structure and S-structure' (1982: 70). On the other hand, she sets out to show that 'word structure has the same general formal properties as syntactic structure and, moreover, that it is generated by the same sort of rule system' (1982: 2). Furthermore, although she remains outwardly loyal to lexicalism by locating the rules of word structure in the lexicon (or lexical component), nothing for her hinges on this decision, and she admits that it is not clear to her what difference it makes where these rules are located in the grammar.

Selkirk's W-syntactic rules resemble S-syntactic rules in two main respects: both are context-free rewriting rules, and both make use of the major categories N, V, A and P. In Chomskyan theory since the early 1970s, S-syntactic rules have projected these categories above the basic level of the word, these projections being distinguished from the word level by 'bars' or 'primes' (X', X'' and so on), up to the level of the **maximal projection**; for nouns, this means that the traditional noun phrase is equivalent to N'' ('N-double-bar'), N''' or possibly even N''''.[3] Selkirk's innovation is to extend this hierarchy of projections for English below the level of the **Word** (which she symbolises X^0, the initial capital highlighting her technical X-bar-theoretic usage) to a level which she calls **Root** (symbolised X^{-1}). A noun Root will be symbolised N^{-1}, an adjective Word A^0, and so on. And, just as according to usual assumptions of X-bar S-syntax any projection X^n must contain a projection one degree lower (X^{n-1}), so according to Selkirk any Word must contain a Root. At this point, however, the principles of S-syntax and of W-syntax begin to diverge.

Let us consider the form of the rewriting rules which Selkirk proposes for English W-syntax (1982: 95, 99) and some of the factual claims which follow from them:

(10)   Word→Word Word
(11)   Word→Word Affix
(12)   Word→Affix Word
(13)   Word→Root

(14) Root→Root Root
(15) Root→Root Affix
(16) Root→Affix Root

Affixes do not belong to any level in the X-bar hierarchy and have no counterpart in S-syntax; the verb-forming suffix *-ise*, for example, is not a V^0 or a V^{-1} but a V^{af}. In this way, it is possible to distinguish between affixes and bound Roots, and between affixally derived verbs, for example, and compound verbs – a desirable distinction, since the former are common in English (formed with the suffixes *-ise*, *-ify*, *-ate*) whereas the latter are rare. (This distinction is not so easily expressed in Lieber's framework, as Selkirk points out.) Rule (10) licenses compounds, which are considered to be at the same X-bar level as simplex words. Selkirk's claim that compounds are Words entails the prediction that affixes which can attach to Words can also attach to compounds. In this respect, Selkirk's framework differs from that of Allen (1979), whose version of level-ordering places all derivational affixation 'before' compounding. Selkirk argues that her own prediction is correct, citing compounds with 'later' affixation such as *pickpockethood*, *un-self-sufficient*, *non-weather-related*, *misbackdate*. Rules (10)–(13) do not, however, allow Words to contain items above the Word level in the X-bar hierarchy; equally, (14)–(16) do not allow Roots to contain Words. These predictions about English follow from a universal principle of W-syntax to the effect that 'a category may not be rewritten in terms of another category . . . higher in the [X-bar] hierarchy' (1982: 8). Selkirk thus espouses what has been called the **No Phrase Constraint**: 'Morphologically complex words cannot be formed on the basis of syntactic phrases' (Botha 1981).[4] Examples such as *ne'er-do-well* and *will-o'-the-wisp*, which seem to contradict the Constraint, are deemed 'not representative of general processes of word formation' (1982: 8).

The No Phrase Constraint highlights a clear difference between W-syntax and S-syntax. In S-syntax it is certainly possible, indeed usual, for a constituent to contain a constituent of the same level or higher in the X-bar hierarchy. For example, according to a standard Chomskyan analysis, *expert on the ozone layer* is a N′ (a projection of N intermediate between a N‴, such as *this expert on the ozone layer*, and a N^0, such as *expert*), yet it contains a P‴ (or prepositional phrase) *on the ozone layer* which in turn contains a N‴ *the ozone layer*. Whether one agrees with Selkirk will depend on one's attitude to expressions like *Monday-morning-ish, do-it-yourself shop*; can they safely be dismissed as marginal? And even if the No Phrase Constraint is correct for

English, Selkirk's claim of universality necessitates investigation of its correctness for other languages.

Selkirk's distinction between Roots and Words serves the same purpose as the Siegel-Allen distinction between Class I and Class II derivational affixes, discussed in chapter 3. Class I derivational affixes are analysed by Selkirk as Root affixes (subcategorised to appear as sisters to Roots, or a subset of them) while Class II ones are Word affixes (subcategorised as sisters to Words). The noun-forming suffix *-ity*, for example, attaches only to certain Roots, so the structure of the Word *scarcity* is as in (17a); the suffix *-ness*, on the other hand, attaches only to Words, so the structure of the Word *scarceness* is as in (17b):

(17)

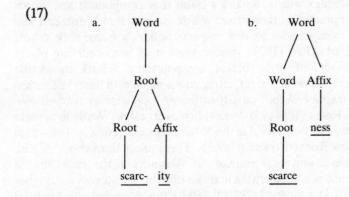

It is important to note that the distinction between Words and Roots has nothing to do with the distinction between bound and free forms. Tentatively, Selkirk proposes a Root-compounding rule (14) to take care of words such as *erythro-cyte* and *intra-mur(-al)*, where the components are certainly bound; but, as the treatment of *scarce* in (17) suggests, all major-category morphemes have a Root projection, even ones which can occur as free forms.

This provokes the question whether Words as well as Roots can be bound. Selkirk does not discuss this issue directly, but her analysis of inflectional affixes as typically attaching to Words and her view of the stem *brok-* in *broken* as a Word (1982: 81) suggest that, in inflected word-forms with special stem allomorphs such as *wives, knelt* and *ridden*, the bound elements *wive-, knel-* and *ridd-* are indeed Words. If so, Selkirk's Words do not have the free-form status ascribed to 'words' by traditional definitions, such as Bloomfield's. Moreover, within S-syntax, the Word level will be the only level in the X-bar hierarchy at which a constituent cannot always by itself head a constituent of the next higher level (namely X'); that is, for example, the N^0 *wives* can head a N' (*wives of the teachers*), but the N^0 *wive-* cannot (**wive- of the teachers*). One alternative might be simply to analyse *wives* as [[wife][s]] in W-syntax, relegating the stem allomorphy to the PF (Phonological Form) component; but Selkirk implicitly rejects such a treatment of nonsuffixed plural forms such as *mice* and *women*, so the familiar question would arise of where to draw the line between 'phonological' and 'nonphonological' alternations. Selkirk avoids such issues by ignoring not only the pervasive nonconcatenative morphology of the Semitic languages (1982: 2) but also most of the kinds of allomorphy that do occur in English.

Siegel and Allen's claim about affix ordering – that a Class II affix can never appear 'inside' a Class I affix – follows in Selkirk's framework from the principle that, within W-syntax, no constituent can contain a constituent of a higher X-bar level. A Class II affix 'inside' a Class I one implies a Word inside a Root, violating this principle. It is therefore as important for Selkirk as it is for Siegel and Allen to demonstrate that such a thing never happens. What about instances where an apparent Word affix such as *-able* or *-ise* (*standardise, reroutable*) appears 'inside' a Root affix (*standardisation, reroutability*)? In her answer, Selkirk points out (1982: 100–6) that *-ise* and *-able* seem to occur sometimes as Root affixes, affecting stress and triggering 'latinate' alternations (e.g. *catholi*[s]*ise, indefen*[s]*ible*); consequently, *standardise* and *reroutable* are open to 'reanalysis' as Roots, and can then be subject to further Root affixation. But, quite apart from the problem of determining where and when such reanalysis can occur, this sort of argument is only as strong as the independent evidence for that dual status of the affix concerned; so a vital task for the Selkirkian W-syntactician must be to check that the appropriate evidence is always available.

One superficially attractive way of handling forms such as *wives* and *knelt* within W-syntax might be to analyse *-s* and *-t* as suffixes which may attach to (or be subcategorised for) Roots but which inherently form Words. This permits us to avoid classifying *wive-* and *knel-* as bound Words. These suffixes would then have to be introducible by a rule such as (18):

(18)   Word→Root Affix

The prefixal counterpart to (18) will of course be (19):

(19)   Word→Affix Root

But (18) and (19) are not among the rules (10)–(16); the only connection between the Root and Word levels is by rule (13) (Word→Root), and Selkirk comments that 'there seems to be no need to posit such rules [as (18) and (19)] in characterizing possible word structures of English' (1982: 95). What sort of behaviour would constitute evidence for such a need? This is another way of asking how (if at all) English is constrained by the absence of such rules. The implicit claim is that there are no Root affixes which intrinsically close off the possibility of further Root affixation; for, if Root affixes can be introduced only by rules (15) and (16), then the existence of a Root affix to which no other Root affix can be added has to be a mere accidental consequence of affixal selection restrictions, not a necessary consequence of the framework or of the grammar. So (setting aside problematic inflected forms such as *wives* and *knelt*) do we find any Root affixes which block further Root affixation? Answering this question involves examining the combinatory possibilities of all Root, or Class I, affixes (of which Selkirk gives a subset on pages 80–1). Certainly, many seem to tolerate further Root affixation, as shown by words such as *glor-ific-ation*, *calam-it-ous*, *curi-os-ity*, *nation-al-ist-ic*, *empir-ic-ist*, *milit-ar-ism*, *inflat-ion-ary*. On the other hand, a few affixes which Selkirk assigns to the Root class do not tolerate it, e.g. *-y* (*decency*), *-th* (*width*), *-a* (*Canadiana*), *-ette* (*suffragette*), *-esque* (*picturesque*) (*picturesqueness* is of course not a counterexample, because *-ness* is a Word affix). Whether these constitute sufficient evidence to warrant incorporating rule (18) into English W-syntax is unclear.

From the point of view of the phenomena which it seeks to explain and the explanations it offers, Selkirk's W-syntax may not appear very different from the level-ordered models discussed in chapter 3, inspired ultimately by *SPE*. What is new in her approach is the emphasis on exploring the extent and nature of the resemblances between word structure and sentence structure. The picture which emerges is inconclusive. The differences between S-syntax and W-syntax in English seem at least as striking as the parallels. Nevertheless, the idea of extending the X-bar hierarchy below the word level, and the associated notation 'X^0' and 'X^{-1}', have won widespread acceptance. More importantly, in raising questions which loyalty to lexicalism had seemed to preclude, Selkirk smoothed the way for more radical departures a few years later.

4.3.2 Heads

In syntax, the term **head** has traditionally been given to that part of any constituent whose own distributional possibilities mimic most closely those of the constituent as a whole, and which can be seen as determining the category to which the constituent belongs. Thus, for example, the phrases *sour milk, that sour milk* and *all that revolting sour milk which I've just poured down the sink* have more or less the same distributional possibilities as the noun *milk* which they all contain; they are all therefore traditionally classified as noun phrases, with *milk* as their head.[5] In morphology, the term is traditionally applied to compounds in a fashion which combines distributional and semantic criteria.[6] *Blackbird* is a noun, just as *bird* is, and a blackbird is a kind of bird; consequently, *blackbird* has *bird* as its head. Compounds with heads are called **endocentric**, by contrast with **exocentric** or (to use the Sanskrit term) **bahuvrihi** compounds such as *pickpocket* or *forget-me-not*. Although *pickpocket* is a noun, just like its right-hand member *pocket, pocket* is not the head of *pickpocket* because a pickpocket is not a (kind of) pocket. And *forget-me-not* is exocentric because its status as a noun is not in any sense derivable from its internal structure, which is that of a verb phrase.

In X-bar syntax, a constituent at any bar-level contains a constituent at the next lower level in the hierarchy, in virtue of the fact that all phrase-structure rules must conform to the schema in (20):

(20) $X^n \rightarrow \ldots X^{n-1} \ldots$

Jackendoff adds (1977: 30): 'The *head* of a phrase of category X^n can be defined in two different ways, either as the X^{n-1} that it dominates or as the lexical category X at the bottom of the entire configuration. . . . Both reflect traditional usages of the term.' Thus, the head of the phrase *our declaration of intent* could be regarded (under a standard analysis) as either the N' *declaration of intent* or the N *declaration*. But what happens when we extend the X-bar hierarchy down into the word *declaration*? Traditionally, since this is a derived word and not a compound, it would not be regarded as having a head at all. But, since X-bar syntax seems to accommodate the traditional notion of head so readily, one expects some natural application of it to be found below, as well as above, the X^0 level in the hierarchy. Unfortunately, this expectation is not fulfilled in any straightforward way. Inspection of the W-syntactic rules (10)–(16) shows that Jackendoff's schema (20) cannot apply generally to W-syntax, since only one of these rules (namely (13)) conforms to it. Our example *declaration*, though a N^0, contains no element N^{-1}, as (20) would seem to require; instead, its structure in Selkirkian terms is $[V^{-1} Af]_N$, where its status as a noun clearly derives from the Affix *-ation* rather than the Root *declar-*. We are confronted with a dilemma. The framework of X-bar theory leads us to expect to find a use for the term 'head' within words as well as phrases, yet the S-syntactic criterion for headhood that X-bar theory provides is of no use in at least some derived words. Should we acknowledge a further difference between S-syntax and W-syntax, namely the characteristic that phrases always have heads but words do not, or should we devise new criteria for headhood within words such that one part of the noun *declaration* (whether the Root or the Affix) shall be deemed its head? The question has not been posed explicitly in these terms, but in practice the second answer has generally been preferred, for reasons which have largely to do with bracketing paradoxes.

As we saw in chapter 2, Lieber's account of how derived words acquire their categorial status involves a notion of feature percolation, whereby the category of a complex word-form is determined in general by the outermost affix; thus, for instance, the category N (interpreted as a combination of feature values) percolates from the suffix *-ation* to the node dominating the whole word *declaration*. One can, if one wishes, call this category-determining affix the 'head' of the word. Williams (1981a) chooses to do so. He observes that the category of derived words is determined much more often by a suffix than by a prefix, and also that in endocentric compounds the head (in traditional terms) is on the right (as in *off-white, greenhouse, bar-tend*). On this basis, he proposes a **Right-Hand Head Rule** for English: any constituent which is on the right-hand edge of a word is a head, so that in *re-education* (which Williams brackets [re[educat+ion]]) both *education* and *-ion* are heads. The Right-Hand Head Rule has exceptions, however; verbs such as *ennoble, enrich, enlarge, entitle* illustrate the systematic formation of verbs from adjectives and nouns by means of a prefix *en-*, so *en-* must be lexically marked as a head, allowing its category V to determine the category of the word as a whole.

What advantages does such an analysis have over an analysis such as Lieber's, which handles the category status of complex words without any direct appeal to the notion 'head'? Williams claims that the percolation of features through heads, as he defines them, makes possible the formulation of a morphological constraint which he calls the **Atom Condition**: 'A restriction on the attachment of af_x to Y can only refer to features realized on Y' (1981a: 253). For example, the fact that the root *-duct* is [+latinate] ensures that the whole word *conduct*, of which *-duct* is the head, is [+latinate] and can therefore have attached to it the suffix *-ion*, which attaches only to [+latinate] bases. This condition is similar though not identical in effect to the Siegel-Allen Adjacency Condition, discussed in chapter 3; both forbid morphological rules to pay attention to the internal constituency of their bases. What is at issue here, however, is not how the two Conditions differ but whether the Atom Condition relies crucially on the notion 'head'. If (as is plausible) the prefix *con-* is analysed as [+latinate], Lieber's main percolation convention will by itself ensure that the feature percolates up to the first branching node dominating *con-*, namely the node which dominates the whole word *conduct*. If, on the other hand, *con-* is unspecified for the feature [latinate], the plus value for this feature will still percolate up to the whole word from the root *duct-*, by virtue of the percolation convention which, in a stem-affix structure, allows the stem to 'fill in' a value for any feature which the affix leaves unspecified. In neither case is any appeal to 'heads' necessary. Especially since the Right-Hand Head Rule is allowed to have exceptions, it is hard to envisage any morphological behaviour which would violate the Atom Condition in its head-related interpretation but which would not also violate Lieberian feature-percolation conventions. So far, therefore, the evidence for the usefulness of the 'head' notion in W-syntax does not appear compelling.[7]

Williams's other main application of the 'head' notion is in the solution of what he calls 'relatedness paradoxes'. We are inclined to call two words 'related' (a) if they share an element of meaning and (b) if one is derived from the other by a morpholexical rule (such as *breath* and *breathe*, perhaps) or by affixation (such as *construct* and *construction*). Problems arise, however, with a word such as *whitewashed* or a compound (or lexicalised phrase) such as *atomic scientist*. We want to say that *whitewashed* is related to *whitewash*; yet, if (as Williams assumes) all affixation precedes compounding, then *whitewashed* must be bracketed [white[wash+ed]], so we cannot say that it is derived from *whitewash* by the suffixation of *-ed*. Even more clearly, if *atomic scientist* is bracketed as [[atomic] [scient+ist]], then it does not contain the constituent [atomic scient-] (or [atomic science]), and is therefore not related to *atomic science*, according to the definition just given. How can we avoid these counterintuitive conclusions? Williams appeals here to the notion 'head' and a related notion **nonhead**: 'the highest left branch of a word' (1981a: 261). Consider the structure of *whitewashed*:

(21)

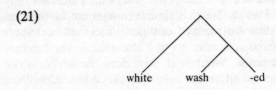

white   wash   -ed

According to Williams's definitions, both *washed* and *-ed* are heads while *white* is the (unique) nonhead. Williams now supplements his earlier definition of relatedness as follows: 'X can be related to Y if X and Y differ only in a head position or in the nonhead position.' This allows us to say that *whitewashed* is related to *whitewash* and *whitewashing*, from which it differs only in a head position (*-ed* versus ∅ or *-ing*) and to *white*, from which it differs only in another head position (*washed* versus ∅). We can also relate *whitewashed* to *washed*, from which it differs only in the nonhead position (*white* versus ∅).

Whitewashed and *atomic scientist* are of course bracketing paradoxes of the kind discussed in section 4.2. What Williams does, in effect, is provide a method whereby we can maintain their 'grammatical' bracketing while still relating them to a constituent of their 'semantic' bracketing. However, as we have seen, at least some bracketing paradoxes are semantically parallel to forms whose relationship with their 'bases' can in no way be described in terms of alternative bracketings, such as *chemical engineer* and *theoretical linguist*; rather, the relationship involves lexical-semantic pressure to provide an entry for some cell within a semantic matrix (in this instance, for a cell labelled 'expert in . . .'). *Atomic scientist* in fact belongs precisely among the 'expert' terms exemplified in (7a), while *whitewashed* can plausibly be analysed as due to lexical-semantic (or 'lexical-morphosyntactic') pressure to provide a past-tense or past-participle form for any verb, whether simple or complex. Certainly, we have not shown that all bracketing paradoxes can be handled in this way. But, to the extent that Williams's notions 'head' and 'nonhead' are motivated by a desire to solve bracketing paradoxes, the existence of a fundamentally different kind of solution for some of those paradoxes must weaken the case for maintaining these notions.

Even if Williams's treatment of relatedness is correct in spirit, details of its implementation are problematic. His definitions require us to say that *whitewashed* is related not only to *white* but to any other word with *white* as its nonhead (*whitebait*, *whiting*, *White House*, *whitest*, etc.), and not only to *washed* but to any other word with *washed* or *-ed* as one of its heads (*brainwashed, unwashed,* etc; *blue-rinsed, confused,* etc.). We quickly find ourselves far removed from the territory of the paradoxes that the head-versus-nonhead distinction was meant to explicate.

There are other problems with Williams's Right-Hand Head Rule, of a more straightforwardly factual kind. Scalise (1988) has pointed out that there is a class of 'evaluative' suffixes in Italian which systematically fail to determine syntactic category, such as *-ino*, which can be added to nouns (*tavolino* 'little table'), adjectives (*giallino* 'yellowish') and adverbs (*benino* 'quite well'). It seems implausible, then, to identify these suffixes as heads. Their category-neutrality reflects a general characteristic of 'evaluative' or 'expressive' affixes, particularly diminutive affixes; in a variety of languages they behave differently in some respects from other kinds of derivational morphology. For example, in Polish, diminutive suffixes are often not subject to blocking (e.g. *triumfek = triumfik* 'little triumph') and can be repeated (e.g. *kot-ecz-ek* from /kot-ek-ek/ 'little kitten') (Malicka-Kleparska 1985; Szymanek 1988); and it is diminutives which constitute the most recalcitrant obstacle to reconciling Breton noun plurals with Anderson's morphological version of the Elsewhere Condition (see chapter 7) (Stump 1989). So one useful spin-off from the Right-Hand Head Rule is the attention which it draws to suchlike 'anomalies'.

In more recent work, Di Sciullo and Williams (1987) maintain the notion 'head' within an X-bar W-syntax, but define it in such a way as to remove it even further from its purported analogue in S-syntax. In languages with more complex morphology (particularly inflectional morphology) than English, problems arise from recognising only a rightmost constituent as head; for example, in the Latin word form *amabar* ([[[amaː]ba]r]) 'I was loved', the head *-r* identifies the form as verbal, 1st person singular and passive, but not as imperfective, past or indicative, which are features realised in the suffix *-ba-*. Di Sciullo and Williams therefore propose a notion **relativised head**: the head of a word with respect to the feature F is the rightmost element marked for the feature F (1987: 26). In *amabar*, *-r* will be head with respect to person-number and voice, *-ba-* will be head with respect to aspect, tense and mood, and *ama-* will be head with respect to argument structure (determining that the verb is transitive, for example; see section 4.4 below).[8] The head with respect to category (that is, the element which determines that *amabar* is a verb-form) could plausibly be identified as any of these three elements. But it is now even less clear than before what difference there is, so far as complex noncompound words are concerned, between an analysis involving heads and one involving feature percolation; and Williams's (1981a) definition of lexical relatedness remains to be reformulated.

4.4 ARGUMENT STRUCTURE OF COMPOUNDS AND DERIVATIVES

In traditional logical semantics, the **arguments** of a predicate are, broadly speaking, positions which must or may be filled by referring expressions in any well-formed proposition containing that predicate. We can distinguish between obligatory arguments, which must be filled, and optional ones, which may be filled. For example, the verb *sleep*, as a predicate, has only a single obligatory argument, as evidenced by the fact that the sentence *John slept*, containing only one noun phrase, *John*, is both grammatical and (in some sense) semantically complete. On the other hand, the sentence *John is a brother*, even if not grammatically ill formed, is semantically incomplete because, as a predicate, *brother* (or perhaps rather *brother of*) has two obligatory arguments (*John is a brother of Sally*). Alongside *sleep*, other verbs with one obligatory argument include *collapse, disappear*; verbs with two include *kick, resemble*; verbs with three include *give, put* (compare the acceptability of *John put the book on the table* with the unacceptability of **John put the book*, **John put on the table*, **John put*). But predicates may differ not only in the number of their arguments but also in the **thematic roles** (or **theta-roles**) which these arguments fulfil – roles such as Agent, Theme, Instrument, Location. For example, in *John kicked the ball* we might say that the subject *John* is Agent and the object *the ball* is Theme, whereas in *John collapsed* the subject *John* is Theme. Thematic roles display their syntactic-semantic usefulness in helping to account for differences in acceptability among examples such as:

(22)   John managed to kick the ball.
(23)   *The ball managed to be kicked (by John).
(24)   ?*John managed to collapse.

What we might say here is that *manage* requires the subject of the sentence embedded below it (or that subject's controller, in Principles-and-Parameters terminology) to be an Agent, not a Theme. Example (24) is thus interpretable only in an ironic sense in which the speaker pretends to think that John, as Agent, collapsed intentionally – an interpretation not available in (23) for pragmatic reasons.

There is clearly vastly more to say about determining the argument structures of predicates and the thematic roles of these arguments. Both notions play a central part in contemporary Chomskyan Principles-and-Parameters syntax. What is important for present purposes is the way in which the grammar should handle the evident parallels between argument-structure relationships in syntax and certain relationships between elements within compounds and some derived words. Consider the following pairs:

(25) [eat meat]$_{VP}$ meat-eater
(26) [drink coffee]$_{VP}$ coffee-drinking
(27) [clear slums]$_{VP}$ slum clearance
(28) [renew a licence]$_{VP}$ licence renewal
(29) [write X by hand]$_{VP}$ hand-written
(30) [go to parties]$_{VP}$ party-going

The items on the right are all **synthetic, verbal** or **secondary compounds** – compounds in which the second element contains a verb stem and the first element appears to have a thematic role in relation to that verb stem identical or very similar to the role it has in a corresponding verb phrase (on the left). This kind of thematic correspondence ensures (or seems to ensure) that the interpretation of synthetic compounds is predictable. In this respect, they differ from **root** or **primary compounds**, in which the second element need contain no verb stem. A particularly common kind of root compound in English is the noun-noun type:[9]

(31)   hair-spray   fly-spray
(32)   mosquito-net   butterfly-net
(33)   teaspoon   tablespoon
(34)   fire-hose   pantyhose

As these examples show, there is no straightforwardly predictable semantic or thematic relationship between the two elements of a root compound. A mosquito-net is for keeping mosquitos away and a butterfly-net is for catching butterflies, but this does not follow from the structure of these compounds or the meanings of *mosquito, butterfly* and *net* individually; if we encounter one of these compounds for the first time, the best we can do is guess its meaning on the basis of pragmatic considerations or analogy with other similar compounds.

The investigation of facts such as these has become one of the most active areas of syntactically oriented morphological research in recent years, in work originating with Roeper and Siegel (1978) and extending through (among others) Williams (1981b), Selkirk (1982), Lieber (1983), Pesetsky (1985), Toman (1987), Di Sciullo and Williams (1987) and Booij (1988).[10]

Roeper and Siegel's (1978) analysis of synthetic compounds is lexicalist in spirit. It involves a kind of movement rule which transforms a representation like $[[. . .]+eat_V+er][meat]$ or $[[. . .] + go_V+ing]$ [to parties] into $[[meat]+eat_V+er]$ or $[[party]+go_V+ing]$. This is not syntactic movement, however, but a **lexical transformation**, a new kind of device to be incorporated in the lexicon alongside Jackendoff's (1975) lexical redundancy rules, or a new kind of word-formation rule in Aronoff's (1976) terms. The structures on which lexical transformations operate are derived directly from the lexical subcategorisation frames, or argument structures, of the verbs which follow the initial 'empty' position. For example, since the noun *meat* can satisfy one of the arguments (the Theme argument) of the verb *eat*, it can move into the empty position in $[[. . .]+eat_V+er]$. According to Roeper and Siegel, lexical transformations for synthetic compounds must conform to the **First-Sister Principle**: 'All verbal compounds are formed by incorporation of a word in first sister position of the verb' (1978: 208). The restriction to words (more specifically nouns, adjectives or adverbs) predicts the nonexistence of synthetic compounds in which the first element is a phrase or clause; we can have *coffee-maker* but not **good dark coffee-maker*, and *history-writer* but not **what-happened-writer*, even though *make good dark coffee* and *write what happened* are well formed as verb phrases. The requirement that the incorporated element be a first sister to the verb is meant to account for patterns of acceptability such as the following:

(35) a. hand-built
      b. factory-built
      c. hand-built in a factory
      d. *factory-built by hand

Roeper and Siegel suggest that the argument structure for *build* (as for transitive verbs generally) will contain optional Instrument and Location arguments (among others), which, if they are both present, must crucially appear in that order. They also assume that a synthetic compound as a whole can **inherit** 'empty' arguments from the verbal element in its head – arguments which must be satisfied 'outside' the compound, in its immediate syntactic context. These factors interact so as permit (35c) and forbid (35d). Consider (36), the input to the lexical transformation which generates *hand-built* in (35c):

(36)   [[. . .]+build$_V$+ed][$_{Instrument}$ by hand][$_{Location}$· · ·]

Ignoring +*ed* and *by*, we can call *hand* the first sister of the verb *build*, because it is the element immediately to its right. Consequently it is available to be moved to the empty position before *build*. The empty Location argument, which is not filled inside the compound, will be inherited by the compound as a whole, and will be available to be filled 'outside' by the phrase *in a factory*. Contrast this with (37), which is what would have to underlie *factory-built* in (35d):

(37)   [[. . .]+build$_V$+ed][$_{Instrument}$· · ·][$_{Location}$ in a factory]

The empty Instrument argument in (37) must be present so that it can be inherited by the whole compound and filled 'outside' by the phrase *by hand*; yet its position as first sister to *build* pushes the Location argument into 'second sister' position, so that the First-Sister Principle prevents *factory* from being moved to the empty slot before *build*. Of course, Instrument is merely an optional argument of *build*, and if it is absent then the Location argument may well be in first-sister position to *build*; this is the case in the structure underlying *factory-built* at (35b).

What happens when a verb has more than one obligatory argument of the kind which would follow it in a subcategorisation frame such as Roeper and Siegel assume – that is, more than one obligatory nonsubject argument? An example is *put*, which, as we noted earlier, has obligatory Theme and Location arguments. Assuming that Theme and Location occur in that order (cf. *put the book on the shelf* versus **put on the shelf the book*), it is clear that the First-Sister Principle predicts that the Location argument cannot be incorporated in a synthetic compound involving *put*, since the Location argument can never be a first sister. This prediction seems correct, as are analogous predictions for other verbs with similar argument structures: **shelf-putter* (*of books*), **children-giving* (*of presents*), **orange-comparison* (*of apples*). But Roeper and Siegel go further, claiming that neither of the two 'post-verbal' arguments can be incorporated. This is a consequence not of the First-Sister Principle but of the way in which they formulate the lexical transformation for synthetic compounds. The compound transformation requires any argument positions other than the first sister to be empty. But this requirement cannot be met by a verb such as *put*, since both its postverbal arguments, being obligatory, must be filled. It follows that a structure such as (38), which is what would underlie (39), is ill formed:

(38) $[[. . .]+put+er][_{Theme}$ book$][_{Location}. . .]$
(39)   *book-putter (on the shelf)

Roeper and Siegel's lexical transformations do not fit into the austere morphological frameworks proposed by Lieber (binary branching structures labelled via feature percolation) or Selkirk (W-syntactic rewriting rules as the sole word-forming mechanism). Furthermore, the 'first sister' notion, with its implication of quasi-syntactic linear order inside the lexicon, is hard to square with frameworks such as have been proposed more recently (see section 4.6 below) in which linear order is banished from syntax to Phonological Form. Even so, the range of facts that Roeper and Siegel chose to examine, and their observations about them, have formed the starting-point for a series of further investigations. Selkirk (1982) and Lieber (1983) agree in rejecting lexical transformations, but they part company over whether the argument structures of the verbs from which the heads of synthetic compounds are derived participate directly in determining their well-formedness. On this matter, Lieber sides with Roeper and Siegel, although her mechanism for filling argument positions is radically different. We will consider Lieber's approach first.

Lieber appeals to a distinction introduced by Williams (1981b) between **external** and **internal arguments**. Every verb has no more than one external argument, coinciding (in active clause-types) with the subject of the clause. The internal arguments of a verb or preposition are all its obligatory arguments with the exception of the external argument. On this basis, Lieber proposes an **Argument-Linking Principle** whose main requirement is that, in any configuration (or binary branching structure) of which either member (or branch) is a verb or preposition and neither member is an affix, that verb or preposition 'must be able to link all internal arguments' (1983: 262); that is, all the internal arguments of that verb or preposition must be satisfiable within that configuration. Let us see how the Principle works with the synthetic compound *truck-driver*. In Lieber's framework, any stem or affix can be inserted at any terminal node in a lexical binary branching structure, provided that its subcategorisation requirements are met (section 2.4). A possible structure for *truck-driver* is therefore as in (40).

(40)

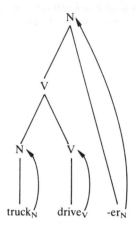

The arrows in (40) mark feature percolation. The agentive noun-forming suffix *-er* is subcategorised to attach to verbs, and the configuration [*truck*][*drive*] satisfies this requirement because, when neither branch is an affix, it is the category of the right branch (in this instance [*drive*]$_V$) which percolates up. (This convention is the closest analogue in Lieber's system to Williams's Right-Hand Head Rule.) In the configuration [*truckdrive*][*-er*] no arguments have to be linked, because [*-er*] is an affix. Within the configuration [*truck*][*drive*], however, the Argument-Linking Principle requires that the internal Theme argument of *drive* must be satisfied – and it is satisfied by the noun *truck*, as left sister to *drive*. The typical synthetic-compound interpretation, with *truck* as the 'object' of *drive*, is thus accounted for. If, however, instead of *drive* we tried to insert a verb with two internal arguments, such as *put*, we could not comply with the Argument-Linking Principle, since we could not have both the Theme and the Location argument filled in the one (left-sister) position available. In this way the Principle accounts for Roeper and Siegel's observation (or claim) that 'double-complement' verbs such as *put* cannot appear in synthetic compounds.

The tree structure at (40) is not the only one compatible with the subcategorisation of *truck, drive* and *-er*. We can also legally insert them in the structure at (41). Here no arguments are linked at all, however – neither in [*drive*] [*-er*], whose second element is an affix, nor in [*truck*] [*driver*], neither of whose elements is a verb or preposition. But this is no drawback. Compounds in which no argument linking takes place are simply root compounds, like *inkwell* or *greenhouse*. So, by making available this second analysis,

Lieber in effect predicts that *truck-driver* is interpretable not only as a synthetic compound ('someone who drives trucks') but also as a root compound, with the usual semantic indeterminacy of root compounds ('driver who makes a noise like a truck', 'driver with a picture of truck on his T-shirt', etc.).

(41)

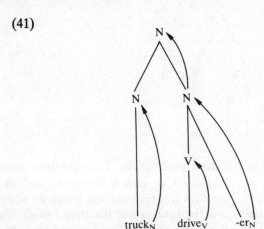

$$truck_N \qquad drive_V \qquad -er_N$$

A possible objection to the structure at (40) is the fact that it incorporates the configuration $[[truck]_N[drive]_V]_V$. Surely this must be wrong, since there is no verb **truckdrive*, and in general very few compound verbs in English with the structure $[N\ V]_V$? It seems strange that one stage in the generation of synthetic compounds, which are numerous and productive in English, should involve a type of compound which is rare and unproductive. Selkirk (1982: 29) and Booij (1988: 67) criticise structures such as (40) on just these grounds. Lieber's answer involves a factor which, jointly with the Argument-Linking Principle, imposes incompatible requirements on any would-be verb of the structure $[N\ V]_V$, if the node which immediately dominates it is S-syntactic (X') rather than W-syntactic (X^0). The argument structure of a simple verb must be satisfied in its immediate syntactic context; for example, *drive* has normally a Theme argument which is satisfied by its direct object (*drive cars*, *drive that huge truck*, etc.). But just as the verbhood of *drive* percolates up to the *truckdrive*, so (according to Lieber) does its argument structure, which must likewise be satisfied in the immediate syntactic context if *truckdrive* is not itself part of a larger word. The trouble is that the Theme argument of *truckdrive* is already satisfied in the compound itself; so we cannot provide another

Theme 'outside' the compound (e.g.*truckdrive cars*, *truckdrive that huge truck*, etc.) without assigning the same thematic role to two distinct arguments, in violation of the Theta-Criterion (which imposes a one-to-one relationship between arguments and theta-roles). There is therefore good reason why *truckdrive* cannot appear as a word in syntactic structure, even though it may appear as a word within a larger morphological structure. On the other hand, if in some [N V]$_V$ structure the N does not satisfy an internal argument, then according to Lieber the structure is at least potentially well formed. This prediction seems correct for at least some such structures, e.g. *spoon-feed* ('feed (metaphorically) with a spoon', not 'feed spoons') and *hand-wash* ('wash by hand', not 'wash hands').

Before considering the merits of Lieber's account further, let us look at Selkirk's (1982) alternative account, substituting as our main example Selkirk's *tree-eater* for Lieber's *truck-driver*. Selkirk's rewriting rules for W-syntax contain no rule V→N V, so there is no way in which she can generate a structure analogous to (40) for *tree-eater*, with [[*tree*]$_N$[*eat*]$_V$]$_V$ as a constituent. Even so, as she acknowledges, *tree-eater* has both a synthetic-compound interpretation ('someone who eats trees') and a root-compound interpretation (perhaps 'someone who likes to sit in a tree while eating'). She relates the two possible interpretations to the fact that the verb *eat* has Theme as an optional, not an obligatory, argument; *She is eating pasta* and *She is eating* are both well-formed clauses, and the deverbal noun *eater* does not have to have a complement (*She is a big eater*). By contrast, *devour* has an obligatory Theme (*She is devouring pasta* versus *She is devouring*), and correspondingly the compound *tree-devourer* appears to have only a synthetic interpretation, with the tree as victim. It is easy to check that this 'semantic' account of the two interpretations for *tree-eater* will also work for Lieber's *truck-driver*, since the Theme of *drive* is not obligatory (*We were driving all night; Jeremy is a good driver*).

Selkirk's method of representing argument structures, taken from Lexical-Functional Grammar (see Bresnan 1981), involves linking thematic roles with grammatical functions:

(42)	a.		SUBJ	OBJ
		devour:	(Agent,	Theme)
	b.		SUBJ	OBJ/∅
		eat:	(Agent,	Theme)

The optionality of the object of *eat* is expressed in the notation 'OBJ/$\emptyset$'. Verbal derivatives (e.g. *eater, devourer* from *eat, devour*) inherit these argument structures. Roeper and Siegel's main observations emerge in Selkirk's terminology as follows:

(43) The SUBJ argument of a lexical item may not be expressed in compound structure.

(44) All non-SUBJ arguments of the head of a compound must be satisfied within the compound immediately dominating the head.

The observation in (43) refers to the unacceptability of, for example, **giraffe-devouring of trees*, with *giraffe* understood as the subject of *devour*; that in (44) reflects the unacceptability of (45) by contrast with (46):

(45) *tree-devourer of pasta
(46) pasta-devourer in trees

In both, *pasta* is the Theme argument of *devour*, but in (46) it is within the compound headed by *devourer* while in (45) it is not. Yet, as Selkirk points out, this fact about compounds is merely an instance of a wider generalisation which also extends to phrases. Compare (47) and (48):

(47) *a devourer in trees
(48) a devourer of pasta

The noun phrase (47), containing no 'object' for *devour*, is considerably less acceptable than (48), which does contain such an object. To facilitate a formulation which will cover phrases as well as compound words, Selkirk defines the **first-order projection** of an item within the X-bar hierarchy as the X-bar category which immediately dominates it in a given S-syntactic or W-syntactic representation. In S-syntax, the first-order projection of a given nonmaximal X^i will always be some X^{i+1}; in W-syntax, however, because of the differences between W-syntax and S-syntax discussed in section 4.3.1, the range of possibilities is larger. Using this definition, Selkirk states a **First-Order Projection Condition** for argument structure: 'All non-SUBJ arguments of a lexical category X_i must be satisfied within the first order projection of X_i' (1982: 37). Let us apply the Condition to examples (45)–(48). In (45) and (46), the first-order projection of *devourer* is the N^0 immediately dominating the compound of which *devourer* is the head; but only in (46) does this N^0 also dominate *pasta*, which satisfies the non-SUBJ (Theme) argument of *devourer*. Similarly, in both (47) and (48) the first-order projection of *devourer* is a N' (dominating *devourer in trees* or *devourer of pasta*), but only in the latter N' is the Theme argument satisfied. And it is easy to check that the First-Order Projection Condition, in combination with Selkirk's W-syntactic structures, entails the by now familiar claim that synthetic compounds cannot be headed by derivatives of verbs, such as *put*, which have more than one non-SUBJ (or obligatory internal) argument.

If we look only at synthetic compounds, it may seem that there is little empirical difference between Lieber's and Selkirk's accounts; they both make similar predictions about acceptability. The difference between them lies mainly in the further facts which they intend their analyses to cover. For Selkirk, as we have just seen, these further facts involve the satisfaction of argument structure within phrases and clauses as well as compounds. For Lieber, by contrast, the further facts include root compounds of certain kinds. Nothing in Lieber's Argument-Linking Principle ties it exclusively to synthetic compounds; in fact, it bears on any compound of which the first or second member is a verb or preposition. For example, it entails the prediction that in any [V N] configuration (which should itself be a noun, according to one of Lieber's feature-percolation conventions) the nominal element must satisfy an internal argument of the verb. It also predicts that in any verb of [V V] structure the first verb should have no internal arguments (i.e. be intransitive), since no such arguments could be satisfied within the compound. Both claims are somewhat problematical, as Lieber herself admits; examples relevant to the first claim include *drawbridge, pickpocket, swearword, whetstone*, and ones relevant to the second include *fly-drive, slip-slide, freeze-dry, stir-fry*. But the important point for present purposes is not their correctness but rather the fact that they have nothing to do with Selkirk's First-Order Projection Condition. So, although Lieber and Selkirk agree that the facts about synthetic compounds flow from some more general principle, they differ as to what this more general principle embraces; for Lieber it embraces further morphological phenomena, while for Selkirk it extends into syntax. On the whole, it is the syntactic tendency which has predominated in more recent work (Di Sciullo and Williams 1987; Booij 1988; Booij and van Haaften 1988; Hoekstra and van der Putten 1988; Roeper 1988). There is also what one could call a 'Logical Form tendency', represented by Pesetsky (1985), who discusses the ill-formedness of **tree-eating* *of pasta* in terms of a 'Quantifier Rule' which maps S-structure to Logical Form by raising *-ing* to become a sister of *tree-eat- of pasta* (see section 4.7.1).

A common feature of all the analyses considered so far is that, for determining what elements either may or must fulfil certain thematic roles in relation to the verbal elements in compounds, they assign a crucial importance to morphological and syntactic structure. But in section 4.2 we found reasons to be sceptical about appeals to structure of that kind, as opposed to lexical-semantic structure, in 'resolving' bracketing paradoxes. So it may be worth exploring an entirely different type of account for synthetic compounds – one which treats them all as essentially no different from root compounds. According to such an approach, the fact that *truck-driver* means someone who drives trucks rather than a driver who owns or sells or paints trucks, for example, is simply that the former interpretation is pragmatically the one most likely to be institutionalised; but it is not the only interpretation possible, as Lieber points out. This seems true even of a compound such as *spaghetti-devouring*, which Selkirk claims can have only the 'synthetic' reading (with *spaghetti* the Theme of *devour*) because *devour* takes an obligatory object. Given a little imagination, we can invent an interpretation for *spaghetti-devouring* such that it can apply to an activity in which no pasta is consumed. Let us suppose that *spaghetti-devour X* comes to mean 'twist strands of X on to a fork and eat it greedily'. Sentences such as (49) and (50), in which the Theme argument of *devour* is not satisfied in its first-order projection, then become acceptable:

(49) The current craze for spaghetti-devouring coleslaw in public is disgusting.

(50) Kellogs have designed a new stringy breakfast cereal which can be spaghetti-devoured.

One thing that is needed for such an account to become a serious contender is a more sophisticated theory of meaning relationships in the lexicon and of possible meanings for newly coined words. Meanwhile, however, one can point to some facts which may count in its favour. An embarrassment for any 'structural' account of thematic roles in synthetic compounds is the frequent divergence in idiomaticity between a compound and its corresponding verb phrase – that is, the verb phrase in which the same words fulfil the same thematic roles. Why should some noun be an appropriate argument for a given verb in a verb phrase but not for the same verb (or a nominal derivative of it) in a compound? In other words, why are selectional restrictions not inherited along with argument structures? The examples (51) illustrate 'synthetic' compounds whose corresponding phrase is less than fully acceptable:

(51) profit-taking ?take profits
slum-dweller ?dwell in a slum
care-giver ?give care
motor-racing ?race (in) motors
door-keeper ?keep the door
time-keeping ?keep time
(i.e. punctuality) (i.e. be punctual)

(Notice that the verb *dwell*, in its literal sense, has an archaic tinge which compounds such as *slum-dweller* and *flat-dweller* lack.) Conversely, one can find acceptable phrases for which the corresponding synthetic compound seems odd:

(52) take offence ?offence-taking
dwell on misfortune ?misfortune-dweller
give a cheer ?cheer-giving
race to the finish ?finish-racer
keep a mistress ?mistress-keeper
deliver a verdict ?verdict-delivery

An advocate of one of the structural analyses of synthetic compounds will probably explain these differences as purely a matter of lexicalisation; just as a verb may lack a derived nominal (e.g. *ignore*) and a 'derived' nominal may lack a verb (e.g. *perdition*), so there may be accidental gaps in the correspondence between compounds and phrases. But, if we adopt the approach mooted here, there is nothing to explain at all; the mismatch is just what we expect, given that the relationship between parts of a compound has nothing to do with the way in which thematic roles are fulfilled in syntax. Here is another avenue to explore, at least.[11]

4.5 INCORPORATION AND THE MIRROR PRINCIPLE

In Principles-and-Parameters syntax, Move-Alpha is firmly established as the sole remaining transformation linking D-structure and S-structure. Move-Alpha moves constituents freely, subject to universal principles (particularly Government, Bounding and Theta Theory) and to language-particular specifications, within a universally defined range, about what constituents may move – that is, about what may count as 'Alpha' for the language in question. One way in which Alpha may differ is with regard to syntactic category and subcategory. For example, in English, Alpha includes noun phrases and *wh*-phrases, but in Japanese Alpha does not include *wh*-phrases as such; from the Principles-and-Parameters point of view, that is why *wh*-phrases get fronted in English but not in Japanese. Baker, however, emphasises that Alpha may also differ with regard to syntactic level, in X-bar terms. The constituents whose movement is most familiar belong to the level of the phrase or, more precisely, the maximal projection (X^{max}). But Baker proposes that, at least in some languages, word-level constituents (X^0) may move too. As to possible 'landing-sites' for X^0 movement, Baker argues that the only options permitted by the various intersecting requirements of Principle-and-Parameters theory are substitution for or adjunction to another X^0 item.

Let us suppose that Move-Alpha affects a N^0 so as to left-adjoin it to a V^0. The structures before and after movement can be represented schematically as follows:

(53)

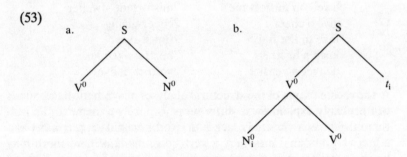

As is normal, adjunction creates a new node at the landing site, so that in (53b) the moved N^0 is both a daughter and a sister of V^0; and, as with 'ordinary' Move-Alpha, the moved constituent leaves behind a coindexed trace (t_i). But what is most important for present purposes is the structure dominated by the higher V^0 in (53b). This is a syntactic structure in the sense that it has been produced by the operation of a syntactic rule (Move-Alpha) linking D-structure with S-structure; on the other hand, it is a morphological structure in the sense that it does not contain any constituent larger than a word (or, in X-bar terms, a X^0). It follows that Baker's account of incorporation is incompatible with most versions of the Strong Lexicalist Hypothesis, in that Baker claims that there is a class of words which are syntactically created. Given Strong Lexicalism, the fact that a structure is labelled N^0, V^0, A^0 or P^0 guarantees that its grammatical analysis is a matter for a word-formation component which, however conceived, is distinct from syntax; but with Baker's approach this guarantee does not hold (Baker 1988b).

Does Baker's proposal represent a strengthening or a weakening of linguistic theory? At first sight, inasmuch as it seems to license syntactic interference in word structure, it must represent a weakening. But things are not so simple. Firstly, Baker argues that his proposal makes for a tighter theory of syntax. A precisely similar process of incorporation handles successfully not only Eskimo-style polysynthesis (he claims) but also a variety of 'grammatical function changing' processes: causative, antipassive and applicative constructions, as well as some passives. If all these processes are construed as involving incorporation of X^0-level constituents into the verb, then we can explain why they behave in the way they do rather than in other conceivable but unobserved ways. This is a large syntactic claim which we need not try to evaluate here; but, assuming it is correct, we may well judge that any consequential weakening of morphological theory is a price worth paying. Even for morphology itself, however, Baker's proposal has some empirically rich consequences. If grammatical function changing processes involve adjunction of X^0-level items to verbs, then in clauses where more than one such process has occurred the syntactic sequence of operations should be mirrored in the order of the corresponding morphological markers with respect to the verb root; markers reflecting processes which take place earlier in the derivational history of the clause should be closer to the root than ones reflecting later processes. And this prediction seems broadly correct (Baker 1985). In contrast, if morphology is handled entirely 'in the lexicon', there is no reason to expect that the order of affixes in a morphologically complex word-form should reflect any sort of syntactic order; the fact that it does so has to be seen as an accident.

By way of illustration, let us consider Baker's treatment of the way in which applicative and passive constructions interact. First we will look at some relevant data in the Bantu language Chichewa, identifying and numbering the facts which Baker claims to be able to explain; then we will summarise his explanations. Baker's account is intricate, and full mastery of it requires a good understanding of Principles-and-Parameters theory in its post-*Barriers* version (Chomsky 1986a). But my emphasis here is on giving a flavour of Baker's approach and in particular indicating the wide range of seemingly disparate facts which it seeks to unify. We can then look more closely at some of its morphological implications.

Compare the following two Chichewa sentences:[12]

(54) Mbidzi zi-na-perek-a msampha **kwa** nkhandwe
      zebras S-Past-hand trap to fox
      'The zebras handed the trap to the fox'

(55) Mbidzi zi-na-perek-**er**-a nkhandwe msampha
      zebras S-Past-hand-to fox trap
      'The zebras handed the fox the trap'

(In the glosses of the verb forms, 'S' stands for 'subject concord prefix'; the aspectual suffix -*a* is left unglossed.) Examples (54) and (55) are essentially synonymous, but differ in that (54) contains a preposition *kwa* 'to', while in (55) the verb has an 'applicative' suffix -*er*-/-*ir*- (according to vowel harmony) (*Fact 1*). When this suffix is present, the position directly following the verb is occupied by the Goal argument *nkhandwe* 'fox' rather than the Theme argument *msampha* 'trap' (*Fact 2*). The applicative construction thus has the effect of changing the grammatical status of some nonsubject arguments of the verb; an Instrument, Location or, as here, Goal argument becomes what we may call the 'applied object'.

In Chichewa, the passive is marked morphologically with a suffix -*idw*-/-*edw*- on the verb, so the passive corresponding to (56) is (57):

(56) Kalulu a-na-gul-a nsapato
      hare S-Past-buy shoes
      'The hare bought the shoes'

(57) Nsapato zi-na-gul-**idw**-a (ndi kalulu)
      shoes S-Past-buy-Pass (by hare)
      'The shoes were bought (by the hare)'

What happens when passive and applicative interact? Example (58) is an active sentence with an applicative verb, syntactically parallel to (55), containing both an applied object *mbidzi* and a 'basic' object *nsapato*. Of these two objects, the applied one can become the subject under passivisation, but the basic one cannot, as (59) and (60) illustrate (*Fact 3*):

(58) Kalulu a-na-gul-**ir**-a mbidzi nsapato
      hare S-Past-buy-for zebras shoes
      'The hare bought shoes for the zebras'

(59) Mbidzi zi-na-gul-**ir**-**idw**-a nsapato ndi kalulu
      zebras S-Past-buy-Pass-for shoes by hare
      'The zebras were bought shoes by the hare'

(60) *Nsapato zi-na-gul-**ir-idw**-a mbidzi ndi kalulu
      shoes   S-Past-buy-Pass-for zebras by hare
      'Shoes were bought for the zebras by the hare'

Notice that in (59) the order of affixes is *-ir-idw-*, not *-idw-ir-*; the passive suffix is 'outside' the applicative one (*Fact 4*). But we might expect the opposite order, at least *prima facie*, in passive sentences where the subject corresponds to a basic, not an applied, object (as in (57)), and where there is also a Goal indicated by the applicative suffix rather than by a preposition such as *kwa* (as in (54)); we might expect, in other words, to find structures glossable as e.g. 'Goat [basic object] was-killed-for chief [applied object]'. As (61) shows, however, this is not possible:

(61) *Mbuzi i-na-ph-**edw-er**-a mfumu (ndi Mavuto)
      goat   S-Past-kill-Pass-for chief (by Mavuto)
      'The goat was killed for the chief (by Mavuto)'

The applicative suffix can never be 'outside' the Passive one (*Fact 5*), even if it is the applied rather than the basic object which is the subject of the passive sentence:

(62) *Mfumu i-na-ph-**edw-er**-a mbuzi (ndi Mavuto)
      chief   S-Past-kill-Pass-for goat (by Mavuto)
      'The chief was killed a goat by Mavuto'

Directly relevant to Fact 1 is Baker's analysis of the applicative suffix *-er-* as a preposition in D-structure, just like *kwa* in (54); for, like Lieber (1981b), Baker treats (at least some) affixes as lexical items, on a par with stems. This analysis ensures compliance with the **Uniformity of Theta Assignment Hypothesis** (UTAH), quoted at (63), which is presented as a constraint on D-structure (1988a: 46):

(63) Identical thematic relationships between items are represented by identical structural relationships between those items at the level of D-structure.

By categorising *-er-* as a preposition, Baker ensures that the thematic relationship between the verb stem *-perek-* and its Goal *nkhandwe* is represented identically in the D-structures of (54) and (55). In (55), *-er-* has been moved from its D-structure position as a sister to the noun phrase *nkhandwe* 'fox' and adjoined to the verb by Move-Alpha, applying in this instance to a X^0-level constituent (more precisely, a P^0) rather than to a phrase. The landing-site for this moved P^0 is precisely identified by its lexical subcategorisation as a verbal suffix. Being a suffix, it does not have the option of remaining in its D-structure position, because that would lead in S-structure to a violation of the **Stray Affix Filter** (Baker 1988a: 147), which bans S-structures containing 'loose' affixes. This Filter is part of **Morphology Theory**, conceived as another set of constraints with which well-formed sentences must comply, alongside Binding Theory, Bounding Theory, Case Theory and the rest.

Facts 2 and 3, concerning the status of applied objects in Chichewa, reflect a generalisation which is true of all languages which have both applicative and passive constructions. *A priori*, one might expect some or even most languages of this kind to allow only basic objects to be movable to subject; but, citing Marantz (1984), Baker claims that this expectation is not correct. Paradoxically, it seems that, in most such languages, basic objects cannot become passive subjects, but in all of them applied objects can. The reason, says Baker, has to do with Case Theory. In Principles-and-Parameters syntax, noun phrases must normally be assigned an (abstract) Case by a verb, a preposition or a tensed Infl (the D-structure locus of 'verbal' inflectional categories such as tense and mood). In (54) the NP *nkhandwe* gets Case from the preposition *kwa*; in (55), however, there is no longer an overt preposition alongside *nkhandwe*, so *nkhandwe* has no choice but to receive 'structural Case' from the verb *zinaperekera*. But 'structural Case' is generally 'absorbed' by passive verbs (which is why passive verbs cannot usually have objects). This in turn means that, since in a sentence such as (59) the applied object *mbidzi* is not only abandoned by its 'preposition' *-ir-* but also prevented from getting Case from the verb by the fact that the verb is passive, it has no choice but to move to subject position, where (according to Case Theory) Case can be assigned to it by Infl.[13] (The alert reader may be wondering where the basic object *nsapato* gets its Case from in (59), since it too lacks any obvious Case-assigner; Baker's attempts to answer this question would take us too far afield, however.)

Fact 4 illustrates the Mirror Principle in Chichewa. If, as Baker claims, applicative constructions involve incorporation (that is, Move-Alpha at the X^0 level), then their syntax and morphology inevitably go hand in hand, with the applicative affix being adjoined to the verb stem by Move-Alpha so as to form a new V^0 constituent. It is therefore natural to expect that any morphological marking of the passive of this new constituent should be 'outside' the applicative affix, not infixed between it and the stem. This is especially so if, as Baker claims, passives typically involve syntactic incorporation too – this time incorporation of the verb (along with any material already incorporated in it) into Infl, as sister to a passive affix located there in D-structure.

This analysis of the passive is crucial to Baker's explanation for Fact 5. Recall that when a constituent is moved by Move-Alpha, a trace is left behind which is coindexed with the moved constituent (see (53) above). On first acquaintance, Move-Alpha looks much too powerful, capable of generating bizarre S-structures in which constituents are inappropriately repositioned wholesale. But a major constraint on the operation of Move-Alpha is the **Empty Category Principle** of Principles-and-Parameters syntax, which requires that all traces left by Move-Alpha must be **properly governed** by a coindexed item – either the moved constituent itself or another of its traces. The exact definition of proper government is highly technical and still the subject of much debate (Baker 1988a: 39, 366–7). In outline, however, A properly governs B provided that:

(a)   A does not dominate B;
(b)   A is at least as 'high up the tree' as B – more precisely, every maximal projection which dominates A also dominates B;
(c)   there is no **barrier** between A and B, that is no maximal projection with a lexical head C closer to B than A is.

On the basis of this definition, it is possible to show that to form an applicative from a passive – in Baker's terms, to incorporate a preposition into a verb which has itself already been incorporated into Infl – will violate the Empty Category Principle. To see this, consider (64), representing schematically a D-structure which is a candidate for both preposition incorporation (i.e. applicative formation) and verb-to-Infl incorporation (i.e. passive, in Baker's analysis) (Baker 1988a: 401, 405–8). If preposition incorporation takes place first (as in the Chichewa example (59)), then P is first adjoined to V, leaving a properly governed trace at its original position, and is then, as part of V, adjoined to the passive suffix in I, leaving another trace at the original V position. This second trace is a crucial link in the chain of government, being properly governed by P (i.e. the applicative suffix) at its final destination, while itself governing properly the first trace at the original 'home' of P. On the other hand, if V-to-I incorporation takes place first, the incorporation of P in V at its new

(64)

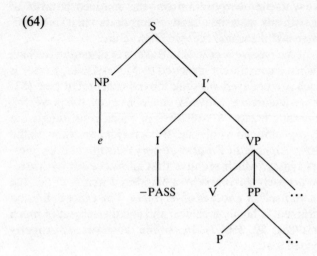

location requires it to move in one leap from its original position into Infl; but this means that its trace is not properly governed, because the VP intervening between Infl and the trace constitutes a barrier.

There is no logical connection between Facts 1–5. According to Baker, however, they are all connected as consequences of the analysis of both applicatives and passives as involving Move-Alpha applied to X^0-level constituents.[14] This analysis therefore unifies an impressive variety of seemingly disparate facts – an even greater variety than we have observed here, because it embraces causative and antipassive constructions too. But it is useful for the morphologist to consider precisely where Baker's explanation stops – that is, what morphological aspects of his data still remain accidental or problematic. In this way, we can see what morphological issues are most pressing within Baker's framework. These issues involve (a) the closeness of the parallel between grammatical function changing and 'ordinary' incorporation, (b) the treatment of morphological alternation, and (c) the closeness of the parallel between syntactic and nonsyntactic morphology.

In response to Fact 1, Baker treats *kwa* and *-ir-/-er-* as basically distinct but (near-)synonymous prepositions in Chichewa, one of which just happens to be an affix and is therefore forced by the Stray Affix Filter to undergo incorporation. But there is nothing in his framework to prevent *kwa* from undergoing incorporation as well as *-ir-/-er-*, and nothing to prevent *-ir-/-er-* from satisfying the Stray Affix Filter by being affixed to a dummy prepositional stem, much as *do* acts as a dummy verb stem in some syntactic contexts in English. Incorporation into the verb of the nonaffix *kwa* would, after all, be exactly parallel to the normal pattern of noun incorporation in languages such as Eskimo; and use of a dummy preposition stem to 'support' *-ir-/-er-* would be exactly parallel to what can happen in Chichewa with the causative suffix *-its-/-ets-*. Consider the following two sentences (Baker 1988a: 21):

(65) Mtsikana a-na-chit-**its**-a   kuti   mtsuko u-**gw**-e
     girl   S-Past-do-cause that   pot   S-fall
     'The girl made the pot fall'

(66) Mtsikana a-na-**gw**-**ets**-a   mtsuko
     girl   S-Past-fall-cause pot
     'The girl made the pot fall'

Baker analyses causative constructions as due to verb incorporation – the incorporation of a lower verb (*-gw-* 'fall' in (66)) into a higher (the causative affix *-its-/-ets-*, analysed as a verb). The D-structure of (66) therefore looks rather like (65). The reason why (65) is allowed to surface as it does, without *-gw-* adjoined to *-its-*, is that *-its-* satisfies the Stray Affix Filter through the support of the dummy verb *-chit-*, glossed as 'do'. So why do *kwa* and *-ir-/-er* not follow these parallels?

At one level, the answer is straightforward and trivial; they just do not happen to work like that. But there is a more serious question underlying this one. If, as Baker suggests, grammatical function changing processes are no different syntactically from 'ordinary' incorporation, we would expect that in ordinary incorporation the distribution of affixes and nonaffixes, both as moved items and as landing-sites, should be roughly the same as we find in grammatical function changing operations. For example, we might expect to find ordinary nouns which, like the Chichewa 'preposition' *-ir-/-er-* and 'verb' *-its-/-ets-*, are affixal. According to Baker, we do indeed find affixal nouns in the 'antipassive' constructions in various languages ('in which a morpheme is added to a transitive verb, and the verb's thematic direct object appears as an oblique phrase instead of as a surface direct object' (1988a: 129)); for he analyses the antipassive affix as a noun compulsorily incorporated into the verb. But this 'noun' is unlike nearly all other nouns in being semantically empty – a mere dummy, forced to move by the Stray Affix Filter. Why do we not find more instances of affixal 'full' nouns – perhaps paired with synonymous nonaffixal counterparts, as Chichewa *kwa* is paired with *-ir-/-er-*? To the extent that we do not find this pattern, we have an awkward observational gap which warrants investigation. Baker hints at a possible reason (1988a: 465, footnote 2): affixes constitute a closed class, whereas nouns are an open class. But the open-class status of verbs does not prevent Baker from including causative affixes among them; and there are many languages in which open-class items are 'bound' in Bloomfield's (1933) sense, in that they require affixal supplementation in order to form words.

The Chichewa 'verb' *-its-/-ets-* has the same shape (barring vowel harmony) in both (65), where no incorporation has occurred, and in (66), with verb incorporation. This fact is cited by Baker as *prima facie* evidence in favour of the verb-incorporation analysis. The corollary is that, where parallel structures such as (54) and (55) exist (that is, in Baker's terms, where incorporation is for one reason or another optional) but there is no such similarity between the relevant morphological markers, this ought to count as *prima facie* evidence against an incorporation analysis. Yet Baker seems reluctant to acknowledge this. He points out, rightly, that 'ordinary' morphology tolerates a considerable degree of allomorphy, with phonological, grammatical and lexical conditioning; so, since the same Morphology Theory applies to all complex X^0 constituents, however formed, we ought to extend the same allomorphic latitude to syntactic morphology too (1988a: 283–5). But, unless there is some constraint on this allomorphy (perhaps on the lines suggested in chapter 7 below), then compliance with the Uniformity of Theta Assignment Hypothesis (63) becomes perilously easy and its empirical content is thereby undermined.

Let us suppose that in some language there is a class of simple (monomorphemic) verbs whose Theme and Goal arguments can be represented in either of two ways, as in (67) and (68) (where P is an arbitrary preposition):

(67)   Verb   [Theme]$_{NP}$ [P Goal]$_{PP}$
(68)   Verb   [Goal]$_{NP}$ [Theme]$_{NP}$

This language clearly poses a problem for the UTAH, because the thematic relationship between the verb and its Goal is expressed structurally in more than one way. However, we can reconcile it with the UTAH by brute force, as it were, if we postulate that in (68) as well as (67) a D-structure preposition governs the Goal argument. Deriving the S-structure of (68) is then a simple matter of incorporating this preposition into the verb (whereupon the Goal argument naturally moves next to the verb in order to acquire Case); and the fact that the verb is 'monomorphemic' is accounted for by specifying that, when affixed to a verb, the preposition is phonologically null. Clearly we want to rule out this kind of analysis if possible, perhaps by building into Morphology Theory some constraint on 'zero morphemes'. Unfortunately, Baker adopts an analysis of precisely this form to handle English 'Dative Shift' verbs such as *give*, whose thematic relationships can be represented in two apparently different structures (*John gave a book to Mary* versus *John gave Mary a book*) (1988a: 286–8). According to Baker, therefore, English resembles Chichewa in having an applicative construction, the only difference being that the 'preposition' in question is never phonologically visible, even as a verbal affix. This analysis is not necessarily wrong; but, if it is accepted, 'Morphology Theory' risks having more to do with syntax than with word structure, rather as 'Case Theory' has more to do with syntax than with morphological case. Is maintenance of the UTAH worth this price?

Baker's Morphology Theory is meant to constrain equally both complex words formed by syntactic incorporation and complex words which, for whatever reason, have to be assigned to the lexicon (or to wherever nonsyntactic word formation takes place). Thus, all X^0 constituents, whatever their origin, have to obey affixal subcategorisation requirements and the Stray Affix Filter, and they cannot contain traces (1988a: 73). Moreover, the same affixes may occur in both syntactically formed and nonsyntactically formed words. For example, certain Chichewa verbs with the *-ir-/-er-* suffix have idiosyncratic meanings, such as *gon-er-* 'lie on' (literally 'sleep for'), *fik-ir-* 'receive' (literally 'arrive for'), *yend-er-* 'inspect' (literally 'walk for') (1988a: 70, 255); they must therefore constitute whole lexical items, even though they contain the item *-ir-/-er-* which also appears on its own as a preposition in D-structure. Similarly, the English passive suffix *-t/-ed/-en* shows the same distribution of allomorphs both in adjectival passives (*The vase seems broken*) and in verbal passives (*The vase was broken to annoy the auctioneer*), even though only the latter are formed syntactically, with the passive suffix appearing at D-structure as a X^0-level item in the Infl phrase. But, in emphasising the parallels between syntactic and nonsyntactic morphology, Baker provokes questions analogous to the ones arising from his emphasis on the parallels between 'ordinary' incorporation and grammatical function changing processes. For example, English is said to have two kinds of X^0 movement: V-to-Infl (in the passive) and P-to-V (in 'Dative-Shift' verbs). English also has various suffixes which form verbs from nouns 'in the lexicon', such as *-ise* (*cannibalise, computerise, Thatcherise, vaporise*). Why, then, does not English exploit these suffixes to form verbs 'in the syntax' by N-to-V movement? As a D-structure affixal V^0 subcategorised for noun stems, *-ise* would be exactly analogous to the 'N-V postbases' of Eskimo such as *-qar-* 'have' and *-si-* 'buy' (1988a: 142), which are always preceded by 'incorporated' objects (see section 4.8). Let us imagine a pseudo-English in which *-ise* can function as an independent D-structure verb in this way, with the meaning 'become' (cf. *vaporise*). In this pseudo-English, S-structures like (69) will be well formed, derived by Move-Alpha from D-structures like (70):

(69)   Ronald president$_i$-ised t_i of the USA
       'Ronald became president of the USA'

(70)

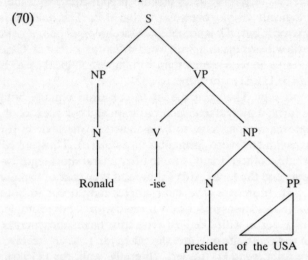

The fact that actual English is not like pseudo-English is presumably an accident in Baker's framework, and to that extent awkward. The overlap between syntactic and nonsyntactic morphology needs more investigation. Assuming that the overlap exists, why is it not greater than it is?

4.6 PARALLEL MORPHOLOGY

Baker aims to show that certain ostensibly morphological phenomena have a purely syntactic explanation, provided that certain affixes are treated as X^0 constituents. The converse of this goal would be to show that certain ostensibly syntactic phenomena have a purely morphological explanation. Borer (1988) offers an explanation on these lines for certain kinds of nominal expression in Hebrew. She calls her framework **Parallel Morphology**, because she posits a Word-Formation (WF) Component which operates in some sense parallel to the syntax. Most words, including all words which are 'listed' because they are semantically noncompositional, are inserted at D-structure; but the Word-Formation Component is also available to manufacture words at 'later' syntactic stages, at or before S-structure, from morphological material already present in the tree. The post-D-structure application of morphological rules (or word-formation processes) is heavily constrained syntactically, however, by her version of the Projection Principle (Borer 1984). This Principle has the effect of preventing the post-D-structure application of any rule which changes category (e.g. deriving nouns from verbs) or changes the linking of thematic roles (Theme, Goal, etc.) with arguments (external and internal) (see section 4.4). The Projection Principle thus imposes a dichotomy between words formed 'before' and 'after' D-structure which recalls in some respects the traditional distinction between derivation and inflection.

Let us suppose that we encounter a constituent which is semantically compositional and whose morphological components are related in such a way as to not violate the Projection Principle. According to Borer's criteria, this constituent need not be listed or inserted as a whole into D-structure, and could be formed 'after' D-structure by either syntactic or morphological rules. How are we to tell which analysis is correct? The answer has to do with the different principles which govern the WF Component and the syntax. Among the principles which Borer ascribes to the WF Component are Lieber's Feature-Percolation Conventions (see chapter 2). We will be concerned in particular with what Borer calls Secondary Percolation: the convention whereby, if the head of a word is not specified for some feature, the nonhead's (or complement's) specification for that feature percolates up to the node dominating the whole word.

Consider the so-called 'construct-state nominals' of modern Hebrew, illustrated in (71) (taken from Borer 1988), paying particular attention to the distribution of the definite article:

(71)   a.   ha-caʕif
            the-scarf
      b.   cəʕif ha-yalda
            scarf the-girl
            'the scarf of the girl'
            '*a scarf of the girl'
            '*the scarf of a girl'
      c.   *ha-caʕif ha-yalda
            the-scarf the-girl
            'the scarf of the girl'
      d.   *ha-caʕif yalda
            the-scarf girl
            'the scarf of a girl'

When unmodified, a noun may bear the prefixed definite article *ha-*, as in (71a). But when modified by an immediately following noun (expressing the possessor, for example), a noun cannot bear the prefixed article, as (71c, d) show. Instead, the definiteness of the whole expression is indicated by a prefixed article on the modifier, and the head noun appears in a special form known as the 'construct state' (*cəʕif* instead of *caʕif*), as in (71b). Notice also that, in regard to definiteness, (71b) has only one interpretation; both the head and the modifier must be interpreted as definite, so that this 'construct state' construction provides no way of expressing the asterisked interpretations of (71 b).

What happens if we wish to modify further the head noun *caʕif* by means of an adjective? The normal position for an attributive adjective is immediately after the noun it modifies, and it must agree in definiteness by carrying the article *ha-* if the head noun does:

(72)   ha-caʕif   ha-yafe
        the-scarf   the-pretty
        'the pretty scarf'

We might therefore expect that 'the boy's pretty scarf' would be expressed as in (73a), with (*ha-*) *yafe* immediately following the head noun *cəʕif*. In fact, however, the grammatical rendering is as in (73b), which is ambiguous as shown:

(73) a. *cəʕif   (ha-)yafe   ha-yeled
          scarf   (the-)pretty the-boy
     b. cəʕif   ha-yeled   ha-yafe
          scarf   the-boy   the-pretty
        'the boy's pretty scarf' *or* 'the pretty boy's scarf'

The construct-state nominal construction thus has two strange characteristics, from the syntactic point of view; definiteness which belongs semantically to the head (or to the nominal as a whole) is expressed on the complement, and the construction is indivisible, tolerating no intervening modifiers. But both these characteristics are expected if construct-state nominals are formed according to the rules of word structure, not syntax. Indivisibility is a widely recognised charcteristic of words, so it is natural that a modifier of the head of the whole word *cəʕif ha-yeled* should have to appear outside it. And so far as definiteness is concerned, Secondary Percolation supplies the answer. The existence of 'definiteness agreement', as in (72), suggests that [±definite] is a feature on nouns in modern Hebrew (according to Borer), and it is a feature for which it is reasonable to expect every noun to be specified; yet a morphological peculiarity of Hebrew prevents nouns in the construct state from having any value for [±definite]. It follows by Secondary Percolation that in a construct-state nominal the value for [±definite] must percolate up to the whole noun not from the head but from the modifier, which is therefore bound to be specified for definiteness if the whole nominal is to be well-formed. By invoking Secondary Percolation, we exploit a property of complex words which is independently attested. By contrast, if we seek a syntactic account of the facts, we run up against the difficulty that 'the percolation of properties from a complement to a maximal projection is syntactically unattested' (1988: 59). (Unfortunately for Borer, this last remark is now controversial; for example, Abney (1987) allows percolation of category status from complements to maximal projections even in syntax.)

The correctness of the percolation analysis is supported by the behaviour of a definite construct nominal which has a construct nominal as its complement, such as [*madaf* [*sifrey* [*ha-yalda*]]] '[the shelf [of the books [of the girl]]]'. As expected, only the complement of the most deeply embedded nominal (*ha-yalda*) may bear the definite prefix. On the other hand, an adjective modifying any of the nouns in the expression must 'agree in definiteness' by bearing the prefix *ha-*, e.g. [*madaf* [*sifrey*ᵢ [*ha-yalda*]]] [*ha-yafim*ⱼ] 'the shelf of the niceⱼ booksᵢ of the girl'. This implies that the feature [± definite] marked on *ha-yalda* percolates up in two stages, via the constituent *sifrey ha-yalda* to the whole nominal (Borer 1988: 59). If this is right, however, we have to concede that in Hebrew a morphologically formed constituent need not be an 'island' or 'syntactic atom', despite the claims of Di Sciullo and Williams (1987).

A central plank of the Parallel Morphology platform is that the same WF processes should be available for words formed 'before' D-structure as for ones formed 'after'. In modern Hebrew, this expectation is confirmed. Alongside construct-state nominals there is a class of 'compounds' which differ from them in being semantically noncompositional, as in (74):

(74) a. beyt xolim
          house sicks
          'hospital'
     b. beyt sefer
          house book
          'school'
     c. beyt safarim
          house books
          'library'

So far as definiteness is concerned, these behave just like construct-state nominals: *beyt ha-sefer* 'the school', *beyt ha-safarim* 'the library'.

Notice, however, that the definiteness which percolates up to *beyt ha-safarim* from the complement does not apply to *safarim* itself, in that a library can be a library without having any definite books in it or indeed any books at all (if they have all been stolen, or if the library has not yet been stocked, for example). But this is just what we expect, according to Borer, on the reasonable assumption that words inserted in D-structure are semantically opaque, interpreted as wholes. The whole 'compound' gets its value for the feature [+definite] from the complement *ha-safarim* because there is nowhere else for it to get it from; but, because *ha-safarim* as such never gets interpreted, *a fortiori* it never gets interpreted as definite or indefinite. It follows that 'compound' is a rather unfortunate term for these items; it implies that they differ from construct-state nominals in their structure, whereas in fact the difference is one of 'listedness'.

What are the implications of this analysis for syntactic and morphological theory jointly? In one sense, it represents a weakening; a structure which would be ill formed syntactically (because it involves feature percolation of a kind forbidden in syntax, for example) is nevertheless permitted, because a morphological analysis is available for it. On the other hand, Borer's approach suggests a way of handling certain kinds of highly productive and semantically compositional word formation which are problematic for most accounts of the interaction of the lexicon, word formation and syntax. We noted in section 4.1 that multiply embedded items such as *law degree language requirement change decision*, even if they are analysed as words rather than phrases, cannot be listed, because the list of them would be infinite. How, then, do they get integrated into syntactic structures? Borer's view of morphology as 'feeding' syntax at more than one level suggests a way. Let us consider how we might analyse in her framework the three expressions *sweatshop*, ˈtoyshop (with primary stress on *toy*) and *toy* ˈshop (with primary stress on *shop*). *Sweatshop*, with the opaque meaning 'factory in which workers (usually mainly women) work long hours for low wages', will be inserted into syntactic structures at D-structure, while ˈtoyshop, with the transparent meaning 'shop associated with (hence, pragmatically, for selling) toys' will be formed 'after' D-structure; both, however, are formed by the WF Component and observe the usual patterns of word formation in English, being of $[NN]_N$ structure and head-final. On the other hand, *toy* ˈshop 'shop which is a toy' will be formed syntactically, as a $[NN]_{N'}$ structure parallel to the more usual $[AN]_{N'}$ structure of e.g. *small shop*. Notice that ˈtoyshop and *toy* ˈshop both have broadly predictable meanings, but different ones; this will be taken care of by the fact that in LF (or wherever the meanings of complex morphological and syntactic units are built up from those of their constituents), the usual interpretation of $[N_1N_2]_N$ will be specified as 'N_2 relating to N_1', whereas one of the usual interpretations of $[N_1N_2]_{N'}$ will be specified as 'N_2 which is a N_1'.

This is clearly only the barest sketch of an approach; in particular, much more needs to be said about the 'usual interpretations' of head – modifier combinations in phrases. Also, Parallel Morphology seems to blur the distinction between morphology and the lexicon in the fashion criticised by Di Sciullo and Williams (1987). Borer provides for both listed and unlisted words (i.e. morphologically formed items), but not for listed items which are formed syntactically; yet clearly such items exist, as phrasal and clausal idioms (*keep tabs on, kick the bucket* etc.). What is needed, perhaps, is not a 'list' from which idiosyncratic items are drawn at the D-structure level but a provision whereby (subject to appropriate structural constraints) an idiosyncratic interpretation can be assigned to any complex item, whether it has arisen morphologically or syntactically. Pesetsky's suggestion of 'rules' for idiosyncratic interpretation at Logical Form may be a candidate (see section 4.7.1 below).

4.7 INTERLEVEL MAPPINGS AND MERGERS

In its morphological aspect, Baker's theory (section 4.5) constitutes a claim that some words are formed in the course of the mapping from D-structure to S-structure by the operation of Move-Alpha. Two other levels of representation recognised in Principles-and-Parameters theory are Logical Form (LF) and Phonological Form (PF), both of which are linked to, or interpret, S-structure; so it is natural to ask whether anyone has ascribed any word-forming role to the mappings from S-structure to LF or to PF. The answer is yes.

One of the roles of LF is to represent the scope of quantifiers (words like *some, any, all, every* and their synonyms) and their interaction with negation, conjunction (*and*) and disjunction (*or*); so LF representations look in some respects like predicate-calculus formulae, in which expressions glossable as 'for some *x*' or 'for every *x*' (with *x, y, z*, etc. as linking variables) cluster at the beginning. The mapping from S-structure to LF therefore involves a Quantifier Rule which, roughly speaking, moves certain expressions to positions higher up the tree, to yield a structure more directly reflecting their semantic relationships (May 1977). This device has been exploited in morphology by Pesetsky (section 4.7.1).

In 'classical' generative grammar, represented by Chomsky's *Aspects* (1965) and Chomsky and Halle's *The Sound Pattern of English* (1968), phonological 'interpretation' was a matter of rendering pronounceable a 'surface structure' conceived as a linear string of morphemes organised into a hierarchy of labelled constituents. In some more recent work in the Chomskyan tradition, including Baker's *Incorporation*, S-structure still does not look much different from that kind of surface structure. But a radical innovation in recent years has been the idea that, at syntactic levels of representation (D- and S-structure), constituents (including terminal elements, or morphemes) are not linearly ordered. According to this view, D- and S-structure and the principles governing them pay attention to **configurationality** (whereby a constituent's mother, sisters and daughters are identified) but not to **adjacency** (whereby a constituent's immediate neighbours, maximally two, are identified from among all its sisters) or to **precedence** (whereby the neighbour which follows is distinguished from the neighbour which precedes). The mapping between S-structure and PF therefore has considerably more to do than the old phonological interpretation of surface structure. As well as accounting for pronunciation, it must also impose a left-to-right order on constituents in accordance with the Head Parameter (which specifies for the language in question the order of heads and complements) and Case Theory (under which some constituents 'assign Case' leftwards or rightwards). And, to the extent that the terminal elements at S-structure include affixes and stems as well as words, it must also combine these affixes and stems appropriately; in Baker's terms, this is necessary to ensure compliance with Morphology Theory. Marantz (1988a) and Sproat (1988) argue that the mapping to PF indeed has a word-forming role on these lines (section 4.7.2).

4.7.1 The Quantifier Rule in morphology

In section 4.2 we looked at some so-called 'bracketing paradoxes'. One example is a negative comparative adjective such as *unhappier*; the phonological restrictions on the bases to which the comparative suffix *-er* can be attached suggest that it should be bracketed [un[happi+er]], whereas its meaning suggests a bracketing [[un+happi]er]. Pesetsky's (1985) suggestion for resolving this dilemma relies on the idea that the subcategorisation requirements of a lexical item need not all be satisfied at one level of representation. The comparative suffix *-er* imposes two requirements on its host stem: (a) that it should be an adjective and (b) that it should be monosyllabic, or else bisyllabic with a weak second syllable. Pesetsky suggests that requirement (b) is satisfied at S-structure (phonologically interpreted), by the bracketing [un[happi+er]], while requirement (a) is satisfied at Logical Form, by the bracketing [[un+happi]er]. This follows from a general principle that it is only at LF that requirements relating to the syntactic category of a constituent's sister need to be satisfied. A consequence of this principle is that, appropriately enough, it is the LF bracketing of *unhappier* which more closely reflects its meaning.

How are the two bracketings related? One mechanism which has already been posited for relating S-structure to LF is the **Quantifier Rule** (QR) which relates (75) to (76) (May 1977):

(75) [$_S$ John likes [$_{NP}$ every girl]]

(76) [$_S$[$_{NP}$ every girl]$_i$ [John likes e_i]]

Although Pesetsky does not rename this rule, he suggests a new formulation to allow it to apply to constituents other than quantifiers (1985: 216)

(77) QR: Adjoin a category [i.e. constituent] C to some node that dominates C.

The way in which this applies to *unhappier* is as follows. Its S-structure is represented as a labelled tree in (78):

(78)

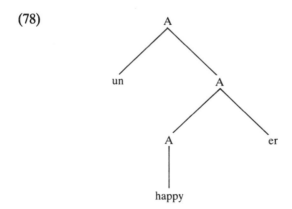

If we now apply rule (77) (QR), the result is as in (79):

(79)

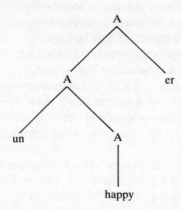

Notice that the linear order and bracketing of the constituents in (79) accord exactly with what Pesetsky suggests should be the LF structure. The Quantifier Rule thus seems to resolve this bracketing paradox in a satisfying way, and Pesetsky extends it to phrasal bracketing paradoxes such as *transformational grammarian*, where it raises the suffix *-ian* so as to yield a LF structure [[transformational grammar]ian]. But can we be sure that QR will not permit undesirable rebracketings as well as desirable ones?

The sort of risk we run is illustrated by the nonword **nationalhood*. In this 'word', the subcategorisation requirements of the affix *-hood* appear to be violated; *-hood* attaches to nouns, not adjectives (*girlhood, priesthood, nationhood; *girlishhood, *priestlyhood, *nationalhood*). But recall that, according to Pesetsky, it is only at LF that the sisters of each constituent are checked for categorial appropriateness. Notice, also, that the S-structure bracketing [[nation$_N$+al]$_A$hood] can be mapped by QR into a LF bracketing [[nation$_N$+hood]al]; and in this LF the categorial requirement of the subcategorisation frame of *-hood* is indeed met. One might object that **-hood-al* is a bad affix combination, because *-al* cannot attach to non-Latinate suffixes such as *-hood, -ship* and *-ness*. But that objection misses its mark; it is at S-structure, not LF, that purely lexical, noncategorial, restrictions need to be satisfied, and at S-structure, we have assumed, *-al* is suffixed not to *-hood* but to *nation*. It follows, seemingly, that **nationalhood* ought to be a possible word, if not an actual one, with the meaning 'pertaining to nationhood'; and **girlishhood* and **priestlyhood* ought to be possible words too, with analogous meanings. How can we rule out this undesirable consequence?

Pesetsky's answer relies on an obvious difference between the words in which we want QR to work (e.g. *unhappier*) and those in which we do not (e.g. **nationalhood*). Only in the latter does QR alter the order of the morphemes in the string, whereas in the former the application of the rule is 'string vacuous', that is it has no such effect. He therefore proposes a **String-Vacuousness Restriction** on morphological QR; it can operate only if 'the terminal string output does not differ from the terminal string input' (1985: 227). The trouble with this restriction, as Hoeksema (1987) points out, is that it does not apply to QR in its original role of relating structures like (75) and (76). It is needed solely in order to get QR to work right in morphology, and therefore seriously undermines Pesetsky's contention that the mechanisms which resolve bracketing paradoxes are independently motivated.[15]

Pesetsky's argument has an at first sight rather surprising by-product, which may prove to have more lasting influence than his treatment of bracketing paradoxes. This concerns the structure of idioms at LF. Pointing out that the word *rarity* has two meanings, a 'compositional' one 'the fact that/degree to which X is rare' and an 'idiosyncratic' one 'something that is rare', Pesetsky claims that the derived noun *unrarity* has only the compositional sense ('the fact that X is not rare') and not the perfectly conceivable 'idiosyncratic' sense 'something that is not rare'. He suggests that, in the idiosyncratic sense, no well-formed bracketing for *unrarity* at LF would be available. The categorial requirement for *un-* to be sister to an adjective at LF imposes the bracketing [[un+rar]ity]. On the other hand, Pesetsky suggests that there is a general property of idioms such that, for two constituents (such as *rar-* and *-ity*) to have jointly an idiosyncratic interpretation, they must be sisters at LF; this imposes the bracketing [un[rar+ity]]. These inconsistent requirements conspire to exclude the idiosyncratic reading for *unrarity*.

This analysis has far-reaching consequences for our notion of the lexicon, at least in its capacity as a repository of information about meanings. The fact that some constituent, whether word or phrase, is semantically noncompositional (e.g. *transmission, lifejacket, keep tabs (on)*) does not mean it has to be picked out as a unit from 'the lexicon' for insertion into syntactic structures; rather, syntax and morphology combine constituents without regard to meaning, and meanings may be assigned at LF to any individual morpheme and also to any pair of constituents related as sisters. Individual morphemes will usually get meanings, but need not do so (e.g. *-ceive, -fer, -mote* from the Latin-derived vocabulary of English); pairs of sister constituents will usually not get idiosyncratic meanings but may do so. This approach recalls in some respects Di Sciullo and Williams's (1987) view of the lexicon as list, independent of both syntax and morphology, but it seems superior in two respects: large complex 'listemes' such as phrasal idioms are not simply 'lawless' but are treated by syntax and morphology just as if they were compositional, so the regularity of their internal structure does not present a problem; and individual morphemes are explicitly allowed to be 'unlisted', so that it is possible for morphologically well-formed combinations of them to be meaningless (e.g. *preceive, perduce, commote*). Both conceptual and empirical issues arise in relation to this approach, of course. How idiosyncratic is 'idiosyncratic'? (As Pesetsky admits, the allegedly idiosyncratic 'something that is . . .' reading of *rarity* has parallels in *peculiarity, absurdity, oddity, impurity* etc., by contrast with *obesity, sanity, purity*, etc.) How does LF combine non-idiosyncratic meanings outside the realm of quantification and scope? Is it really true that non-sisters cannot have a joint idiosyncratic interpretation? But these issues seem worth pursuing – even if QR as a solution for bracketing paradoxes is abandoned (see section 4.2).[16]

4.7.2 Mapping between S-structure and Phonological Form

Marantz (1988a) and Sproat (1988), like Pesetsky (1985), suggest an analysis for bracketing paradoxes which involves different structures at different levels of representation. But they say that it is PF, not LF, which is the level concerned, alongside S-structure; and their treatment of these paradoxes links them not with quantifiers but with clitics. Marantz's and Sproat's approach differs from Pesetsky's in another, subtler, fashion. Their Mapping Principles are not rules or set of rules which derive PF from S-structure or vice versa; rather, they are conditions on pairs of representations, one at S-structure and one at PF, which determine whether any given pair can count as mutually corresponding. It follows that one S-structure can have more than one valid PF counterpart, and vice versa.

For both Marantz and Sproat, constituents at S-structure are arranged hierarchically but not linearly ordered. An S-structure representation tells us whether constituent A is a sister of constituent B, a daughter of B, or neither. Consequently, we can tell from S-structure whether A dominates or governs B in Principles-and-

Parameters terms, but not whether A is adjacent to B or whether A precedes or follows B. 'Adjacent to' and 'precede' are terms which apply to phonological representations, not to syntactic ones. Now, these terms differ logically in a fashion which is crucial for the way in which the Mapping Principle works. It is clear that if A precedes B, B does not precede A; or, if '(A^ B)' is used to mean 'a structure in which A immediately precedes B', then (A^ B) ≠ (B^ A). On the other hand, if (A^ B) immediately precedes a constituent C, it is clear that B immediately precedes C; using Sproat's notation, ((A^ B)^ C) = (A^ (B^ C)). In the terminology of algebra, the precedence operator ' ^ ' is not commutative but is associative. By contrast, adjacency has exactly the opposite characteristics; it is commutative but not associative. If '(A*B)' means 'a structure in which A is adjacent to B', then (A*B) = (B*A). On the other hand, the fact that C is adjacent to (A*B) does not guarantee the existence of a structure (B*C) adjacent to A; notationally, ((A*B)*C) ≠ (A*(B*C)).

We are now in a position to define Sproat's **Mapping Relation** (1988: 344). It states simply that, if two morphemes are sisters in S-structure, then their phonological representations must be adjacent in PF. Crucially, neither precedence nor bracketing (i.e. hierarchical structure) is mentioned. This means that, in a PF representation corresponding to any given S-structure, the morphemes can be in any order, provided only that (a) S-structure sisters are adjacent (in compliance with the Mapping Relation) and (b) there is compliance with any linear ordering imposed by other grammatical principles (such as Case Theory) and, in particular, the requirement that affixes are attached to appropriate stems. It also means that morphemes can be rebracketed into new constituent structures in PF, as the associativity of precedence allows. Let us look at how this works in practice with the familiar example *unhappier*. We posit an S-structure for this word which reflects its 'meaning' (just as Pesetsky's LF representation was meant to do), so *happy* is a sister of *un-* and [*happy, un-*] is a sister of *-er*: [[*happy, un-*], *-er*]. By the Mapping Relation, S-structure sisterhood is translated into adjacency: [[*happy*un-*]* *-er*]. Now, since adjacency is commutative, this is equivalent to [*-er*[*happy*un-*]], [[*un-*happy*]*-er*] and [*-er*[*un-*happy*]]. But in PF we must specify the linear order of morphemes, not just their adjacency; and clearly these four expressions are not equivalent when we translate '*' into '^'. Which, if any, of the four possible orderings are 'good'? Here, the status of *un-* as an adjectival prefix and *-er* as an adjectival suffix comes into play. Jointly, they ensure that [[*un-*ˆ*happy*]ˆ*-er*] reflects the only possible ordering. But, because precedence is associative, this is equivalent to [*un-*ˆ[*happy*ˆ*-er*]]. Again the question arises which, if either, of the two expressions is 'right'. This time the relevant consideration is the fact that *-er* does not attach to trisyllabic stems. It follows that [[*un-*ˆ*happy*]ˆ*-er*] must be ruled out in favour of [*un-*ˆ[*happy*ˆ*-er*]]. We thus conclude that there is precisely one well-formed PF counterpart to the S-structure representation of *unhappier*. Notice in particular that, although the bracketing at the two levels of representations differs, the Mapping Relation is complied with; nothing at PF separates the S-structure sisters *happy* and *un-* or the sisters [*happy*, *un-*] and *-er*. One can indeed think of the Mapping Relation as imposing a 'Sisterhood Vacuousness Restriction' on rebracketing at PF.

Both Sproat and Marantz are keen to exploit their Mapping Principles to account for the behaviour of **clitics** – elements with word-like properties from the point of view of syntax (even 'surface' syntax) but affix-like properties from the point of view of morphology and phonology.[17] The attraction of this idea lies in the fact that, just like bracketing paradoxes, clitics seem to involve mismatches between bracketings at different levels of representation. Consider, for example, the English modal *-'ll* as in *I'll go to Milwaukee*. Syntactically and semantically, it seems to be a sister of the material to its right: [[I] [will [go to Milwaukee]]]. Phonologically, however, it belongs with the material to its left: [[I'll] [go to Milwaukee]]. In terms of Klavans's (1985) classification of clitics on the three dimensions initial/final, before/after and proclitic/enclitic, it is *initial* in its phrase, comes *before* the peripheral constituent of its sister within its phrase, and is *enclitic*, i.e. phonologically part of the preceding word. From Sproat's point of view, this behaviour involves straightforward rebracketing in PF, just like *unhappier*. The Mapping Relation imposes in PF the adjacency requirements [[I]*[-ll*[go . . .]]], which are consistent with the structure [[I]ˆ[-ll ˆ[go . . .]]]; but, by associativity, this is equivalent to the bracketing [[Iˆ-ll]ˆ[go . . .]], which is imposed in preference to the first bracketing by the fact that *-ll* is a suffix.

But how are we to cope with **second-position clitics** – ones which, in Klavans's terms, are phrase-*initial* but come *after* the peripheral constituent? An example is provided by the following Papago sentence, containing an auxiliary clitic *-'o* (Marantz 1988a: 253, 262, citing Pranka 1983):

(80) [[[pi+'o]   iam-hu   cikpan]   g   Huan]
        Neg+Aux   there   work   Art   John
      'John is not working there'

Marantz argues that, in S-structure, *-'o* should be analysed as a sister to the rest of the clause:

(81) ['o   [s[v′   pi   iam-hu   cikpan]   g   Huan]]
       Aux   Neg   there   work   Art   John

But, because *-'o* is a suffix, it has to move to second position in PF in order to have something to be suffixed to. The drawback of this analysis from Sproat's point of view is that it violates his Mapping Relation; *pi* and *iam-hu* are sisters in S-structure, yet they are not adjacent in PF. And any such 'movement-in-PF' analysis of a second-position clitic will involve a similar violation. Not surprisingly, therefore, Sproat is keen to show that, with most if not all second-position clitics, the peripheral material which precedes the clitic has been moved there in the mapping between D-structure and S-structure, so there is in S-structure no longer any sisterhood relationship between this peripheral material and the material which follows the clitic. This kind of analysis is unattractive in Papago, however, because of evidence that the constituent labelled V′ in (81) is particularly resistant to syntactic disruption. The Papago facts therefore remain a stumbling-block for Sproat. How, then, does Marantz handle them?

Marantz's Mapping Principle is more elaborate than Sproat's but in relevant respects similar; it provides for linear adjacency as one of the possible PF counterparts of an S-structure relationship between two constituents. What is important so far as second-position clitics are concerned is his separate principle of **Morphological Merger** (1988a: 161):[18]

(82) At any level of syntactic analysis: (D-structure, S-structure, phonological structure), a relation between X and Y may be replaced by (expressed by) the affixation of the lexical head of X to the lexical head of Y.

Marantz invokes this principle to handle many of the syntactico-morphological phenomena which Baker describes in terms of X^0 movement (see section 4.5). Despite its title, the principle clearly has applications well outside morphology in the traditional sense (Marantz 1984). We are concerned here only with morphological

applications, however. The S-structure configuration ['o [[pi iam-hu
. . .]]] in (81) is mapped into a phonological structure with adjacency
constraints ['o*[[pi*iam-hu* . . .]]]; this in turn is compatible with an
ordering ['oˆ[[pi ˆiam-huˆ...]]] which, because of the associativity
of precedence, is equivalent to [['o ˆpi]ˆ[iam-hu ˆ...]]. Now,
applying Morphological Merger to the constituent ['oˆpi], we
derive [pi+'o], with -'o adjoined to *pi* in the normal fashion,
that is as a daughter of (a copy of) the node directly dominating
pi:

(83)

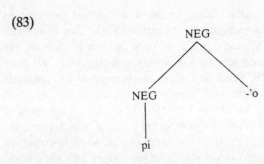

The adjunction structure is the key to Marantz's answer to the problem
of how *pi* and *iam-hu* can remain adjacent even after -'o has been
suffixed to *pi*: 'any adjacency relations borne by the root word
will be satisfied by adjacency relations of the whole derived word'
(1988a: 263), so *pi-'o* is just as much adjacent to *iam-hu* as *pi* was.
On the other hand, Merger will disrupt the adjacency relationship
between -'o and anything to its left in S-structure; it is therefore
predicted (correctly, says Marantz) that -'o will not be cliticised to
the first element of V' if a constituent has been fronted to the left
of Aux.

This analysis appears to take care of the Papago data while
also explaining why second-position clitics are generally in second
position in the whole sentence, not in some clause-internal phrase.
Nevertheless, there is evidence that Morphological Merger is too
powerful a device. Consider again the nonword *nationalhood* meaning 'pertaining to nationhood' (section 4.7.1). Pesetsky's problem was
to prevent the derivation from S-structure [[nation+al]hood] of a LF
representation [[nation+hood]al] by the morphological Quantifier
Rule. These two bracketings are close to what in a Marantz – Sproat
analysis will be PF and S-structure representations respectively.
At (84) we see how the two can be related in the Marantzian
framework:

(84)   S-structure (unordered):   [-al, [-hood, nation]]
                                     'pertaining to nationhood'
       Mapping Principle: [-al*[-hood*nation]]
       Commutativity of adjacency:[-al*[nation*-hood]]
       Precedence: [-al^[nation^-hood]]
       Associativity of precedence: [[-al^nation]^-hood]
       Morphological Merger: [[nation+al]^-hood]
       Morphological Merger: [[nation+al]+hood]

There is therefore a well-formed correspondence between [-al, [-hood, nation]] and *nationalhood*, and it is predicted that the latter should be at least a possible word with the meaning 'pertaining to nationhood'. Notice that, because *-al* is merged with *nation*, *nation* still counts as adjacent to *-hood*, in accordance with the Mapping Principle.

The implications for morphology of relegating linear order to Phonological Form are considerable, so it is hardly surprising that current versions of Morphological Merger and the Mapping Principle do not resolve all difficulties which arise. One way forward might be to distinguish between morpheme orderings which are determined by a Mapping Principle shared with syntax, and ones which are fixed 'beforehand'. If it could be shown independently that *national*, *girlish* and *priestly* must function as wholes in S-structure (perhaps because the affixes *-al* and *-ish* are purely 'local' in scope, unlike the Papago auxiliary marker *-'o*), then Morphological Merger could not have the unwanted consequences just outlined. But this suggestion has yet to be explored.

4.8 COANALYSIS AND AUTOLEXICAL SYNTAX

In sections 4.5 and 4.7, we have looked at some morphological implications of mappings between different structures at different levels of representation (D-structure, S-structure, LF and PF). In this section, we will be concerned with the morphological implications of the idea that the same structure may, in some sense, have two distinct but simultaneous representations. In the Principles-and-Parameters model and in work close to it, this phenomenon is generally labelled **coanalysis**. It is also a central feature of the Autolexical Syntax model developed by Sadock (1985; 1988). There are various versions of coanalysis, classifiable as follows:

(a)   Two distinct structures, one wholly syntactic, the other partly syntactic and partly morphological (Zubizarreta 1985; Zubi-

zarreta and van Haaften 1988;[19] Di Sciullo and Williams 1987).
(b) Two distinct structures, one syntactic and one morphological
(Sadock 1985; 1988).

Zubizarreta's concern is with Romance causative constructions, some
of which we can illustrate from French as follows:

(85) Pierre fera   travailler Marie
      Pierre will-make   work   Marie
      'Pierre will make Marie work'

(86) Pierre fera   nettoyer la chambre à   Marie
      Pierre will-make   clean   the room   to Marie
      'Pierre will make Marie clean the room'

The salient fact is that, whereas the English construction can plausibly
be analysed as biclausal ([*Pierre will make* [s*Marie clean the room*]]),
such an analysis is much less evidently correct in the Romance
examples. In (85) and (86), *fera* forms a tight unit with its following
infinitive, allowing no noun phrase to intervene, and the Agent of the
'lower' verbs *travailler* and *nettoyer* (*Marie* in each instance) surfaces
not as the subject of a lower clause but either in the normal 'object'
position, as in (85), or else (when the 'lower' verb has an object of
its own) in a prepositional phrase, as in (86). The data are more
complex than this brief sketch suggests, and Zubizarreta's argument
is elaborate; but her conclusion is that a causative sentence such as
(85) has two simultaneous S-structure bracketings, as follows:

(87)

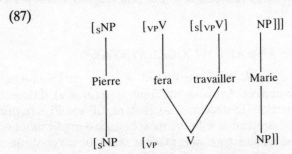

These bracketings differ in that one of them treats *fera travailler* as
a sequence of two verbs while the other treats it as a single verb.
The second bracketing raises the question: what is the status of the
verb's two constituents, *fera* and *travailler*? Zubizarreta's answer is
that *travailler* is a stem to which *fera* is 'affixed' (the inverted commas
are hers). Neither *fera* nor any inflected form of *faire* 'make' is an
affix in the ordinary sense, of course; but Zubizarreta introduces a

distinction between **morphosyntactic** and **morphophonological affixes**. Morphophonological affixes are affixes in the traditional sense, e.g. the Person-Number suffix *-a* in *fera* and the Infinitive ending *-er* in *travailler*. Morphophonologically, *fera* is not an affix but a word; but from the point of view of some aspects of the syntax of French causatives (Zubizarreta claims), it behaves like a bound morpheme – a morphosyntactic affix – and it is the unit *fera travailler* which behaves like a word.

Di Sciullo and Williams (1987: 88–106) adopt a similar analysis of French causative constructions. The main differences between their approach and Zubizarreta's stem from their insistence that 'morphology and syntax are different sciences about different objects', with partially distinct vocabularies and obeying different principles (46–7). The kind of interpenetration between syntax and morphology that Zubizarreta and Baker allow is therefore forbidden. This commits Di Sciullo and Williams to the claim that coanalysed structures, in their morphological guise, must display all the characteristics of **morphological objects**, in their terminology; for example, the Right-Hand Head Rule (1987: 26; cf. section 4.3.2), which entails that the category of a word is determined by the category of the rightmost constituent whose category is specified. This condition is satisfied by [*fera travailler*] $_V$ inasmuch as *travailler* is a verb. Unfortunately, it is not satisfied in all the other putative coanalyses that Di Sciullo and Williams propose. For example, they suggest that one can maintain the generalisation that an object NP always follows its verb in French if one analyses a postverbal adverb as part of the verb:

(88)   Il   [mange   rapidement]$_V$ [ses   pâtes]$_N$
       he   eats   quickly   his   pasta
       'He eats his pasta quickly'

But *mange rapidement* is then a verb whose 'head' is an adverb – an impossible 'morphological object'. In fact, the differences between morphology and syntax as 'sciences' would seem to restrict severely the circumstances under which coanalysis is possible – a conclusion that Di Sciullo and Williams may welcome, in view of their dictum that 'coanalysis is not core grammar, it is simply the best you can do under the circumstances' (1987: 91).

Analyses on Zubizarreta's lines have been suggested for constructions in other languages which are broadly similar to the Romance causatives in that they involve pairs of verbs which are adjacent in surface structure (e.g. Bok-Bennema and Groos 1988: 51–4; Coopmans and Everaert 1988: 88–100). Clearly, this sort of coanalysis is a powerful tool for the syntactician. What are its consequences for morphological theory?

For Principles-and-Parameters morphologists, an obvious problem is that it is hard to reconcile 'morphosyntactic affixation' with the Stray Affix Filter of Baker (1988a) (see section 4.5). In Baker's framework, having determined that some X^0-level constituent is an affix, we know at once that it must be combined (morpho-) phonologically with some other X^0 constituent in order to yield a well-formed S-structure; for otherwise the Stray Affix Filter will be violated. Moreover, Baker assumes tacitly that affixhood is an inherent, lexically determined property of an item; that is, if a given item is an affix in one context, it is an affix in all contexts. But if morphosyntactic and morphophonological affixes are distinct, neither of these assumptions can be made. An affix may be of the purely morphosyntactic kind, in which case it undergoes a new kind of 'affixation' requiring it to be adjacent to its 'stem' while permitting it to remain morphophonologically a 'stray'. And a lexical item such as French *faire* must be allowed to be an affix in some contexts (as in the lower analysis in (87)) and a free form in others (as in the upper analysis in (87), or in contexts such as *Pierre fera tout* 'Pierre will do everything'). So, quite apart from its syntactic implications, this kind of coanalysis creates morphological difficulties which (so far as I know) have not yet received attention.

Sadock's oddly named **Autolexical Syntax** (1985) resembles Di Sciullo and Williams's approach in that it distinguishes morphology rigidly from syntax. It differs from theirs, however, in that it disallows bracketings which are partly syntactic and partly morphological, like the lower bracketing for *Pierre fera travailler Marie* in (87). Rather, syntax and morphology are autonomous components, each of which imposes an independent set of requirements to be met by every well-formed sentence. A simple illustration is provided by the English sentence *John's here*:

(89)

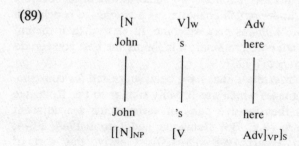

Here the upper bracketing is morphological (with W standing for Word) while the lower is syntactic. Notice that the sentence is analysed into the same basic constituents both morphologically and syntactically, and that they appear in the same order (so that the 'association lines' between the two representations do not cross). Neither of these characteristics applies to all autolexical analyses, although the second is much more general than the first. Mismatches between syntax and morphology in basic constituency are common; for example, the item *Americanise* will be analysed as a single basic constituent (labelled V) in syntax, but as two constituents, *American-* (N) and *-ise* (V) in morphology, bracketed as [NV]ᵥ (1985: 388). Notice also that the category labels attached to the three elements (N, V and Adv) are the same in both analyses; Sadock suggests that this may always be the case, whenever an element in the string is a basic constituent of both morphological and syntactic structure.

Whereas for Di Sciullo and Williams morphological and syntactic coanalysis is an expedient which the grammar resorts to only when all else fails, so to speak, for Sadock it is central, as a consequence of the distinction between morphology and syntax. But to what extent, and in what ways, can the two analyses diverge? Sadock answers this question mainly by reference to West Greenlandic Eskimo. Consider the West Greenlandic sentence *Hansi illoqarpoq* 'Hans has a house', segmentable as *Hansi illu-qar-poq*. This contains the 'postbase' *-qar-* 'have', which is syntactically a verb but morphologically an affix:

(90)

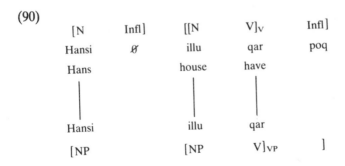

Inflectional affixes are represented solely in the morphology, and the constituent *illu-qar-*, though a constituent in both analyses, has different labels: it is a complex word morphologically but a phrase syntactically. A more radical mismatch between the two analyses occurs in sentences where, in Baker's terms, noun incorporation has occurred. Consider the sentence *Hansi ataatsinik qamuteqarpoq* 'Hans has one sled'. Here *qamut-* 'sled' has been incorporated with the verbal postbase *-qar-*, leaving its modifier *ataaseq-* 'one' stranded (and subsequently modified morphophonologically). To cope with this, Sadock posits a difference in ordering between the basic constituents in morphology and syntax:

(91)

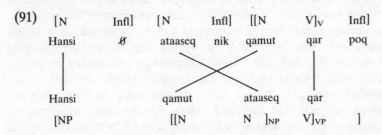

But what legitimises this reordering? If association lines between syntactic and morphological analyses are allowed to cross indiscriminately, then clearly the theory is much too powerful, authorising mismatches of kinds which never occur. Sadock's answer is reminiscent of Marantz's Morphological Merger. The morphological order in (91) is the only one which is consistent with the two requirements that (a) *-qar-* is morphologically an affix and so must be attached to some stem, and (b) the stem to which *-qar-* is affixed must be the head, not the modifier, of the NP which *-qar-* governs. Let us leave aside the question whether requirement (b) reflects any general principle, and focus on requirement (a). The fact that it is satisfied, so that the 'surface' order of elements in the sentence reflects the morphological rather than the syntactic analysis, implies that morphology has in some respects priority over syntax. Sadock expresses this as the principle that 'constraints on morpheme ordering are inviolable' (1985: 408). At the same time, he suggests, the ordering mismatch is kept to the minimum necessary in order to satisfy this principle; if it can be satisfied with only one pair of crossed association lines, then any alternative orderings with more than one line-crossing will be rejected.

Di Sciullo and Williams do not discuss data of this kind, so one cannot compare their approach with Sadock's directly.[20] Baker (1988a) certainly does discuss such data, but he posits quite different factors from Sadock as relevant to determining when a noun can incorporate into a verb. For Sadock, it is a matter of meeting the requirements of morpheme ordering with the fewest possible line-crossings; for Baker, however, it is mainly a matter of ensuring that the trace left by the 'moved' noun is properly governed. On the face of it, Autolexical Syntax imposes a tighter 'locality' requirement on incorporation than Move-Alpha does. But research is clearly needed to test which explanation better fits a wider range of facts.

4.9 A RECURRENT PROBLEM: ALLOMORPHY

In his review of Di Sciullo and Williams (1987), Baker (1988c: 260) comments: 'Virtually every topic of current research [in generative morphology] is addressed to some degree: compounding, the relationship between derivation and inflection, productivity and semantic transparency of affixes, argument structure operations, anaphoric islandhood, affix ordering, polysynthetic constructions, bracketing paradoxes, and phrases "reanalyzed" as words.' One topic omitted from this list is allomorphy; but Baker is right to omit it, because allomorphy is not at the centre of any generative morphologist's concerns, and we have already noted Baker's own ambivalence about it. In fact, there is at present an unresolved contradiction in the generative attitude towards allomorphy. On the one hand, if several affixes with the same meaning or function are distributed more or less arbitrarily, then a word formed with one of these affixes is to that extent idiosyncratic and is therefore usually analysed as being listed in the lexicon rather than constructed syntactically. On the other hand, the various shapes which an affix displays in different contexts may be merely a matter of Phonological Form, and no obstacle to treating that affix as a syntactic constituent, combining with stems syntactically (e.g. by Move-Alpha). But how do we tell when we are dealing with several synonymous affixes, and when we are dealing with one affix with several phonological shapes? At present, similar patterns of alternation are analysed in either of these two ways.

Here are some analyses of the first type. The variety of nominalising suffixes in English (-*ion*, -*ment*, -*ance*, -*al*, etc.) constituted one of the reasons why Chomsky (1970) placed derived nominals 'in the lexicon'; none of these suffixes displays the kind of productivity typical of syntactic operations. Sproat (1985: 97) uses a similar argument to account for the unacceptability of would-be bracketing paradoxes such as *symphony orchestrate* and *white elephantine*. Because -*ate* and -*ine* are not productive suffixes, he says, words containing them must be lexically listed, so these suffixes are not available to combine with phrases such as *symphony orchestra* and *white elephant*. Evers (1988: 123) argues on similar grounds that the formation of past participles in Dutch 'takes place in the lexicon'. He points out that some past participles have a prefix *ge-* while others do not, some are suffixed *-t* while others have *-en*, and some display vowel change while others do not.

Here now are a couple of analyses of the second type. Sproat (1985: 274) argues that an item NOM, or 'nominalisation', is motivated syntactically in English; 'NOM is a real syntactic entity, and spells itself out phonologically with the affixes *-ing*, *-tion*, *-ment*, *-ance*, . . ., each depending on the particular verb chosen.'[21] Fabb (1988a) argues on grounds of Case Theory that English passive participles like *dropped*, *broken* and *sung* are to be analysed as verbs containing noun phrases: syntactically, they are $[drop_V\ en_{NP}]_V$, $[break_V\ en_{NP}]_V$, $[sing_V\ en_{NP}]_V$.[22]

The contradiction between the two types of analysis is evident. The idiosyncrasies which seem to Evers to show that the affixes which form past participles in Dutch are not separate syntactic entities are precisely similar to the idiosyncrasies displayed by English passive (or past) participles, yet Fabb in effect ignores Evers's argument. And Sproat's analysis of nominalisations in English is not only incompatible with Chomsky's (1970) but also hard to square with his own analysis of *elephantine* and *orchestrate*. If the unproductivity of *-ine* and *-ate* shows that these words are lexically listed, why does not the unproductivity of at least some nominalisation suffixes (cf. section 2.7) show that the words formed with them are lexically listed too? One may argue, of course, that in some circumstances the arguments for a lexical analysis can be overridden by syntactic considerations. But, as yet, proponents of syntactic affixation within the Principle-and-Parameters framework (including Baker, as noted in section 4.5) have not specified what these circumstances are. For the time being, allomorphy remains for them something of an embarrassment.

Part III

Other Impetuses in
Morphological Research

5 Typological and diachronic issues

5.1 INTRODUCTION

Languages have been assigned to distinct types on the basis of two main sets of criteria: morphological and syntactic. The classification of languages according to their morphological structure has a long history, extending back to the early nineteenth century. Typology based on word order (or 'the order of meaningful elements', in Greenberg's phrase (1963)) is much more recent.[1] But both kinds of classification, if they provide criteria for identifying the characteristics of a language which are inconsistent with its dominant type, can generate expectations about morphological change. Whether these changes take place or not therefore contributes to deciding whether the typology in question is sensible or useful. Phonology is relevant here too, since a language's morphology can be affected by phonological change in far-reaching ways. A standard example of this is the neutralisation and loss of many unstressed vowels in Early Middle English, which is traditionally seen as a major factor in destroying the English case system and radically simplifying English verb morphology. Such changes can in turn impinge on syntax, as when loss of case leads to more rigid word order. These syntactic changes can then generate new expectations about morphology, and so on. Theories of linguistic types ought, therefore, in principle to have plenty to contribute to at least some kinds of theory about morphology, and vice versa, with language change as the main testing ground for the mutually relevant predictions.

Section 5.2 discusses the morphological relevance of typologies based mainly on syntax; section 5.3 looks at more traditional morphological typology. My assessment of the suggestions about morphology which have followed directly from this work up to now is rather negative. But that is not to say that further investigation on these lines is bound to be unfruitful. More importantly, typological claims underlie much of the theoretical work on morphology which we will be discussing in later chapters.

5.2 GREENBERG'S UNIVERSALS

Among English-speaking linguists, the main inspiration for recent typological work has been Greenberg (1963), who in turn gives credit to Jakobson.[2] Greenberg proposes forty-five **universals** of an implicational kind: if a language has characteristic X, then it will have (or is overwhelmingly likely to have) characteristic Y. The basis is a sample of thirty languages, supplemented with observations about others; so, although Greenberg states some universals without qualification and some of them hold for all the languages which he knows about, they are statistical rather than absolute, not intended as direct claims about an innate language faculty or Universal Grammar in the Chomskyan sense. Of the forty-five, twenty (Universals 26–45) concern morphology specifically; yet some of his syntactic universals have morphological relevance too, as we will see in the next section.

The twenty morphological universals can be divided into four groups. Some relate to the position and nature of morphological markers; others to morphological categories (number, gender and so on) and their mutual relationships; others to the distribution of morphological categories among word-classes and to agreement patterns; and still others to the relationship between categories and their inflectional exponents. All are quoted here, even though not all have been equally influential.

The first group of universals concerns morphological markers:

Universal 26. If a language has discontinuous affixes, it always has either prefixing or suffixing or both.

Universal 27. If a language is exclusively suffixing, it is postpositional; if it is exclusively prefixing, it is prepositional.

Universal 28. [Where both derivational and inflectional elements are found together,] if both the derivation and inflection follow the root, or they both precede the root, the derivation is always between the root and the inflection.

Universal 29. If a language has derivation, it always has inflection.

Of these, Universal 28 (or a version of it) is cited in almost every discussion of the difference between derivation and inflection.

The second group concerns categories and their relationships to one another:

Universal 34. No language has a trial number unless it has a dual. No language has a dual unless it has a plural.

Universal 36. If a language has the category of gender, it always has the category of number.

Universal 37. A language never has more gender categories in non-singular numbers than in the singular.

Universal 41. If in a language the verb follows both the nominal subject and nominal object in the dominant order, the language almost always has a case system.

Two of the universals so far cited, 27 and 41, explicitly link a morphological characteristic with a syntactic one. We will return to the implications of this in the next section.

The third group concerns categories and their distribution:

Universal 30. If the verb has categories of person–number or if it has categories of gender, it always has tense–mode categories.

Universal 31. If either the subject or object noun agrees with the verb in gender, then the adjective always agrees with the noun in gender.

Universal 32. Whenever the verb agrees with a nominal subject or nominal object in gender, it also agrees in number.

Universal 33. When number agreement between the noun and verb is suspended and the rule is based on order, the case is always one in which the verb precedes and the verb is in the singular.

Universal 40. When the adjective follows the noun, the adjective expresses all the inflectional categories of the noun. In such cases the noun may lack overt expression of one or all of these categories.

Universal 42. All languages have pronominal categories involving at least three persons and two numbers.

Universal 43. If a language has gender categories in the noun, it has gender categories in the pronoun.

Universal 44. If a language has gender distinctions in the first person, it always has gender distinctions in the second or third person, or both.

Universal 45. If there are any gender distinctions in the plural of the pronoun, there are some gender distinctions in the singular also.

The fourth group concerns categories and their exponents:

Universal 35. There is no language in which the plural does not have some nonzero allomorphs, whereas there are languages in which the singular is expressed only by zero. The dual and the trial are almost never expressed only by zero.

Universal 38. Where there is a case system, the only case which ever has only zero allomorphs is the one which includes among its meanings that of the subject of the intransitive verb.

Universal 39. Where morphemes of both number and case are present and both follow or both precede the noun base, the expression of number almost always comes between the noun base and the expression of case.

Much of the work described in later chapters can be thought of as a search for links between these universals belonging to different groups.

5.2.1 Greenberg's syntactic universals and morphology

It was undoubtedly Greenberg's twenty-five universals of word order, not his twenty morphological ones, which had the most immediate impact on the linguistic community. He pointed out that in the vast majority of languages the dominant word order conforms to one of the three patterns VSO, SVO and SOV (where S, O and V stand for subject, object and verb respectively); furthermore, that this dominant order has implications for the relative order of other elements, such as modifiers and heads in noun phrases and auxiliaries and verbs in verb phrases, and for the choice between prepositions and postpositions (that is, for what we may call 'adpositional preference'). These observations led to a considerable upsurge in work on word-order typology in the 1970s, attempting in particular to account for syntactic changes in various languages in terms of pressure to do away with characteristics which rendered the language in question typologically inconsistent – that is, which caused it to violate some universal.[3]

For morphologists, it is SOV order and adpositional preference which are most important. If a language has SOV order, we expect it to have morphological case, through Universal 41, quoted above. Adpositional preference has links with the choice between prefixes and suffixes ('affixal preference') via Universal 27; it also ties in with dominant word order, through Universal 3 and 4, quoted below:

Universal 3. Languages with dominant VSO order are always prepositional.

Universal 4. With overwhelmingly greater than chance frequency, languages with normal SOV order are postpositional.

As an example of how these universals are interlinked, consider a hypothetical language which has suffixation as its only morphological process. (In this respect, it resembles Turkish.) By virtue of Universal 27, it is predicted to have only postpositions, no prepositions; consequently, by Universal 3, it cannot be a VSO language, so it must be either SOV or SVO. Now suppose that, perhaps through borrowing, this language acquires some transparently prefixed lexical material and at the same time, through phonological attrition, it loses its distinct case suffixes, whose function is fulfilled instead by prenominal adverbs or particles which come to be reinterpreted as prepositions. (This last development resembles what has happended in English and many other Indo-European languages since their Proto-Indo-European origins.) Before these developments took place, the language might have had SOV as its dominant order; but, after these developments, Universals 4 and 41 predict that the language will almost certainly switch to SVO or even VSO.

The point of this hypothetical example is to show how Greenberg's typology can give rise to a chain of expectations about change, including morphological change, and so to show how in principle his universals can be tested by diachronic evidence, morphological as well as syntactic. The next step in the enquiry would therefore seem logically to be to find various languages for which there is solid evidence of change in one or more of Greenberg's parameters (basic constituent order, adpositional preference, the presence of case and so on) and check whether these changes are consistent with what his universals lead us to expect. Some purely syntactic universals have certainly been checked diachronically in this way (e.g. Hawkins 1983: 215–32, 258–9), especially Universal 41. From this it follows that if a language shifts from SVO to SOV order, or if a language retains SOV order despite losing its original case markers, then that language should either (a) acquire (new) case markers or (b) switch (back) to SVO order.

Prediction (a) is relevant to Chinese and to certain west African languages, and has been tested for them by Li and Thompson (1974) and by Givón (1975). The outcome of these tests is mixed. For example, Archaic Chinese had a clear SVO structure. This pattern still occurs in modern Mandarin (or Putonghua), and is exemplified in (1); but the language is now moving towards a verb-final pattern, exemplified in (2) (examples from Li and Thompson 1974 and 1975, with tone marks omitted):

(1)   Wo   da   Zhang-san   le
      I   hit Zhang-san   Aspect
      'I hit Zhang-san'

(2)   a.   Wo   ba   Zhang-san   da   le
           I   Object   Zhang-san   hit Aspect
           'I hit Zhang-san'

      b.   Haizi   ba   shu   mai   le
           child   Object   book   buy   Aspect
           'The child bought the book' (or: 'What the child did
           to the book was buy it')

      c.   Shu   bei   haizi   mai   le
           book   Agent   child   buy   Aspect
           'The book was bought by a/the child'

In (2), where the verb is final (but for the aspect marker), the second noun phrase is marked for 'case' by a preposition *ba* (glossed 'Object') or *bei* (glossed 'Agent'), just as Universal 41 predicts if SOV is now the dominant order. (*Ba* and *bei* happen in fact to be derived historically from verbs.) But (2) does not exhaust the verb-final patterns of colloquial Chinese, since there are also 'topicalised' sentences such as in (3), without any 'case' marking:

(3)   a.   Shu,   haizi   mai   le
           book   child   buy   Aspect
           'As for the book, the child bought it'

      b.   Haizi,   shu   mai   le
           child   book   buy   Aspect
           'The child bought the book'

Furthermore, even the pattern in (2) is inconsistent with one of Greenberg's statistical universals, namely Universal 4, which favours postpositions rather than prepositions in SOV languages.

Prediction (b) receives clear *prima facie* support from the drift towards SVO order in most of the Indo-European languages which have lost overt case marking (e.g. English and the modern western Romance languages). A traditional view of this change is that it maintains communicative efficiency by substituting order for morphological marking to signal syntactic function. The trouble is that many languages adopt a 'belt and braces' strategy in that they have SVO order while still retaining morphological case; Vennemann (1975: 295) cites Russian, Finnish, Old English and (in main clauses) modern German. If these all have SOV ancestors (a widespread though not universal view for both Proto-Indo-European and Proto-

Finno-Ugric), then they must have changed their dominant word order for a reason which has nothing to do with the loss of case marking; so even in the languages which did lose morphological case it is questionable how far we are entitled to attribute the development of SVO order to that cause. Vennemann pleads that the case system of Old English was 'not dependable' (one marker could have many functions), 'nonuniform' (one function could be fulfilled by many markers) and 'largely inconspicuous' (being often dependant on ablaut of an unstressed vowel), and so was inadequate to meet the requirement that Universal 41 imposes on SOV languages. But this argument brings into the typological debate considerations of semiotic 'naturalness' (to be discussed in chapter 8), whose ramifications will have to be explored more fully before Vennemann's plea can be accepted. Besides, it is not clear how justly the same accusations can be levelled against case marking in other SVO languages such as Russian and in particular Finnish, which is much closer to the canonical agglutinative pattern than Old English is and is therefore semiotically better behaved.

The upshot for the morphological theorist is frustrating. Of the Greenbergian universals relating to morphology, two seem not to have been checked against diachronic data at all (Universals 3 and 27) and for one (Universal 4) the Chinese facts are discouraging. Even for Universal 41, which has been checked diachronically, the outcome is unclear. Loss of case marking may contribute to word-order changes, but it is hard to disentangle its effect from that of other factors. It is also hard to justify the claim that a shift towards SOV can engender case as a morphosyntactic category. Quite apart from the 'topicalised' Chinese sentences at (3), where 'case' is not marked at all, what we observe in (2) is not so much morphological case as prepositional marking of direct object and agent. In fact, Universal 41 might be better formulated as follows:

Universal 41 (revised). If in a language the verb follows both the nominal subject and nominal object in the dominant order, the language almost always distinguishes subject and object by overt marking (morphological or other).

This version is consistent with the Chinese facts but evidently less interesting to the morphologist.

5.2.2 Morphology as evidence in syntactic reconstruction

Work in Greenbergian typology has not been restricted to testing and refining the universals by application to *états de langue* for which data are available. Universals of the Greenbergian kind have also been used to help reconstruct prehistoric *états de langue*. The pioneer of this technique in syntactic reconstruction was Lehmann (1973). The logic of the technique is as follows: one assumes that some relevant set of universals is correct and, in the light of this assumption, one tries to deduce what some prehistoric language (or *état de langue*) must have been like in order for its attested descendants to have evolved from it. This procedure is risky. Its validity clearly depends on how solidly the universals in question have been established and on how firmly one can rule out interfering factors such as language contact. There is a less obvious danger too. By no means all attested languages are typologically totally consistent – indeed, the very idea of using Greenbergian universals to explain language change presupposes inconsistency, which will generate pressure for change. We have therefore no right to suppose that any stage of any protolanguage will be typologically consistent either. The best that can be hoped for is that the universals may point us towards characteristics which the protolanguage must have had at some stage or another, not necessarily all at the same time.

For the morphologist, what is most interesting is Lehmann's use of word structure in syntactic reconstruction (1969; 1975), carrying on an established tradition in Indo-European philology. He sums up his assumptions and aim as follows: 'If compounds in some way reflect sentence patterns, by examining types of compounds which we may assume for PIE [Proto-Indo-European] we may gain further information for our revised views on PIE sentence patterns' (1969: 4). Vedic (early Sanskrit) has a certain number of synthetic compounds of the type *madhu-pa* 'honey-drinking', where the second element (*-pa* 'drink(ing)') is verbal and (in the terminology of chapter 4) the first element is the object or the Theme of the verb. This type of compound becomes less frequent in later Sanskrit and is therefore probably old, inherited from Proto-Indo-European. In 1969, Lehmann cites these compounds as evidence that Proto-Indo-European was an OV language, on the basis that the OV structure of this old compound-type in Sanskrit reflects earlier sentence structure. In 1975 the argument is somewhat more subtle. Why should earlier embedded clausal structures of the type *madhu pa-* '(one who) drinks honey' have become combined into compound words? Let us assume that in late Proto-Indo-European the original OV pattern was changing towards a VO pattern. In that case there would be pressure for an embedded clause like *madhu pa-* to change in the direction of *pa- madhu*; the only way for the original order to be preserved would be for the clause to cease to be a clause – to become a syntactic atom, analysable now only morphologically, as a compound word. The *madhu-pa* type of compound is therefore evidence not for the syntactic pattern of the language at the time when it was productive ('late' Proto-Indo-European, changing to VO) but for the immediately preceding period ('early' Proto-Indo-European, still rigidly OV).

These morphologically based reconstruction arguments must be treated with the same caution as arguments based on purely syntactic evidence. But there is a further difficulty; their fundamental assumptions are flawed. Against Lehmann's 1969 argument, it is easy to show that the order of elements in compounds, even compounds of productive kinds, bears no direct relationship to the contemporary order of elements within the sentence. A highly productive kind of synthetic compound in modern English is illustrated by *hedge-cutter*, *painkiller*, *nit-picking*, while the kind represented by *cutpurse*, *killjoy* and *pickpocket* is fossilised and unproductive; yet it is in the second type, not the first, that the order of elements parallels normal sentence order. So, from the likely productivity of compounds of the *madhu-pa* type in Proto-Indo-European, one can conclude nothing about its contemporary syntactic pattern. What is wrong with the 1975 argument, on the other hand, is not that it directly contradicts some known facts outside the Proto-Indo-European field to which Lehmann applies it, but rather that there is no warrant for Lehmann's assumption that any given morphological pattern, such as the *madhu-pa* type of synthetic compound, must have a syntactic ancestor, such as an embedded clause of the type *madhu pa-*.

This assumption has the feel of a hang-over from the early nineteenth century. It was widely believed then that (a) the methods of historical linguistics applied to available materials can lead us significantly closer to the origins of language, and (b) the 'isolating' type of linguistic structure, in which all morphemes are free forms, is the most primitive or basic type. From these assumptions it follows that the bound forms (stems and affixes) of attested Indo-European languages are necessarily descended not just from free forms but from free forms which are conceivably discoverable by comparative linguistic investigation. Neither of these assumptions is respectable today. The time depth for which we know anything at all about what human languages have been like is tiny compared with the total period during which human languages have been spoken; and no one now pictures language change as a once-for-all 'ascent' from the isolating type through the agglutinating to the fusional, represented by the older attested Indo-European languages, followed by a 'decay' towards the modern state. And an important consequence of abandoning those two assumptions is that there is now no reason to insist that a morphological phenomenon must have a nonmorphological ancestor within the timescale accessible to our investigation – in other words, there is no reason why a form which is bound today should not always have been bound, where 'always' means 'for as long as human language has existed in its present form'.

Givón (1971), however, makes the same assumption as Lehmann, although he motivates his claim explicitly by invoking typological consistency. 'Today's morphology is yesterday's syntax', so that the nature and order of the morphemes in a word is always a guide to the nature and order of free forms in a syntactic construction at some earlier stage. But why should a syntactic structure become fossilised – in other words, why should its erstwhile free forms become bound? Givón's answer is that changes in word order (such as a shift from OV to VO order) render that structure inconsistent with the language's new dominant pattern, so that (just as with Sanskrit *madhu-pa*, according to Lehmann in 1975) the only way in which the order of elements in the old structure can be maintained is for the structure to become morphological. Clearly, if it can be shown that a substantial proportion of attested morphology does originate in this way, then the nonmorphological ancestry of bound forms has a basis quite independent of nineteenth-century assumptions, and we also have the sort of tool for syntactic reconstruction that both Lehmann and Givón seek. It is certainly true that some affixes derive from free forms. The modern Swedish passive suffix *-s*, as in (4), is derived from a Proto-North-Germanic reflexive pronoun, still surviving as the third-person reflexive pronoun *sig*, as in (5):

(4) han höra-s 'he is heard'
(5) han hör sig 'he hears himself'

And it is well known that the person–number endings of the future-tense endings in most Romance languages are derived from free forms of the Latin verb *habere* 'have', as in French:

(6) French:
     (je) chanter-ai '(I) will   cf. (j')ai '(I) have',
       sing', etc.   etc.
     chanter-as   as
     chanter-a   a
     chanter-ons   av-ons

chanter-ez	av-ez
chanter-ont	ont

But, to establish Givón's claim, it would be necessary to show that in all such attested 'morphologisations' the original syntactic order of the elements is faithfully preserved. Unfortunately, this is not the case, as is demonstrated by the development of preverbal clitic pronouns in Romance, discussed below. It follows that one cannot safely use the order of pronominal prefixes on verbs in Bantu languages as evidence for an OV pattern in Proto-Bantu, as Givón tries to do.

In Italian, like most modern Romance languages, object noun phrases regularly follow finite verb-forms, but bound or cliticised object pronouns regularly precede them:

(7) a. Maria offre i garofani a Giovanni
        'Mary is offering the carnations to John'

      b. Maria **glie-li** offre
        Mary him-them is-offering
        'Mary is offering them to him'

(8) a. Giovanni accetta due garofani
        'John accepts two carnations'

      b. Giovanni **ne** accetta due
        John of-them accepts two
        'John accepts two of them'

According to Givón, the synchronically anomalous position of these bound pronouns must result from their being stranded by a change in dominant word order, from OV to VO. This seems plausible inasmuch as OV order was certainly common and perhaps the dominant order in Italian's ancestor, Classical Latin. Unfortunately, however, the consistently preverbal position of these pronouns is a comparatively recent development, established only long after VO order became dominant. In medieval Italian, bound pronouns were positionally freer than they are in modern Italian, and in particular they seldom preceded the verb if they would thereby occupy the first position in the clause (Rohlfs 1949: 204–6). One cannot therefore attribute their preverbal position today to 'yesterday's syntax'.

I have been careful not to attribute to Givón the nineteenth-century view that the earliest form of language must have had only free forms. But his view of morphology evidently rests on a feeling that the existence of bound forms somehow needs explaining, while the existence of free forms does not. Now, it is true that no language lacks free forms while some languages may lack bound forms (namely languages such as Vietnamese which are most purely isolating in type). But this does not justify insisting that all bound forms must be derived historically from free forms, any more than the lack of the vowel sound [e] in a few languages justifies insisting that [e] must everywhere be derived historically from [i] or [a].

Attempts at word-order reconstruction on morphological grounds have so far been overambitious. But the enterprise has been premature rather than misguided. It may perhaps be true that some types of inflection – person–number inflection in verbs, say – do always involve historically the phonological attrition and cliticisation of originally free forms. If so, then a new question arises: what factors determine the positions in which these erstwhile free forms come to rest (so to speak)? The fact that Givón's answer is oversimplified does not mean that the question has no interesting answer. In the case of the Italian bound object pronouns mentioned earlier, it is clear that a relatively vague determinant of position (roughly: 'next to finite verb-form, but not clause-initial') has given way to a relatively precise one ('immediately preceding finite verb-form'). Perhaps this progress towards greater precision can be linked with something like the semiotic principle of uniformity (see chapter 8). So far, this is speculation. But, if speculations of this kind prove accurate, we may at last be able to use morphology in syntactic reconstruction with confidence.[4]

5.3 MORPHOLOGICAL TYPOLOGY AND GRAMMATICAL CHANGE

The classification of languages on the basis of their morphological structure originated in the early nineteenth century with the Schlegel brothers and was continued by Humboldt and Schleicher.[5] But it fell into disfavour with the rise of the Neo-Grammarian view that the only truly scientific classification of languages is genetic. Sapir's elaborate typology (1921) was never successfully applied or developed by other scholars, and the resurgence of interest in language universals since 1957 has not provoked any serious re-examination of the old classification. Yet the old labels 'isolating', 'agglutinating', 'inflecting' (or 'fusional') and 'polysynthetic' continue to be widely used. They therefore have a peculiar status in contemporary linguistics. They are not part of the technical vocabulary of any currently influential theory of grammar except Natural Morphology (see chapter 8). Moreover, they encourage oversimplification in that, as introductory textbooks always explain, nearly all languages have characteristics of more than one of these types. On the other hand, these labels do provide a convenient shorthand for clusters of morphological characteristics which are implicitly assumed to go together. If we are told that a language we know nothing about is agglutinating, we expect to find (a) that it has word forms which are segmentable into strings of morphs each with a single 'meaning' or grammatical function; but we also expect to find (b) that it lacks grammatical gender and (c) that it lacks clear-cut distinct inflection classes ('declensions' and 'conjugations'). Yet there is no logical connection between characteristic (a), on the one hand, and characteristics (b) and (c), on the other. Why should they go together? Or is our assumption that they do go together a mere prejudice built on the behaviour of a couple of well-known European languages, Turkish and Hungarian? This question is not addressed as such in any prominent current approach to morphology, so there are no answers for us to summarise and discuss here. But morphological typology is still relevant to current concerns, because of its role both in Natural Morphology (chapter 8) and in attempts to account for morphological change.

The scholar who has done most to codify the characteristics of the various morphological types is Skalička (1979), and it is his version of morphological typology which Dressler incorporates into Natural Morphology. Skalička recognises five ideal morphological types or **typological constructs**: agglutinating (e.g. Turkish, Hungarian, Eskimo), fusional (e.g. Czech, Latin, Bantu languages), isolating (e.g. English, Hawaiian), polysynthetic (e.g. Chinese, Yoruba) and introflexive (e.g. Semitic languages)[6]. Of these, it is the first two which have figured most prominently in theoretical discussions, and Skalička's characterisation of them is as follows:

Agglutinating (e.g. Turkish, Hungarian, Finnish, Armenian, Basque, Georgian, Eskimo): Word-forms consist of a root surrounded by affixes, each with a single 'meaning' or function. Word formation is by means of affixation, and the distinction between derivational and inflectional affixes is hard to draw. Both nominal and verbal affixes can be attached to any root, so that roots are not assignable to word-classes or major categories. There are neither homonymous affixes (syncretisms) nor synonymous affixes (lexically or grammatically conditioned alternants), and no distinct inflection classes. Grammatical agreement is lacking and word order is rigid. Instead of finite subordinate clauses we find infinitive, participle and gerundive constructions. Closed-class items (pronouns, conjunctions, articles, prepositions) are nonexistent.

Fusional (or inflecting) (e.g. Czech, Latin, Greek, Bantu languages): Word-formation morphology and inflection are sharply distinguished, and every word has just one inflectional affix, realising all its inflectional properties in fused or cumulative fashion. These affixes vary according to lexical, syntactic and semantic properties of the stem (e.g. gender, inflection class, transitivity). Homonymy among affixes is common. Grammatical agreement is widespread and word order is free. Finite subordinate clauses exist.

The ideal nature of these constructs is evident; in Latin, for example, nouns do conform to the fusional pattern of having just one inflectional affix, but verbs do not.

The traditional morphological typology has figured in accounts of grammatical change, just as Greenbergian word-order typology has. The simplest account on these lines posits a sort of circular or spiral development involving the isolating, agglutinating and fusional types. Skalička (1979: 159), citing von der Gabelentz (1901), describes the development as follows (my translation):

A language of the isolating type shows a tendency towards an ever closer attachment of formal (grammatical) elements to elements with lexical-semantic content. Thereby long words arise and the language becomes agglutinating in type. The formal elements attach themselves still more tightly and fusional characteristics arise. Words then get shortened, suffixes disappear and new form words have to be used. Thus the language reverts to the isolating type again.

The factors usually held responsible for the drift from agglutination to fusion and from fusion to isolation are phonological. Assimilatory changes blur the clear-cut boundaries between morphs which are characteristic of the agglutinative type, and further reductive changes (neutralisation and syncope) either remove grammatically relevant affixes altogether or render them insufficiently distinct from one another. This spiral model has an obvious common-sense appeal, and Vennemann (1975) has combined it with word-order typology to create an adventurous model of language change; SOV order with agglutinative case marking distinguishes subject from object satisfactorily, but phonological changes which obscure the morphological contrast between subject and object necessitate a shift in order to SVO, which encourages the drift from agglutination to fusion and thence to isolation. But before we can use the spiral model to explain or predict change, we need to find solid evidence that it is correct

– that is, we need to show that languages with long attested or solidly reconstructable histories do in fact develop spirally. Attempts to establish this have been only modestly successful so far, however.

For the drift from fusion to isolation, developments in the western European Germanic and Romance languages in historical times are traditionally held up as evidence, with perhaps some corroboration from Chinese (for which some scholars posit an early inflected stage). But the other two segments of the spiral cannot be illustrated from Indo-European by any wholesale typological shift between two historical stages of one language; the Indo-European evidence consists of piecemeal innovations such as the Romance future forms and the Scandinavian suffixal passive, discussed in section 5.2.2. The language family within which wholesale shifts from agglutination to fusion have been most carefully examined is Uralic. The results are not particularly encouraging for the spiral model.

Hungarian and most of the Uralic languages of the Soviet Union are generally regarded as belonging squarely to the agglutinating type, with more or less luxuriant case systems, clear-cut boundaries between number and case affixes, and suffixed person–number markers for possession. Finnish, however, is seen as having advanced further down the road towards fusion, with considerable allomorphy in both suffixes and stems, while Estonian and some Lappish dialects have become fully fledged fusional languages, with case–number cumulation and with stem alternation as the sole exponent of certain cases in many nouns (Korhonen 1969; 1979; 1982: 193):

(9) Proto-Lappish   Modern Lappish
     Nominative singular *koːleː 'fish'   kuolli
     Genitive singular   *koːleː-n   kuoli

Here the case contrast, realised agglutinatively by the presence versus absence of a suffix in Proto-Lappish, is realised in modern Lappish by consonant gradation (*-l-* versus *-ll-*) in the stem. It is tempting to try to relate this development to the change in dominant word order in Baltic Finnic languages (Finnish, Estonian, Veps and Livonian) and in most Lappish dialects, which have become predominantly SVO, forsaking an earlier reconstructed SOV pattern. Is the change in word order a natural consequence of the change in morphological type, as Skalička's characterisation of the agglutinating and fusional constructs would suggest? Or can we relate it to a weakening of the morphological contrast between subject and object, as Vennemann's model suggests? This second possibility seems to be supported by the fact that in Finnish there are no cases peculiarly associated with the subject and object functions; the subject may, according to context, be in either the nominative or the partitive, while the object may be in the nominative, the partitive or the genitive. Unfortunately, however, SVO order establishes itself not only in Finnish but also in Lappish dialects where the subject and object continue to be quite distinct morphologically. Moreover, an alternative explanation for the word-order change is available, namely contact with Germanic languages (Korhonen 1980). So, although an agglutinating language certainly can drift towards fusion, the Uralic evidence does not support the idea that it must do so. Even a language which undergoes dramatic phonological changes can preserve its agglutinating character by, for example, reinterpreting parts of stems as inflectional suffixes; in this way the Uralic language Zyryan has remained agglutinating, even though it has undergone the same kinds of phonological change as Lappish has (Korhonen 1982).[7]

The attempts that we have described so far to explain grammatical change through morphological typology have been relatively clumsy; our criticisms may not necessarily apply to a more subtle approach. In von der Gabelentz's spiral model, an agglutinative language may display (morpho) phonological alternations in stems triggered by neighbouring inflectional affixes, and these alternations may acquire the status of fused inflections if subsequent phonological changes destroy the affixes in question, as in the development from Proto-Lappish to modern Lappish illustrated at (9); but these latter changes are independent of the earlier stem innovations. Is there any reason to claim that the two phenomena are not independent after all? If there is, then typology may actually help to explain, not merely describe. Korhonen (1969: 303–42) answers yes to this question, invoking information theory in an ingenious fashion. First, he discusses measurements of the relative levels of redundancy and 'entropy' (roughly, unpredictability) in texts in a variety of languages, tending to show that the balance between redundancy and entropy is about constant; roughly, there has to be a certain amount of redundancy in the linguistic signal, but neither too much nor too little. He then points out that stem alternations of the kind just referred to tend to increase redundancy, to the extent that they and the affixes which trigger them are mutually predictable. If this increase is small, nothing need happen. But Korhonen calculates that the stem changes which took place in Proto-Lappish increased redundancy to such an extent that the proper balance between redundancy and entropy was thrown awry. To restore the balance, the language had no choice but to either abandon the new stem alternations (as happened in southern

Lappish dialects) or else blur the distinctness of the affixes so as to increase the entropy of the stem alternations (as happened in all other Lappish dialects).

For this kind of argument to be totally convincing, both the redundancy constant itself and the mode of calculating changes in redundancy would have to be more firmly established, as Korhonen admits. Nevertheless, a start has been made which deserves to be followed up. The idea that languages do not tolerate too much redundancy looks intriguingly like a syntagmatic counterpart of the idea that they do not tolerate too much synonymy in the paradigmatic dimension. The latter idea is at the root of Pinker's (1984) Uniqueness Principle and Clark's (1987) Principle of Contrast: 'Every two forms contrast in meaning.' Perhaps a principle which has at first sight nothing directly to do with either syntactic or morphological change may prove to be relevant to both in unexpected ways.

6 Meaning-based approaches to morphology

6.1 INTRODUCTION

American structural linguistics was notorious for its neglect of meaning. In the generative tradition semantics has in principle been brought back within the fold, in that knowledge of meanings, in some sense, is deemed to be part of linguistic competence; yet the generativist community still handles it warily, and has devoted to it only a fraction of the attention devoted to syntactic and phonological structure. Even the generativist concern with the lexicon, in its morphological aspect, has concentrated more on how 'morphemes' are combined than with the search for generalisations about the kinds of meaning that are expressed morphologically and the kinds of expression that these meanings receive. This search is the focus of the work described in this chapter.[1]

In view of American theoretical linguists' distrust of semantics, one might have expected work on morphological meanings to be centred in Europe. Paradoxically, however, two of the main workers in this field, Joan Bybee and Robert Beard, are Americans. They have developed their approaches independently, and there are considerable differences between them; but, in the context of this book, the differences are overshadowed by their common interest in meaning. For Bybee, the main focus is on inflection – that is, on identifying which meanings are most commonly expressed inflectionally, as opposed to derivationally or lexically, and finding out to what extent the set of inflectional meanings to be expressed in a given word-form influences the mode of expression (i.e. the choice between affixal and nonaffixal inflection, and the order of affixes). Bybee also has things to say about the structure of inflectional paradigms; her views here parallel in some respects the 'Morphological Economy' reaction against the Natural Morphology school, so will be discussed in chapter 8. Beard is more ambitious, in that he seeks a universal set of principles governing all meanings expressed morphologically, whether derivationally or inflectionally, and he claims that the semantic side of morphology obeys principles which are to a large extent independent of its formal, or morphophonological, side. In the first of these two concerns, Beard has been joined by the Polish scholar Bogdan Szymanek.

The relationship of competing morphological expressions for the same 'meaning' is the topic of the Domain Hypothesis proposed by the Dutch scholar Jaap van Marle. Again, however, he has developed his ideas independently of both Bybee on the one hand and Beard and Szymanek on the other.

6.2 INFLECTIONAL VERSUS NONINFLECTIONAL EXPRESSIONS OF MEANING

Bybee's hypotheses about inflection are based on a sample of fifty languages chosen by Revere Perkins and 'designed to be as free as possible of genetic or areal bias' (1985b: 25). This sample was not specially designed for work on morphology, and so contains languages with little or no inflection; but this has the advantage that no bias on the part of morphological researchers has influenced it. The use that Bybee makes of this sample places her in the typological tradition (see chapter 5), but differentiates her from those typologically oriented morphologists who rely on comparing just two or three languages viewed as exemplifying contrasting 'types'.

In the lexical item *kill*, we can distinguish 'at some level of analysis' the **semantic elements** DIE and CAUSE; similarly, *walked* and *brought* both express the semantic element PAST, while the phrase *come to know* expresses the semantic elements INCHOATIVE and KNOW (Bybee 1985b: 11). What determines whether a given semantic element is likely to be expressed **lexically** (like CAUSE in *kill*), **morphologically** (like PAST in *walked*) or **syntactically** (like INCHOATIVE in *cause to know*)? And if the expression is morphological, what determines whether it is more likely to be inflectional or derivational, and whether it is likely to be **fused** morphophonologically with the surrounding morphological material? How precisely these questions can be answered depends in part, as always, on how precisely the relevant terms are defined. But it is worth noting at the outset that, no matter how precise one's definitions, it is quite conceivable that a sample of fifty languages should yield no interesting answer to these questions at all; that is, it is quite conceivable that no coherent pattern should emerge about what kinds of meaning are expressed morphologically and how. One could call this the null hypothesis on morphology and meaning. Probably few if any morphologists today would explicitly defend the null hypothesis as correct. What Bybee tries to do, however, is show explicitly that the null hypothesis is incorrect; and despite some defects in her argument (to which we will return), her attempt seems successful. We will look in turn at her hypotheses about (a) what meanings are most likely to be expressed inflectionally, (b) the order in which inflectional meanings are expressed, and (c) what determines the degree of fusion in morphological expression.

Bybee concentrates on verbs and on some of the semantic elements that they express. Of course, the range of meanings of verbs is vast, and so is the range of relevant semantic elements, however they are determined. But Bybee is interested in those semantic elements which are at least sometimes expressed inflectionally in the languages of her sample. The distinction between inflection and derivation is not clear-cut; nevertheless, one can identify the main characteristic of inflection as obligatoriness. Let us define a **morphological** or **morphosyntactic category** (in the sense of Matthews 1972) as a set of related but mutually contrasting semantic elements expressed morphologically.[2] A morphological category is **inflectional** in a given language if some member of the category is obligatorily expressed in all words of a given syntactically defined class. For example, Tense is inflectional in English because all verbs (in finite clauses, at least) are either Past (e.g. *walked, brought*) or Present (*walk(s), bring(s)*). Applying these criteria to her sample, Bybee identifies as relevant the familiar verbal morphological categories of Voice, Aspect, Tense, Mood, Number, Person (agreeing with the subject), Person (agreeing with the object), and Gender, as well as the perhaps less familiar Valence, which 'refers to differences in the number or role of arguments that the verb stem can take' (1985b: 28); for example, the semantic element Causative (or CAUSE, as in *die* above) belongs in the Valence category.

Before we can examine Bybee's first hypothesis, we must define and illustrate two further notions: relevance and generality. 'A meaning element [= semantic element] is **relevant** to another meaning element if the semantic content of the first directly affects or modifies the semantic content of the second' (1985b: 13). For example, the semantic element (or combination of elements) THROUGH WATER affects the semantic element WALK more directly than do the semantic elements ON A SUNNY DAY, inasmuch as walking through water differs from walking on dry land much more than walking on a sunny day differs from walking on a cloudy day. It is not surprising, therefore, says Bybee, that for WALK THROUGH WATER there is in English a lexical expression *wade*, but there is no lexical expression for WALK ON A SUNNY DAY. Relative relevance is not universal, however; it 'depends on cognitive and cultural salience', so that for example English and Romance verbs of motion differ in that in the former the category MANNER is salient (*walk, swim, fly, slide, roll, swirl* etc.) whereas in the latter PATH is salient (Spanish *entrar* 'go in', *salir* 'go out', *bajar* 'go down', *subir* 'go up', *volver* 'go back', etc.) (Talmy 1985). Notice that a semantic element may be highly relevant to another semantic element without being widely, or generally, applicable; THROUGH WATER is applicable to WALK and also to RUN, PUSH, FALL (cf. the lexical item *sink*), but not to PLAY, SLEEP, TALK, FORGET. This brings us to Bybee's notion of **generality**. An inflectional category is, by definition, obligatorily expressed (via one of its members) in all word-forms of a certain syntactically defined class; it follows that inflectional categories (or the semantic elements which compose them) must be widely applicable and so highly general. Gender is an inflectional category of verbs in Russian, which (in the Past Singular) must be marked as Masculine, Feminine or Neuter in agreement with the subject (compare *on pisal* 'he was writing' with *ona pisala* 'she was writing'), and Gender is clearly general in Bybee's sense; on the other hand, it is not highly relevant, in the sense that for nearly all actions (or states) the grammatical Gender and even the sex of the agent (or experiencer) do not affect or modify the action (or state) itself. In this respect, verbal Gender differs from nominal Gender, in that the sex of the referent of an animate noun, which Gender often helps to express, is highly relevant.

We are now in a position to state Bybee's first hypothesis: a category is most likely to be expressed inflectionally (i.e. will be so expressed in a relatively high proportion of the languages in her sample) if it is both highly general and and highly relevant. From this point of view, let us compare Gender, Valence and Mood as verbal categories. Gender, as we have seen, is general but not highly relevant. At the other extreme, Valence (embracing semantic elements such as Causative) is highly relevant but (Bybee claims) of only limited generality:

> Causatives may serve as an example here. The causative meaning is highly relevant to verbs, since it affects quite directly the event or state being described by the verb stem. However, a causative meaning combined with a verb stem describes quite a different action than the verb stem alone does. For example, dying and causing to die (killing) are two quite different activities. . . . This can easily lead to a situation in which the products of a morphological causative process could become unpredictable sem-

antically and therefore lexicalized. When many of the words resulting from a morphological process become lexicalized, it becomes more and more difficult for speakers to learn to apply the process productively, and the process might eventually lose its productivity.

(1985b: 17–18)

This exemplifies Bybee's dictum that 'high relevance tends to *detract* from generality' (1985b: 17; her emphasis). Mood (embracing Indicative, Imperative and so on) occupies a middle position between Gender and Valence; it is high in both relevance and generality. So, according to Bybee's hypothesis, Mood is more likely to be expressed inflectionally in verbs than either Gender or Valence. Is this correct? Bybee says yes; Mood is an inflectional category in 68 per cent of the languages in her sample, whereas Gender is inflectional in 16 per cent and Valence in only 6 per cent. This emerges from the chart in (1) (1985b: 30–1):

(1)   Languages expressing category by means of:

	A Inflection (%)	B Derivation (%)	C Total (A+B) (%)
Valence	6	84	90
Voice	26	30	56
Aspect	52	22	74
Tense	48	2	50
Mood	68	0	68
Number	54	12	66
Person	56	0	56
Person (object)	28	0	28
Gender	16	0	16

The categories are listed in (1) in descending order of relevance (1985b: 20–4). Column A shows that those most likely to be expressed inflectionally are those towards the middle of the hierarchy of relevance. According to Bybee, this is because, to be commonly inflectional, a morphological category 'must be highly relevant to the meaning of the stem to which it attaches', but it must also be 'very generally applicable . . . or it simply will not apply to enough different items' (1985b: 19). Gender and Valence are relatively seldom expressed inflectionally because they do not meet the first and second conditions respectively; Mood is relatively often inflectional because it meets both conditions. What column B shows is that, for highly relevant categories, derivational expression is an alternative to inflectional, and with the most highly relevant ones (Valence and Voice) derivation predominates.

How significant is the connection that Bybee alleges between inflection, generality and relevance? At first sight, the statistical tendencies revealed in (1) are quite striking. But two problems arise with 'relevance'. The first has to do with the relevance hierarchy. If relevance is partly a matter of cultural salience, as we are told when the notion is introduced (1985b: 13), then there is something odd about devising a universal hierarchy of relevance, as in (1). In a language where Tense is expressed morphologically but Aspect is not, for example, one could argue that Tense is culturally more salient, and therefore more relevant, than Aspect, just as Path is more relevant than Manner in Romance verbs. If so, what entitles us to classify Aspect as universally more relevant than Tense (1985b: 22)? What is needed is some theory of 'unmarked' and 'marked' orderings of categories with respect to relevance. This would involve a considerable complication of the framework that Bybee presents, but is probably compatible with its spirit. The second and more serious problem has to do with the relationship between relevance, generality and 'lexicalisation'. Recall that the inflectional expression of semantic elements is contrasted by definition with lexical, derivational and syntactic expression (1985b: 11–12). Any hypothesis which associates inflection with relevance and generality in some way will therefore lose much of its empirical character if the relevance and generality of any given semantic category is determined in part by whether or not it is likely to be expressed lexically; for the hypothesis will then be in part reducible to the truism (in Bybee's terms) that a category which is likely to be expressed lexically is to that extent unlikely to be expressed inflectionally. Unfortunately, Bybee's first hypothesis does appear to suffer from just this flaw; for one of the factors which contribute to the high relevance and low generality of the semantic element Causative, in the discussion quoted at length above, is the fact that Causative verbs are in many languages 'lexicalised', with an unpredictable meaning alongside or instead of the expected one. Just how serious the circularity here is depends on whether 'lexicalised' expression implies 'lexical'. At first sight, it cannot do so, because the 'lexical' expression of two or more semantic elements is inherently 'monomorphemic' (1985b: 11), unlike 'lexicalised' expressions with Causative affixes. But the picture is complicated by the fact that the lexical and derivational expression are said to belong to a continuum without clearcut divisions (1985b: 81–109).

Bybee's notion of relevance is crucial to her second hypothesis also.

This hypothesis concerns the order in which inflectional categories are expressed relative to the stem. On the basis of the ways in which Aspect, Tense, Mood and Person are expressed inflectionally in the fifty languages of her sample, she argues for 'a "diagrammatic" relation between the meanings and their expression, such that the "closer" (more relevant) the meaning of the inflectional morpheme is to the meaning of the verb, the closer its expression unit will occur to the verb stem' (1985b: 34–5). But how solid is the evidence for this claim? Consider, for example, the expression of Mood and Person in the twenty-six languages where they are both inflectional categories, remembering that Mood is more relevant than Person: '*Mood* markers occur closer to the stem than *person* markers in 13 markers out of 26. In 5 languages the opposite order appears.' In the remaining 8 $(26-(13+5))$ languages, Person and Mood are presumably realised either cumulatively or on opposite sides of the stem. These two categories are therefore consistent with Bybee's claim, provided that it is interpreted as probabilistic. Are there any pairs of categories where the 'diagrammatic relation' is observed more consistently? Bybee says yes; in the ordering of Aspect and Tense with respect to the other categories and to each other, 'there are almost no counter-examples to the predicted ["diagrammatic"] ordering' (1985b: 35). As this implies, the allegedly more relevant category Aspect is always expressed closer to the stem than Tense is, if a relative ordering is determinable. But, if Aspect really is more relevant than Tense, the figures for Aspect and Tense in column A of (1) appear anomalous. The first hypothesis leads us to expect, on grounds of generality as well as relevance, that inflection for Tense should be more, not less, common than inflection for Aspect. The predictions of the two hypotheses do not always mesh exactly, it seems.

Bybee's third hypothesis has to do with degrees of fusion in the expression of inflectional categories and verb stems; 'if the meaning of an inflectional morpheme is highly relevant to the verb, then it will often be the case that their surface expression units will be tightly fused'. This is illustrated by the fact that, in her sample, '*Aspect* conditions changes in the verb stem more frequently than any other inflectional category' (1985b: 36). Here, unfortunately, the difficulties with relevance are compounded by difficulties with 'fusion'. Sometimes Bybee uses 'fusion' to refer to 'morphophonemic effects that have gone beyond the point of being phonologically conditioned' (1985b: 36). Sometimes, on the other hand, she relates 'degree of fusion' directly to the rival types of expression for semantic elements, including lexical, inflectional and derivational, in such a way that lexical expression is by definition the most fused and inflectional expression the least fused of the three (1985b: 12). This equivocation is encouraged, perhaps, by the fact that (as we have noted) 'lexical' sometimes implies 'monomorphemic' in Bybee's usage (1985b: 11); it follows that, if two semantic elements are maximally fused in the second sense, they will also be maximally fused in the first sense, although the converse is not the case. Bybee's equivocation makes it hard to assess her claim that, in terms of 'degree of fusion', 'derivational processes tend to have a greater effect on the root than inflectional processes do' (1985b: 97). In the second sense of fusion, this is trivially true. In the first sense, however, it is probably not true. It is easy to find in English examples to show that the status of a semantic element as inflectional or noninflectional has no direct connection with how fused its expression is morphophonologically, as shown in (2):

(2)

		Type of expression		
		morphophonologically fused	not fused	not morphological ('syntactic')
a.	PAST	took	baked	did . . . bake
b.	PLURAL	men	boys	pieces of toast (*cf.* *French* toasts)
c.	FEMALE	queen	princess	woman driver
d.	YOUNG	shoat	piglet	baby pig

By most people's criteria, including Bybee's, PAST and PLURAL are inflectional semantic elements (or properties or features) in English, while FEMALE and YOUNG are not; yet for all of them English provides a similar range of expressive options.[3]

Bybee's descriptive work on Perkins's sample confirms that some verbal categories are far more commonly realised inflectionally than others and that, broadly speaking, ones which are more commonly inflectional are expressed closer to the root than ones which are less commonly inflectional. Her attempts to explain these observations are less successful, so far; in particular, the attempt to unify the observations by recourse to the notion of 'relevance' seems at this stage to dissolve in vagueness and circularity. But, as we shall see in chapter 8, relevance plays a role for Bybee in yet another hypothesis, concerning the organisation of inflectional paradigms; so some such notion, more carefully formulated, may indeed turn out to play a central role in a network of related morphological constraints.

6.3 CHANGES IN INFLECTIONAL MEANINGS

The semantics of inflection has a diachronic as well as a synchronic angle. The diachronic angle brings in wider questions of semantic and also syntactic change, so we will not discuss it at length here; but, since it complements Bybee's synchronic, sample-based work, it deserves to be mentioned.

It has often been observed that, in a variety of languages, some meanings which are not logically connected are nevertheless expressed by the same syntactic or morphological means. This is particularly noticeable in the area of modals. As is well known, the English sentence *He must live in London* has two readings: a 'true modal' reading ('He is obliged to live in London') and an 'epistemic' reading ('It must be the case that he lives in London'). Other modals like *may* and *should* are ambiguous or vague in a comparable way. Now, other languages, non-Indo-European as well Indo-European, display the same sort of ambiguity; moreover, wherever we can establish the order in which the 'true modal' meaning and the epistemic meaning arose historically, the former always appears to precede the latter. Similarly, an expression may be ambiguous between volition and futurity, such as *I won't come* ('I refuse to come' or 'It is not the case that I will come'), and in this instance it always seems to be the volitional meaning which is historically prior. It is as if there is a universal propensity to extend the meaning of certain expressions metaphorically in certain particular directions.

Fleischman's (1982) study of the development of future-tense forms in Romance languages makes clear the considerable variety of source constructions from which new future forms developed to replace the Latin inflectional futures in *-b-* or *-e-* (*ama-b-it* '(s)he will love', *reg-e-t* '(s)he will rule'). The best-known of these innovations involves the Latin infinitive and forms of the verb *habere* 'have', e.g. French (*il*) *aimera* '(he) will love' < (*ille*) *amare habet*, where *amare habet* had originally the sense of obligation which its English gloss 'has to love' would imply (Fleischman 1982: 58–9). But other old Romance future innovations include the Romanian construction with a descendant of the Latin *velle* 'wish' and the parallel Sardinian use of *debere* 'must, owe'; and more recently there has been a widespread growth of 'go-futures' as in French *il va pleuvoir* 'it's going to rain'. From the point of view of the source expressions, one can see this as a kind of semantic bleaching, possibly combined with agglutination of the expression of futurity to the infinitive, as in *aimera* and the colloquial American Spanish *vadormir* 'will sleep' (Fleischman 1982:

116). But Bybee and Pagliuca (1985) look at the phenomenon from the point of view of the endpoint. Why should changes in the meaning of so many different expressions in a variety of languages converge on futurity as their 'destination'? It is as if, in the course of 'grammaticalisation' (whether or not inflection is involved), the lexical meanings of the ancestors of modals are funnelled into a relatively small set of universally available 'grammatical meanings' (cf. the repertoire of morphological categories for verbs listed in section 6.2).[4] Emphasis on the narrowness of the range of meanings which can be expressed morphologically is a feature of the work of Beard and Szymanek, to which we now turn.

6.4 LEXEME–MORPHEME-BASED MORPHOLOGY AND THE COGNITIVE GROUNDING CONDITION

In illustrating his famous account of the linguistic sign, Saussure used an oval diagram divided into two with a horizontal line, above which was a picture of a tree (the **signified**) and below which was the word *arbre* 'tree' (the **signifier**). In this example it so happens that, given either the signifier or the signified, there is no difficulty in identifying the other; *arbre* has no rival in French as the usual label for trees, and there is nothing else which the phonological entity *arbre* designates. There is thus an unambiguous one-to-one relationship, in this instance, between signifier and signified. Apparent exceptions to the one-to-one pattern do occur more or less frequently in the lexicons of most, perhaps all, languages; they are instances of synonymy (*bucket* and *pail*) and homonymy (*bank* 'money depository' and *bank* 'river's edge'). Nevertheless, if we look only at open-class items, these exceptions are sufficiently infrequent for us to feel justified in forcing them into the one-to-one mould of de Saussure's *arbre* example. Perfect synonymy between open-class items is notoriously rare, perhaps nonexistent, and when we find perfect homonymy we simply posit two or more items (or signs) which happen to be phonologically identical. But if both homonymy and synonymy were a great deal commoner, then the Saussurian sign, as a combination of a single signifier and a single signified, would be much less evidently apt as an analytical tool for the linguist.

The starting-point of Beard's investigation is the observation that for some closed-class items and in particular for affixes in at least some languages, notably Serbocroatian and English, precisely this sort of rampant homonymy and synonymy exists. For example, there is no single well-behaved past-participle sign in English, because the past participle may be formed by affixing *-en* (*driv-en*), *-ed* (*paint-ed*) or zero (*hit-∅*). Conversely, the suffixes *-en* and *-ed* are not parts of well-behaved signs, because each has two or three disparate derivational and inflectional functions, as in *enliv-en*, *ox-en*, *wood-en*, *paint-ed* (past tense), *beard-ed* (Beard 1981: 333). Of course, we can force these observations into the Saussurian mould by positing distinct but homonymous affixes, or by positing a single past-participle morpheme with lexically determined allomorphs, or both; but this simply obscures the central point (as Beard sees it), namely that the pattern of the relationship between affixes and the meanings of the words they help to form is quite different, and much less 'Saussurian', than the pattern of the relationship between simple open-class items (or simple lexemes) and their meanings.

From this observation, two questions arise. If the Saussurian theory of the sign is not a suitable framework for analysing the semantic contribution of affixal morphology, what is? And given that affixes constitute a closed inventory of elements in any language, is there any evidence that the inventory of 'meanings' that they can express is also closed in any interesting sense?

So far, we have avoided using Beard's own terminology, whose idiosyncrasy has almost certainly hindered discussion of his ideas. Even so, we need to come to terms with it. For the semantic relationship between a simple open-class lexeme such as *bake* and a related complex word such as *baker*, Beard uses the term **derivation** (or **L-derivation**, where L stands for 'lexical'), whereas their morphological relationship is one of **affixation**. In traditional terms, *baker* and *typist* are the agent nouns corresponding to *bake* and *type*; in Beard's terms they both exhibit the same 'agentive derivation', although they differ affixally. Conversely, *baker*, *hotter*, *cooker* and *Londoner* all involve affixation of exactly the same **morpheme -er**, but exhibit different derivations: agentive, comparative, instrumental and 'delocative ablative agent' (Beard 1981: 196). A **lexeme** such as *bake* or *type* generally has an identifiable meaning, and can be thought of as a Saussurian sign; on the other hand, a morpheme has no meaning, except in the sense that it signals that a derivation has taken place. There is, in fact, a clear-cut **separation** between derivation and affixation, without any parallel in the semantics of lexemes. In view of this separation, it is not surprising that derivation should sometimes occur with no concomitant affixation (as in *cook*$_N$ from *cook*$_V$), or vice versa; Beard has no need to postulate 'zero affixes', and 'empty morphs' do not constitute a problem.[5]

To the first of the questions posed above, Beard's answer is: we need a model of affixal morphology which gives pride of place to the separation between derivation and affixation, and to the semantic difference between lexemes and morphemes. The name he now proposes for this model is **Lexeme–Morpheme-Based Morphology** (LMBM) (Beard 1988; 1990). His answer to the second question is yes; and, in developing it, he invokes in an at first sight rather surprising fashion the nominal case systems of the more conservative Indo-European languages.

If we compare the morphology of a selection of Indo-European languages (say, English, French, Serbocroatian and Urdu), we clearly see many affixal differences. But, since affixation and derivation are separated (in Beard's technical sense), this tells us nothing about their derivational differences, if any. Do English *read-er*, French *lis-eur*, Serbocroatian *čital-ac* and Urdu *paṛhne-wala* differ derivationally as well as affixally? Beard says no; they all exhibit the same agentive derivation, which (he says) is common to all Indo-European languages, since 'the rate of diachronic change for agentive L-derivations is remarkably slower than that of their affixes' (1981: 111). Furthermore, nearly all the derivations which form nouns and adjectives can be plausibly linked to one of a set of 'grammatical functions': Nominative, Accusative, Dative, Genitive, Ablative and Locative. For example, the agentive derivation combines characteristics of the Nominative and of the Instrumental case, by means of which the agent is still expressed inflectionally in passive clause-types in Slavic languages.

It is worth comparing Beard's claims with Bybee's (section 6.2) and Lieber's (chapter 2). Beard concentrates on derived nouns and adjectives rather than verbs, and his data are almost exclusively Indo-European; but his conclusion is quite similar in character to Bybee's, namely that there is only a limited range of meanings that affixal morphology can express (in his terms, a limited range of L-derivations). On the other hand, he differs fundamentally from Lieber about the relationship of affixes to the lexicon. Lieber (1981a; 1981b) treats affixes as lexical items on a par with stems, differing from simple free forms only in being subcategorised for attachment to items of specific categories. For Beard, Lieber's stems are lexemes, and can be regarded as signs, whereas Lieber's affixes are morphemes, and cannot. Her parallel treatment of them is therefore ruled out. The kind of two-way mismatches that we noted earlier, in so far as they are commoner with affixes than with stems, tend to support Beard's position as against Lieber's. On the other hand, Beard is determined to allow morphemes not only no consistent meaning but also no morphosyntactic category such as Gender, since he sees such categories as peculiar to lexemes. Potentially problematic for Beard, therefore, is the fact that some affixes do appear to have Genders of their own; for example, in German, nouns formed with the diminutive suffix *-chen* are always Neuter, irrespective of the Gender of the noun from which they are formed, so that Masculine *Bart* 'beard', feminine *Haut* 'skin' and Neuter *Haus* 'house' all have Neuter diminutives in *-chen*: *Bärtchen, Häutchen, Häuschen*.

Beard's line in dealing with all such apparent counterexamples to separation (in its strongest version) is to argue that the meaning or feature in question belongs not to the morpheme but to the derivation (1988: 34–41). Thus, he argues that in German it is not *-chen* which is Neuter but rather the diminutive L-derivation which imposes Neuter Gender, however it is expressed affixally; so nouns with other diminutive suffixes (*-lein*, dialectal *-(e)l*) are always Neuter too. It seems doubtful whether this line can always be maintained; but it is worthwhile to investigate how far it can be.

If derivation is a matter of forming words with specific meanings relative to their bases, irrespective of how these meanings are expressed affixally, then it would seem that all derivation should be perfectly 'productive' in the sense of being semantically predictable ('régulier' in Corbin's terminology; see section 2.3). Beard does indeed claim that the notoriously 'gappy' character of derivational morphology substantially melts away if we focus on derivation in his sense (1981: 336):

> Once separated from affixation, lexical derivation becomes much more predictable (= productive?). Lexical extensions such as *knowledgeable, grassy, bearded, two-headed, nodose, modular, youthful, temperamental, harmonious, elegiac, dilemmatic, methodical, burdensome* all share one common, highly active and wholly regular derivational source: the possessional adjective . . . variant of the case relation rule.

At the same time, however, Beard seems reluctant to abandon affixal identity entirely as a clue to lexical derivation. As (3) illustrates, the single Serbocroatian suffix *-ina* is associated with a range of apparently quite diverse meanings: 'meat from', 'skin from', 'fat from', 'tusks from', 'wood from':

(3)

svinja	'pig'	svinj-et-ina	'pork'
jelen	'deer'	jelen-ov-ina	'venison, buckskin'
dabar	'beaver'	dabr-ov-ina	'beaver fur, fat'
slon	'elephant'	slon-ov-ina	'ivory'
hrast	'oak'	hrast-ov-ina	'wood from oak'

But Beard does not conclude that (3) involves a set of different derivations, all of which just happened to be signalled morphologically by *-ina* (as is the case with the different 'meanings' of English *-er*). Rather, he concludes that all the examples in (3) exemplify a single derivation linked to the Indo-European 'ablative of origin' (1981: 193–6). How is it, then, that *slonovina* does not mean 'elephant meat' and *svinjetina* does not mean 'pig's tooth', for example? The answer is that the differences belong not to the derivation itself but to 'pragmatic reference', which comes under 'performance theory'. Performance theory contains 'performative rules', one of which (in its application to the 'ablative nominalisation' of Serbocroatian animate nouns) 'designates the referent as the most widely used product from the animal' in Yugoslav society (1981: 333). Similarly, pragmatic factors explain why the 'possessional adjective' *nogat* 'legged' is interpreted sometimes as simply 'having legs' (as in the phrase *nogati vodozemci* 'amphibians with legs'), sometimes as 'having long legs' (as in the phrase *nogata devojka* 'long-legged girl'); some amphibians normally lack legs but no girls do (1981: 117). Thus, both ablative nominalisations and possessional adjectives can be regarded as productive; their deviation from a perfectly mechanical kind of semantic predictability is accounted for by the theory of performance.

There remain, however, some morphologically complex words which cannot be regularized in this way. An example is *transmission* in the sense of 'mechanism for changing gears'. Assuming that this is derived by nominalisation from *transmit*, there is nothing in either the derivation itself or our experience of the world which might tell us that it relates to the transmission of power from the engine to the wheels in cars, rather than (say) the transmission of a message from the speaker to the hearer in a telephone conversation (whereby *transmission* might mean 'handset'), or the transmission of an inherited characteristic from one generation to another (whereby *transmission* might mean 'gene'). What must have happened is that some individual decided at some point to apply the word to a particular referent in the field of motor mechanics (rather than telephony or genetics), and this application has become institutionalised. Beard (1987) uses **lexical**

stock expansion as the name for the relatively haphazard process of assigning unpredictable new senses to existing words, as well as to coinings such as *smog* or *gazump*. In its haphazardness, lexical stock expansion differs from the rule-governed process of **lexical extension** by derivation.

Szymanek's approach to morphological semantics (1988) differs from Beard's in that the limit on the range of 'meanings' which morphological processes can express is attributed not to some inherited repertoire of Indo-European cases or syntactic functions but rather to a supposedly universal repertoire of **cognitive categories**, for whose existence Szymanek cites such authorities as Smith and Medin (1981), Lakoff and Johnson (1980) and Jackendoff (1983).[6] The requirement that derivational meanings should reflect cognitive categories is called the **Cognitive Grounding Condition**. But in practice this does not make as much difference as one might expect, because the cognitive categories include ones such as OBJECT, SUBSTANCE, POSSESSION, ACTION, AGENT and INSTRUMENT, which parallel many of Beard's Indo-European case functions. For instance, the Serbocroatian possessional adjective *nogat* '(long-)legged' exemplifies for Beard a possessional adjective derivation related to the 'primary case' Genitive (1981: 205), whereas for Szymanek it exemplifies derivation based on the cognitive category POSSESSION.

Beard and Szymanek both have difficulty with diminutive and augmentative forms, which are particularly common in Slavic languages.[7] These are problematic for Beard because they do not correspond to any plausibly reconstructible case function; so, because of their extreme productivity in Slavic languages, he assigns them to a limbo 'somewhere between lexical and purely inflectional forms' (1981: 180; cf. 201). For Szymanek, the problem is that they do not reflect exactly any of the cognitive categories; DIMENSION (or SIZE) may seem a plausible candidate, but that omits the attitudinal or expressive overtones which accompany diminutives especially. He therefore relegates them to an 'expressive periphery' of derivation, which does not have to be cognitively grounded (1988: 106–9). Whether this is more than a dodge to save the Cognitive Grounding Condition depends largely on whether there is any independent difference between 'expressive' and 'cognitively grounded' derivation. Some evidence that such a difference exists may be found in the fact that 'expressive' suffixes can be piled on one another (e.g. Polish *kot* 'cat', *kotek, koteczek* 'kitten') and that 'rival' formations do not block one another (*kotunio, kociunio, kotuś, kociuś*, etc. are all available as diminutives for *kot*) (cf. Malicka-Kleparska 1985). But the diminutive problem is just one aspect of a large question which the ambitious explanatory hypotheses of Beard and Szymanek provoke. We are encouraged to expect a parallelism between primary cases, or cognitive categories, on the one hand, and derivational 'meanings', on the other. Can nonarbitrary reasons be produced for all mismatches? Mismatches may be of two kinds: derivational patterns without a case or category base, and cases or categories which never appear to be relevant to derivation. Examples of the former are the productive Polish suffix *X-ówka*, which means 'type of vodka made from X' (Szymanek 1988: 114), and the English suffix *-ism* (Beard 1981: 225). Examples of the latter are the categories COLOUR and SHAPE; we seem never to encounter a suffix which, when added to a stem X, means 'blue X' or 'round X'. Accounting for these mismatches must be a high priority for the Beard–Szymanek enterprise.

Despite these reservations, let us grant for the moment the basic hypothesis that only a limited repertoire of meanings can be expressed derivationally. The question remains: how is this repertoire of derivationally expressible meanings related to the range of meanings (or meaning-contrasts) which can be expressed lexically? For example, the agentive sense expressed derivationally in *writer* and *typist* also occurs in the simple word (in Beard's terms, the lexeme) *thief*. Conversely, the recurrent lexically expressed semantic relationship exhibited by the pairs *horse/foal, cow/calf* and *sheep/lamb* receives derivational expression in *pig/piglet* and *duck/duckling*. In view of Beard's insistence on the separation of derivation from affixation, one might have expected him to attribute to the pairs *steal/thief* and *horse/foal* precisely the same productive 'derivational' relationships as to the pairs *write/writer* and *pig/piglet* respectively. But Beard explicitly rejects this option, arguing that 'suppletive' forms are always separate lexemes, which may be related to each other semantically but not 'derivationally' (1981: 75–81, 206). Similarly, for Szymanek (1988: 138–45), the existence of monomorphemic items with an agentive sense, such as *thief* and *pilot*, demonstrates the 'lexical relevance' of the category AGENT, which in turn reinforces the status of agentive derivation as a 'prototypical' morphological process; but he still classifies 'lexical' relationships such as *thief/steal* as distinct from 'morphological' ones such as *write/writer*. Yet, as was suggested in section 2.7, there is evidence that at least some of the relationships which are traditionally seen as morphological are better seen as primarily lexical-semantic, the morphological similarity being a clue to the meaning relationship rather than the determinant of it – very much in the spirit of Beard's separation hypothesis, if consistently applied. Almost certainly the Beard–Szymanek enterprise would benefit from a more sophisticated theory of the kind of semantic matrices illustrated by the domestic-animal terms in section 2.7. It is paradoxical that, despite their emphasis on the role of meaning in morphology, Beard and Szymanek still share Jackendoff's (1975) and Aronoff's (1976) reluctance to equate meaning relationships which are expressed morphologically with ones which are not.

6.5 THE DOMAIN HYPOTHESIS

In Szymanek's framework, one **derivational category**, such as Agent Noun ('grounded' in the cognitive category AGENT), may subsume more than one **derivational type**, defined as 'a group of complex lexemes characterized by a singleness of derivational function and of its formal exponence (e.g. all English Agent nouns which end in *-er*)' (1988: 60). English in fact has Agent Nouns of at least four derivational types, illustrated by *paint-er*, *inform-ant*, *escap-ee* and *cook-∅*. In Szymanek's framework this 'meaning–form asymmetry in derivation' (42–59) is of relatively marginal interest, as a hindrance to the identification of derivational categories. But certain questions arise if derivational types are promoted to centre stage. For example, what factors determine the membership of each type, and what characteristics (if any) do more general, or regular, types share by contrast with less general, or more irregular, ones? At first sight, these are simply restatements of questions about productivity which arose in chapter 2; but in the context of this chapter they are questions not just about how certain word-formation processes apply but about how certain meanings (derivational categories, in Szymanek's sense) are realised.

In answer to these questions, van Marle (1985; 1986) offers his **Domain Hypothesis**, not as a firm prediction about what can and cannot happen, but as a 'heuristic principle, with the help of which a further investigation of morphological systems can be undertaken'; it 'indicates which phenomena are "problematic" and which are not' (1985: 228). We must first introduce some of van Marle's terminology. A possible source of confusion at the outset is the fact that Szymanek's derivational types correspond to what van Marle calls 'categories'. For example, van Marle cites three 'derivational categories of [+female] personal names in modern Dutch' associated with the suffixes *-in*, *-es* and *-ster* respectively, as in e.g. *boer-in* 'woman farmer, farmer's wife', *onderwijzer-es* 'woman teacher', *herbergier-ster* 'woman inn-keeper'; a fourth [+female] 'category', illustrated by *adviseuse* corresponding to *adviseur* 'adviser', is rather oddly classified as 'non-derivational' because there is in Dutch no free form *advis-* to which the suffix *-euse* is added (1985: 216–17). But in Szymanek's terms, these would all four be derivational types belonging to the category Female Noun; and, for present purposes, no harm will be done if we continue to use Szymanek's term 'types' for what van Marle calls 'categories'.

Other crucial terms for van Marle are **domain, general case** and **special case**. The domain of a derivational type is the set of items to which it applies – the set of bases which come within the scope of the relevant WFR, in Aronoff's terms. For example, the domain of all the four [+female] types just mentioned will be [+human] nouns, or a subset of them. A special case is a type which applies to only a minority of exceptional or irregular items, so that specifying the domain of a special case is usually relatively complicated and may involve simply listing the items concerned. In English noun plurals, the vowel-change type represented by *teeth* and *mice* is a special case, whereas the majority type in *-s*, represented by *cats, dogs* and *horses*, is the general case (1985: 196–9). Furthermore, the domain of the vowel-change type is **restricted**, in that it has to be defined in terms of a 'positive domain demarcation' involving (in this instance) lexical listing (1985: 221); by contrast, the domain of the *-s* type is unrestricted in the sense that it cannot be characterised insightfully in positive terms, but only negatively, as the 'elsewhere' type. Finally, the domain of a type is **paradigmatically determined** if it is determined solely by the fact that it is 'not within reach of any of the related special cases' (1985: 225), where 'related' means 'synonymous' or 'subsumed under the same derivational category, in Szymanek's sense'. A type with a paradigmatically determined domain will thus, as it were, fill all the gaps left by the special-case types, ensuring that its category is realised by some type or other for bases of the relevant kind (nouns, [+human] nouns, or whatever).

We are now in a position to give in (4) van Marle's statement of the Domain Hypothesis, which is the climax of a long discussion of Dutch plural and female noun formation (1985: 227):

(4) (a) The domains of special cases are (i) restricted, and (ii) not determined by paradigmatic forces; whereas

    (b) the domains of general cases are (i) unrestricted, and (ii) entirely paradigmatically determined.

Van Marle admits that this is 'far too strong' as an empirical claim, but we will concentrate here on the sort of phenomena which it characterises as problematic in its 'heuristic' capacity.

Because of the sense which van Marle assigns to 'restricted', parts (a.i) and (b.i) of the Hypothesis are virtually tautological. The domain of a special case could be unrestricted only if it required no 'positive domain demarcation'; but then it would constitute the 'elsewhere' case, and would be highly unlikely to have the minority status which would justify calling it 'special' rather than 'general'. Conversely, the domain of a general case could be restricted only if there were no possibility of stating it in 'elsewhere' terms, which is scarcely compatible with its being general. The meat of the Hypothesis is therefore in parts (a.ii) and (b.ii). Let us see how it applies to English female nouns and to nominalisations of Latin-derived verbs in -*mit* and -*fer*, mentioned in section 2.7.

Various derivational types of English female nouns are illustrated in (5):

(5) a. hero   heroine
     b. aviator   aviatrix
     c. raconteur   raconteuse
     d. waiter   waitress
         actor   actress
         host   hostess
         deacon   deaconess

It is clear that (5a–c) constitute special cases while, if there is a general case, it is the -*ess*-suffixed type illustrated in (5d). But then, according to the Domain Hypothesis, the domain of -*ess* should be determined purely paradigmatically – that is, it should extend to every [+human] noun which is not explicitly included in the domain of one of the special cases. This means that as well as *waitress*, *actress*, *hostess* we should also find (for example) *cookess, *writress, *guestess. But this expectation is not fulfilled. English contrasts in this respect with Dutch, which, according to Koefoed and van Marle (1987: 132), is 'extremely rich in morphological processes by means of which female personal names may be coined'; Dutch seems, in fact, to make available a specifically female equivalent for every male or sexually neutral personal noun, so that, for example, it is possible to coin unselfconsciously *astronaut-e* as the female counterpart of *astronaut*, using the 'general case' suffix -*e*. The numerous gaps in the English pattern are therefore problematic, from the point of view of the Domain Hypothesis. One possible conclusion might be that in English, as opposed to Dutch, '[+human] noun' is too wide a specification for the bases of the derivational category of female nouns. The challenge then is to specify these bases more accurately.

One plausible exclusion, for example, might be all [+human] nouns with the suffix -*ist*, since e.g. **typistess* and **physicistess* appear to be systematic rather than accidental gaps (contrast Dutch *typist-e* 'woman typist' alongside *typist*); but **guestess* and **writress* still look irredeemably accidental. Another possibility is that 'female noun' just does not exist as a derivational category in English. But clearly that jeopardises the establishment of any universal or quasi-universal set of categories, on the lines proposed by Beard and Szymanek.[8]

A further consequence of the Domain Hypothesis is that, if a special-case female noun exists, such as *heroine* or *aviatrix*, the corresponding general-case noun (**heroess*, **aviatress*) should not exist alongside it, since the paradigmatically determined domain of the general case restricts it to filling in gaps left by the various special cases. So far as English female nouns are concerned, this seems to be correct. But problematic examples can be found in other derivational categories. If we take it that -*er* suffixation is the general case for agent-noun category, then the existence of *informer* and *escaper* alongside the special-case *informant* and *escapee* is a problem. This raises questions about the existence and definition of the agent-noun category itself. Should we exclude *informant* from the category on the ground that an informant is not simply someone who informs? But then similar considerations should lead us to exclude many apparently prototypical agent nouns – for example, *writer* and *teacher*, on the ground that their senses include a factor of professional status which goes beyond 'pure' agentivity.

Van Marle's 'general-case' derivatives will in Aronoff's framework (chapter 2) be classified as formed by productive WFRs, while most of his 'special-case' derivatives (certainly those whose domain specification contains an arbitrary list) will count as lexicalised. So van Marle's prediction that general-case derivatives should not exist in competition with special-case synonyms contradicts Aronoff's claim that productively formed words cannot be blocked by lexicalised rivals. The evidence from English and Dutch female noun formation, so far as it goes, seems to support van Marle, whereas the pattern illustrated by *glory* and *gloriousness* versus **gloriosity* seems to support Aronoff. Here, then, is another problem thrown up by the Domain Hypothesis.

A knot of problems arises when the Domain Hypothesis confronts English deverbal abstract nouns. As noted in section 2.7, nouns from the latinate verbs in -*mit* and -*fer* are formed in a variety of ways (e.g. *commitment, pérmit, remittance; preferment, tránsfer, referral*), but two generalisations stand out; all verbs in -*mit* have a corresponding noun in *-mission* (*commission*, *permission*, *remission*, etc.) and all verbs in *-fer* have a corresponding noun in *-ence* (*preference*, *transference*, *reference*, etc.). The fact that each verb has more than one nominalisation shows that none of the derivational types concerned has a paradigmatically determined domain – not even *-ion* and *-ence*. But this implies that *-ion* and *-ence* must be special, not general, cases. That is consistent with the fact that their domain is not simply 'elsewhere' but must be positively specified in terms of stems in *-mit* and *-fer* respectively. The best candidate for 'general case' status among the various nominalisation types would seem to be *-ing*. But then the Domain Hypothesis predicts that *-ing* nominalisations should not exist alongside special-case ones; and this prediction is wrong, because *John's committing of the crime* and *the magistrate's committing of John for trial* are not blocked by *John's commission of the crime* and *the magistrate's committal of John for trial*. Notice, however, that we have been assuming that abstract-noun formation is indeed a derivational category in English. If this assumption is wrong, then the problems which these nominalisations seem to pose for the Domain Hypothesis disappear, because the various derivational types are not 'related special cases' (van Marle 1985: 225). Evidence against this assumption might be the fact that the shared element in abstract nominalisations is a purely syntactic category-changing operation, whose cognitive grounding is at best doubtful (Szymanek 1988: 31–9, 104–6).

Van Marle is right in seeing the Domain Hypothesis as a provoker rather than a solver of problems. Whether these problems have interesting answers remains to be seen. Meanwhile, however, he has pioneered a rapprochement between semantically oriented approaches to morphology, such as Beard's and Szymanek's, and more formal approaches, such as that of Aronoff and most of the other scholars discussed in part I.

7 Morphosyntactic properties and their realisation

7.1 INTRODUCTION: DEVIATIONS FROM THE ONE-TO-ONE PATTERN

This chapter summarises various searches for constraints on how inflectional morphology operates. Inflection has of course been mentioned often already, particularly in chapters 2, 4 and 6. But the work described here differs from that described in chapters 2 and 4 in that its starting-point, so to speak, is the other side of the morphological sign: the signified rather than the signifier. Scholars such as Jackendoff, Lieber and Baker, despite their disagreements, all focus first on relatively concrete aspects of word structure – the division of words into stems and affixes, and alternations in the shape of these elements – and proceed to try to account for these in lexical or syntactic terms. By contrast, linguists such as Stephen R. Anderson, Arnold Zwicky and Andrew Carstairs take as their starting-point relatively abstract aspects of how words function syntactically – the contrasting syntactic categories, such as Case or Tense, which may be expressed in different forms of the same lexical word (or lexeme) – and then consider how these categories (or the properties belonging to them) are expressed inflectionally. Zwicky's work is part of a wider **Interface Program**, exploring the interfaces between different components of grammar (phonology and syntax, phonology and morphology, syntax and morphology) (Pullum and Zwicky 1988; Zwicky 1990); but all three are more or less explicitly concerned with the search for constraints on how inflection works. This search is closer in spirit to Bybee's enterprise, described in chapter 6, than to the concerns of chapters 2 and 4. But, whereas that work of Bybee's concerns mainly the semantic aspect of inflection (identifying which 'meanings' are most typically expressed inflectionally rather than derivationally, and why), the scholars discussed here concentrate more on formal issues:

how the clusters of morphosyntactic properties which a given word-form expresses are structured internally, and how they are 'spelled out' inflectionally (through affixes, stem changes or whatever).

These questions are implicitly raised by Chomsky's treatment in *Aspects* (1965: 171) of word-forms such as German *Brüder* 'of (the) brothers'. As mentioned in chapter 2, Chomsky envisages a surface syntactic structure in which Plural and Genitive are not separate terminal elements but rather 'values' of the 'features' [Number] and [Case] associated with the terminal element *Bruder* and interpreted phonologically as umlaut. So it may seem odd that this chapter is not included in part I. Certainly, some, if not all, the scholars discussed here would see their work as part of the generative enterprise, seeking to explicate aspects of Universal Grammar as an innate mental faculty. But, perhaps by mere historical accident, the workers on morphology (at MIT and elsewhere) who have remained in closest touch with concurrent developments in Chomsky's own views on syntax have chosen not to develop the hints on inflection contained in *Aspects*. The investigations discussed here have therefore been pursued with little direct stimulus from the Chomskyan mainstream, and are therefore to that extent 'non-Chomskyan'.

We noted in chapter 6 that one inflectional affix may have several meanings and one meaning may be expressed by several different affixes, according to context. This kind of mismatch typically affects nonaffixal processes as well as affixation. De Saussure's notion of the sign presupposes for its usefulness that lexical items should generally conform to a pattern of one-to-one relationships between meaning and expression; but, in inflection, divergence from the one-to-one pattern is very widespread. Superficially, this fact may seem discouraging for the would-be inflectional theorist. If inflection can deviate from the one-to-one pattern quite unconstrainedly, then the pattern of deviation exhibited by any one language will be merely a set of language-particular idiosyncrasies, conforming to no general principles. Carstairs (1987a) has therefore suggested that the fundamental question for inflectional theorists can be posed as follows: what is the extent and nature of the constraints, if any, on deviation from the one-to-one pattern of inflectional realisation? All the linguists discussed in this chapter agree that some such constraints exist, even if they disagree about what they are.

Carstairs (1987a: 12–18) proposed classifying deviations from the one-to-one pattern under four headings. One inflectional property (say, Perfect Tense in Classical Attic Greek) may have several realisations in a single word-form; for example, the Tense (or

Tense–Aspect) contrast between the Perfect form *le-lu-k-a* 'I have loosed' and the Present form *lu-o:* 'I loose' shows up in three places (the reduplicative prefix *le-*, the suffix *-k-* and the special Perfect form of the 1st Person Singular suffix, *-a*). This is the phenomenon which Matthews (1972; 1974) calls **extended exponence**. One property may also have several alternative realisations which show up not in the same word-form but in different ones; in our Greek example, the combination of properties 1st Person Singular is realised as *-o:* in the Present form and *-a* in the Perfect form. Exploiting de Saussure's dichotomy between the syntagmatic and the paradigmatic (or associative) dimensions of language, we may call these two deviations 'one-to-many syntagmatic' and 'one-to-many paradigmatic' respectively, and label them as follows:

Deviation I: one-to-many syntagmatic
Deviation II: one-to-many paradigmatic

Many-to-one deviations, by contrast, will involve several distinct inflectional properties sharing a single realisation. Where the single realisation is in a single word-form, we have what Matthews calls **cumulative exponence**. This can be illustrated by contrasting the Ablative Plural forms of the Turkish and Latin words *ada* and *insula*, both meaning 'island'. In the Turkish form *ada-lar-dan* 'from (the) islands', the Ablative suffix *-dan* is clearly separable from the Plural suffix *-lar*, so there is no deviation from the one-to-one pattern. On the other hand, in the Latin form *insul-i:s* the single suffix *-i:s* realises both Ablative and Plural simultaneously, or cumulatively. We can call this a many-to-one syntagmatic deviation. A many-to-one paradigmatic deviation will involve the identical inflectional realisation of two or more distinct inflectional properties – inflectional homonymy, in other words. We can illustrate this again with the Latin word-form *insul-i:s*. In our example just now, this was interpreted as the Ablative Plural form of *insula* (contrasting with the Ablative Singular form *insul-a:*). But *insul-i:s* can also be interpreted as the Dative Plural form of *insula* 'for (the) islands', contrasting with the Dative Singular form *insul-ae*. We can now complete our list of the four types of deviation:

Deviation III: many-to-one syntagmatic
Deviation IV: many-to-one paradigmatic

Any conceivable deviation from the one-to-one pattern must fall into one of these four types, so it is at first sight discouraging that one can so easily find examples of all four. But the fact that all the deviations are instantiated does not mean that all can occur freely. They may be linked, in the sense that the occurrence of one deviation in some word-form or set of word-forms may turn out to require, to favour, to discourage or to prohibit the occurrence of another. Most of the proposed constraints which we will be considering in this chapter involve implications of this kind, so the fourfold classification of deviations provides a map, so to speak, on which the constraints and their interrelationships can be plotted.

7.2 THE STRUCTURE OF MORPHOSYNTACTIC REPRESENTATIONS

The approaches described here share an important characteristic with the traditional Word-and-Paradigm model of inflection (see chapter 1) – indeed, Anderson sometimes calls his approach the **Extended Word-and-Paradigm** model.[1] In traditional British school Latin teaching, a complex verb-form like *ama:vera:mus* 'we had loved' is analysed not as a sequence of 'morphemes' (say, *am-a:-v-er-a:-mus*) but rather as a grammatical word: 'the first-person plural pluperfect indicative active of *amo:*'. In Matthews's (1972) terminology, the items in this string are **morphosyntactic properties**, which he identifies as such typographically with an initial capital (Plural, Indicative, Active, etc.), each of which belongs to a **morphosyntactic category** or set of mutually contrasting properties, also with a capital (Number, Mood, Voice, etc.). The complex of morphosyntactic properties associated with a lexical item to form a grammatical word can be called its **morphosyntactic representation**, following Anderson (1982). Section 7.2 is concerned with the internal structure of morphosyntactic representations and the ways in which they can be altered or manipulated 'before' they are realised, or spelled out, inflectionally. The relationship between properties and their realisations is discussed in later sections.

The terminology in this area is not settled, unfortunately. In this chapter we will use '(morphosyntactic) representation', 'category' and 'property' consistently in the senses just given, and we will also follow Matthews's convention on initial capitals. But corresponding to our 'property', Anderson uses 'feature', and writes, for example, '[−passive]' and '[+plural]' for our 'Active' and 'Plural'. Zwicky (1985c) follows Chomsky (1965) in using 'feature' to correspond to our 'category', while his term for our 'property' is 'value'; thus, plural is one value of the feature NUMBER. Zwicky (1990) also uses the term 'grammatical category' to embrace both categories and properties, in our terms (his 'features' and 'values'). The only issue of substance here is implied by Anderson's plus–minus notation; he assumes that morphosyntactic properties can be analysed in terms of binary features, so that, for example, 1st Person is [+me, −you], 2nd Person is [−me, +you], 3rd Person is [−me, −you] and the combination [+me, +you] will represent the so-called 'inclusive' 1st Person Plural. Evaluating this kind of binary analysis is a matter of investigating whether it groups together helpfully those (nonbinary) morphosyntactic properties which share either syntactic characteristics or inflectional realisations or both. In its favour, Anderson cites the behaviour of Potawatomi and other Algonquian languages (1977). However, this issue is independent of the ones that we will be mainly concerned with here.

Deciding whether a property is morphosyntactic rather than derivational or purely syntactic in a given language involves essentially devising criteria for distinguishing inflection from derivation – a task also faced by Bybee (see chapter 6). Anderson (1982: 587) announces that 'inflectional morphology is what is relevant to the syntax', where being relevant to the syntax means being 'assigned to words by principles which make essential reference to larger syntactic structures' such as phrases and clauses. By this criterion, for example, Number is clearly inflectional in English but probably not in Afrikaans, which has lost all Number agreement. That said, Anderson and Carstairs are generally content to take for granted the morphosyntactic categories relevant to a given word-class in a given language; none of their major proposals so far entails any radically new view of what is inflectional as opposed to derivational or purely syntactic.

Zwicky's situation is different, in that his insistence that syntax is 'phonology-free' commits him to analysing as morphological certain phenomena which might otherwise be regarded as syntactic. As part of his Interface Program, Zwicky is concerned to show that syntactic phenomena cannot pay attention to the phonological shape of constituents. The debate on this issue involves phonologically conditioned alternations which appear superficially to be analysable either syntactically or morphologically. For example, the Spanish feminine article *la* is generally replaced by (what looks like) the masculine *el* before feminine nouns, but not adjectives, beginning with stressed *a* (*el agua* 'the water', not **la agua*, but *la alta casa* 'the tall house', not **el alta casa*), and the French feminine possessive adjectives *ma* 'my', *ta* 'your', *sa* 'her/his/its' are replaced by (what look like) the masculines *mon, ton, son* before all vowel-initial words, whether nouns or adjectives (Plank 1984; Posner 1985; Zwicky 1985d; cf. Dressler 1985d). To handle such instances, Zwicky's framework commits him to allowing the shape of the realisation of some morphosyntactic property to be conditioned by phonological factors outside the same 'word', in some sense. A current problem for the Interface Program, then, is to determine precisely when and how such conditioning can occur.

7.2.1 Layering within representations

In the traditional British school analysis of Latin verb-forms, the properties are conventionally listed in a consistent order: Person, Number, Tense, Mood, Voice. This happens to yield something like an order of increasing relevance, in Bybee's terms. One could, in fact, see relevance as imposing a hierarchy on the various properties within a morphosyntactic representation. For their purposes, however, Anderson and Zwicky see no need to order the properties within a representation; in Anderson's notation, for example, [+me, +past] and [+past, +me] are equivalent representations for 1st Person Past. But the need for some internal structure becomes evident when one encounters a word-form which is inflected for two or more properties within the same category. This occurs in a Turkish form such as *ellerimiz* 'our hands', where comparison with *ellerim* 'my hands', *ellerin* 'your (Singular) hands' and *elleriniz* 'your (Plural) hands' points towards an analysis as in (1):

(1)	el-	ler-	im-	iz
	hand	Plural	1st Person	Plural

Zwicky (1986a) sketches a treatment which distinguishes between **inherent** and **imposed** morphosyntactic properties; the Plural realised by *-ler* will be inherent, whereas that realised by *-iz* will be imposed by agreement with the possessor ('we'). Anderson's solution is rather different, and constitutes the main justification for the internal structure which he proposes for some morphosyntactic representations. To understand it, we need to look at some aspects of Person–Number agreement in Georgian verbs.

Georgian has three sets of verbal Person–Number agreement markers, which we can call the V-set, the M-set and the H-set, as set out in (2) (Anderson 1984: 161, 177):

(2)

	V	M	H
1st Singular	v-	m-	m-
2nd Singular	∅	g-	g-
3rd Singular	-s	∅	h-
1st Plural	v-. . .-t	gv-	gv-
2nd Plural	-t	g-. . .-t	g-. . .-t
3rd Plural	-en	∅	h-

(Various details are omitted here; the 3rd Person Singular affixes in both the V-set and the H-set display allomorphy governed by combinations of lexical, grammatical and phonological factors.) The function of these sets varies, partly according to Tense and partly according to lexical characteristics of the verb stem. With ordinary transitive verbs and in most Tenses, the V-set, M-set and H-set indicate agreement with the subject, direct object and indirect object respectively. However, in the Tenses traditionally labelled 'Perfect', the H-set marks the subject and the V-set the direct object, while affixal marking of the indirect object (usually the task of the H-set) is impossible. This phenomenon is known as 'inversion'. There is also a class of verbs which show 'inverted' Person–Number marking in all Tenses. Inversion can be thought of as a complex instance of Deviation II; the available sets of Person–Number inflections distinguish subject and object, but not in a one-to-one fashion.

Anderson suggests that inversion is not a syntactic but a morphological phenomenon. He points out that one cannot simply distinguish the various 1st Person affixes, for example, as [+me subject] versus [+me object], because the morphosyntactic relationship between them is then lost; the fact that the property labels both contain [. . . me . . .] is just an accident, so far as his framework is concerned. Rather, precisely the same Person–Number properties are involved in all three agreement functions, but in different **layers**, or levels of embedding, within the morphosyntactic representation.[2] If the verb acquires Person–Number properties first from its 'nearest' complement (or argument) and last from its 'furthest' one, then the most deeply embedded Person–Number properties will be those of the direct object and the most superficial will be those of the subject (the external argument, in Williams's framework (chapter 4)), with the indirect object (if any) in between. We can represent this with bracketing, as in (3):

(3)   [Person–Number [Person–Number [Person–Number]]]
        Subject   Indirect Object   Direct Object

Properties of Tense and Voice, for which a verb will be marked only once, will not need to be layered; we can think of them as parallel with the outermost, or shallowest, Person–Number layer (although this is not crucial). Since Georgian verbs cannot agree with more than three arguments, Georgian morphology will ban representations with more than three layers, as in (4) (Anderson 1984: 197):

(4)   *[W[X[Y[Z]]]]

Consider now the morphosyntactic representation of a transitive verb with a subject and direct object but no indirect object. It will have only two layers of Person–Number properties, as in (5):

(5)   Verb
      [Person–Number X [Person–Number Z]]

The properties on the deeper layer (Person–Number Z), deriving from direct-object agreement, will be expressed by the M-set of affixes while the properties on the shallower layer (X), deriving from subject agreement, will be expressed by the V-set. In fact, for ordinary transitive verbs, at least, we can associate each layer of bracketing with one of the three sets of affixes, as in (6):

(6)   [[[   ]]]
      V-set   H-set   M-set
      (obligatory) (optional)   (obligatory)

But what happens when this verb is in one of the Perfect Tenses? Recall that in these Tenses subject agreement is expressed with the H-set of affixes and direct object agreement is expressed with the V-set. Now, on the basis of the layering displayed at (3) and (6), this effect can be achieved if in these Tenses the Person–Number properties for the direct object move to the outermost layer and those for the subject move to the intermediate layer, while the deepest layer is stipulated to be empty – or, equivalently, 3rd Person, since a glance at (2) will confirm that 3rd Person has no overt realisation in the M-set of affixes which is associated with this layer. All we need is a morphological rule which, as in (7), adds a layer of structure in Perfect contexts and moves Person–Number properties (abbreviated X and Z) from one layer to another (see Anderson 1982: 600; 1984: 192):

(7)   [X [Z]]
      →   [Z [X [3rd Person   ]]]

(The spacing in (7) is not significant, but serves as a reminder that before the rule applies the intermediate layer, normally indicating indirect-object agreement, is absent.) If rule (7) tries to apply to a morphosyntactic representation in which the indirect-object layer is present, it will fail, because the filter in (4) will block the creation of a fourth layer of structure.

The full range of relevant facts in Georgian is highly complex, and (7) does not represent Anderson's last word on the inversion. Moreover, a strong syntactic rival to Anderson's morphological solution exists, in the shape of Alice Harris's analysis in the framework of Relational Grammar (1981). But (7) does illustrate the freedom with which, in Anderson's framework, properties can be layered within morphosyntactic representations and the representations themselves can be manipulated. Is this freedom a desirable contribution to morphological theory?

At first sight, the freedom looks dangerously generous. Can we, for example, take Person–Number properties from one layer of embedding and swap them with Tense properties from another layer? What difference this will make, if any, will depend on how morphosyntactic bracketing affects realisation rules (see section 7.3 below); still, it is a possibility that the theory should probably exclude. In fact, it is easy to see how it might be excluded. The property combinations X and Z which rule (7) relocates both involve the same categories (Person and Number); and it would be natural to require of all rules such as (7) that they should similarly affect only one category or category combination. But, oddly enough, when one looks at some of the Person–Number phenomena in other languages which are superficially similar to what goes on in Georgian, one is struck by how seldom rules such as (7) are useful. In Latin, there is a class of so-called 'deponent' verbs which are traditionally described as 'Passive in form but Active in meaning' (see the discussion of *utebantur* in section 3.1.3). Since realisation of Voice (Active and Passive) in Latin verbs is generally cumulative with Person–Number, this amounts to saying that deponent verbs are syntactically Active but have the Person–Number markers normally found on Passive verb-forms. But, because Latin verbs agree in Person–Number only with subjects, there is no justification here for positing distinct layers of structure. There is therefore no scope for invoking a 'relayering' rule on the lines of (7); rather, what seems to be needed is a rule which changes Active into Passive, for morphological purposes only. As the next section will show, rules of this kind have independent justification. The question therefore arises whether the Georgian facts would not be better handled by this kind of rule than by Anderson's relayering. If the answer is no, it would still be good to find applications for the relayering mechanism beyond the two (Georgian and Potawatomi (Anderson 1977)) where it has so far been invoked.

7.2.2 Homonymy, syncretism and rules of referral

Normally, the spell-out rules, however they are conceived, will match a property with its realisation directly. Zwicky (1985c) and Carstairs (1987a: 93–106), however, point out that there are occasions where one property is always or usually realised in the same way as another, and this homonymy does not seem to be merely accidental – where, in other words, Deviation IV occurs systematically. We noted in section 7.1 that in Latin the Dative and Ablative Plural of *insula* 'island' are identical (*insulis*); this is not an idiosyncrasy but rather a characteristic shared by all Latin nouns, pronouns and adjectives without exception. In English, if a verb has a Past Tense form with a coronal (*-t* or *-d*) suffix, whether 'regular', like *peeled* or *tended*, or 'irregular', like *thought, felt* or *spread*, then its Past Participle form is identical with its Past Tense form; by contrast, most verbs with a noncoronal Past form (e.g. *sang, gave*) have a distinct Past Participle (*sung, given*). Carstairs and Zwicky would therefore treat the Latin Ablative–Dative Plural homonymy as clearly systematic and the English coronal-suffix homonymy as very probably so, whereas the homonymy between some English non-coronal Past and Past participle forms (e.g. *clung, dug*) is probably accidental. Refining the criterial for the systematic-accidental distinction remains a problem. Meanwhile, however, the question arises: how should systematic inflectional homonymies be handled in morphological description?

One possibility is that the spell-out rules (to be discussed in section 7.3) should be constructed in such a way that the homonymies emerge automatically. For example, all Feminine nouns in German have the same form throughout the Singular, without any Case ending; this might be taken care of by simply failing to supply any spell-out rules for Feminine Singular Cases. But, as Zwicky points out, this will not work for all systematic homonymies. If Latin merely has two distinct spell-out rules covering the Dative–Ablative Plural, one yielding *-is* for nouns like *insula* and another yielding *-ibus* for nouns like *urbs* 'city' (*urbibus*), then the fact that the homonymy occurs in both classes of nouns appears accidental. What we need is a statement that the Dative and Ablative Plural are always alike, however they are spelled. Zwicky calls such statements **rules of referral**, and illustrates them with German material. German nouns, adjectives and determiners usually have identical forms in the Nominative and Accusative, both Singular and Plural, so *das gute Buch* 'the good book', *ein gutes Buch* 'a good book', *die guten Bücher* 'the good books', *eine gute Zeitung* 'a good newspaper', *diese guten Zeitungen* 'these good newspapers' are all Case-wise ambiguous, despite the fact that several different inflectional endings are involved (*-e, -en, -er, -es* and zero). Using 'nounal' to mean 'noun, adjective or determiner', Zwicky expresses this in his notation by means of the rule of referral at (8):

(8)   In the context of [CATEGORY: Nounal], [CASE: acc] has the same realisation as [CASE: nom].

If rule (8) applied everywhere, there would be no ground for distinguishing Nominative and Accusative as morphological Cases; and indeed, in some Masculine Singular contexts, rule (8) does not apply, so that *der gute Mann* 'the good man (Nominative)' is distinct from *den guten Mann* 'the good man (Accusative)'. But this is partly taken care of by the fact that rule (8) is less specific than, and is therefore automatically overridden by, Zwicky's rule (9) (in which 'adjectival' means 'adjective or determiner'):

(9)   In the context of [CATEGORY: Adjectival], [CASE: acc, GEND: masc, NUM: sg] is realised by the suffixation of /en/.

A further override affects some Masculine nouns, like *Präsident* with its distinct Accusative *Präsidenten*. We will have more to say about overrides in the next section. Meanwhile, what are the implications of the referral mechanism?

Zwicky does not suggest any restrictions on what can be referred to what. Yet, if unconstrained, the mechanism is suspiciously powerful. In fact, restrictions of two kinds have been proposed, relating to meaning and to the form of the relevant spell-out rules.

Any inflectional homonymy creates at least a superficial ambiguity; but one cannot straightforwardly cite this as a factor inhibiting homonymy because the tolerance of ambiguity in natural languages is notoriously high. However, Frans Plank (1980) argues that a specific kind of Case homonymy may indeed be disallowed. If in some language the relationship between a head noun and a possessive nominal modifier in a noun phrase is expressed by a morphological Case contrast, noun phrases in which this Case contrast is neutralised in both the head and the modifier are not normally acceptable. Thus, in German, the phrase **Benachteiligungen*

Frauen 'discrimination against women' (literally 'discriminations of-women') is unacceptable because (Plank suggests) both the head *Benachteiligungen* and the modifier *Frauen* fail to distinguish the head Case-form (Nominative) from the modifier Case-form (Genitive), but *Benachteiligungen Andersgläubiger* 'discrimination against unortho-dox people' is acceptable because the suffix *-er* on *Andersgläubiger* renders it unambiguously Genitive. This entails that a noun whose meaning is such that it frequently functions as both head and modifier in noun phrases, such as most nouns denoting humans, should not follow a pattern of inflection in which the relevant Cases are syncretised. In the light of this generalisation, Plank seeks to explain certain developments in noun inflection in late Latin. The possibility of applying this kind of semantic argument to other actual or potential homonymies has yet to be explored.

Carstairs (1984b; 1987a: 107–24) proposes a constraint of quite a different kind, involving cumulative exponence. In any instance of inflectional homonymy, one can distinguish between the properties which are homonymously realised and the property or properties which provide the context in which this occurs (the **dominant** prop-erties, in Hjelmslev's (1935) terms). In the Latin Dative–Ablative Plural example, the homonymously realised properties are Dative and Ablative and the contextual property is Plural. One can then ask how the homonymous properties are realised in relation to the contextual property or properties: simultaneously (cumulatively) or not? In the Latin instance, the realisation is cumulative, since neither *-i:s* nor its rival *-ibus* can be divided into a Plural part and a Dative–Ablative part. For this kind of homonymy Carstairs rather unfortunately proposes the label **syncretism**, although this term more usually means any inflectional homonymy, or else in particular one which arises through phonological change; a better label for homonymies of the Latin kind might therefore be 'cumulative homonymy'. An example of noncumulative homonymy is supplied by the 1st Person Singular Past Indicative of Hungarian verbs. In the Present Indicative, a Hungarian verb such as *olvasni* 'read' distinguishes an Indefinite 1st Person form *olvas-ok* 'I am reading' and a Definite 1st Person form *olvas-om* 'I am reading it' (where Definiteness depends on agreement with a 3rd Person object). In the Past, however, the 1st Person Singular Definite and Indefinite are homonymous: *olvas-t-am*. This homonymy is noncumulative because the realisation of the contextual property Past (the suffix *-t-*) is clearly separate from that of the homonymous properties (*-am*).

Looking at a variety of inflectional homonymies in several

languages, Carstairs makes three observations: (a) cumulative homonymies are much commoner than noncumulative ones; (b) in noncumulative homonymies, the realisation of the homonymous properties nearly always looks like the one which is usual for just one of these properties in other contexts, and (c) in noncumulative homonymies, at least one of the contextual, or dominant, properties is, in Bybee's terms, less relevant than the homonymous properties. Thus, in our Hungarian example, the homonymous 1st Person suffix -*am* of the Past Tense 'looks' Definite (compare Definite -*om* versus Indefinite -*ok* in the Present), and, although Definiteness is rare as a verbal category and is not given a position by Bybee in her hierarchy of verbal relevance, one could argue that (subject) Person should retain the bottom position which Bybee assigns to it. Carstairs's observations might be just an accidental fact about the homonymies in his sample; but they seem likely to be more than this, because a kind of functional explanation can be invoked for the preference for cumulative contexts. In a language with cumulative exponence of Case and Number, such as Latin, a syncretism between two Cases in the Plural reduces by one the total number of Case-forms which have to be learned. On the other hand, in a language with no such cumulation, like Turkish, a Case syncretism increases what has to be learned: not only the exponent of Plural and the exponents of the two Cases in the Singular, but also the fact that something special happens with one or both of these Cases in the Plural. Correspondingly, Carstairs and Stemberger (1988) argue that inflectional homonymies of the rarer, noncumulative, kind are more difficult to simulate in a certain kind of 'connectionist' model of morphological structure. Carstairs therefore puts forward a **Systematic Homonymy Claim**, to the effect that any systematic homonymy must either be cumulative or else have characteristics (b) and (c) above.[3]

From the point of view of Carstairs's question about possible deviations from one-to-one exponence, this claim constrains Deviation IV by linking it in a certain fashion with Deviation III. It may therefore seem to have more to do with how morphosyntactic properties are realised than with how they are structured in morphosyntactic representations. But that is not quite so. From Zwicky's point of view, the Systematic Homonymy Claim constrains rules of referral. This means that, when a morphosyntactic representation is manipulated by a rule of referral, information must already be available about the aspect of the representation that is most vital to the Systematic Homonymy Claim, namely about which morphosyntactic properties are to be realised cumulatively. So the claim indirectly supports Warburton's proposal (1973) that a morphosyntactic representation is 'unpacked' into a linear sequence of properties and property bundles, reflecting the order of their exponents, before these properties are spelled out; for it is on this linearised representation that rules of referral operate, if Carstairs is right. We must therefore set Warburton's linearisation alongside Anderson's relayering and Zwicky's referral as a third kind of manipulation which morphosyntactic representations may undergo.

7.3 SPELL-OUT OF MORPHOSYNTACTIC PROPERTIES

Factors of several kinds appear to affect the way in which a given property in a given morphosyntactic representation is spelled. Some, discussed in section 7.3.1, involve the relationship between spellout rules themselves; others (section 7.3.2) involve the syntagmatic context in which the property is realised. The factors summarised here are quite various, yet most of the proposals relating to them are precise and readily testable. It seems fair to guess, therefore, that increased research effort in this area of morphology would be especially rewarding.[4]

7.3.1 The Elsewhere Condition and disjunctive ordering

What happens when the grammar of a language appears to provide two or more ways of spelling out the same morphosyntactic property in one word? Can all the rules concerned apply? If not, how do we choose between them? It could be that there is no general answer to these questions. If this pessimistic conclusion is correct, then the choice between competing rules will always be a matter of language-particular stipulation – something for which Univeral Grammar provides no help to the language learner. But all recent researchers in morphology share the hope that this conclusion is wrong. Anderson in particular has laid stress on a criterion for identifying which rule should take precedence in such situations (the **Elsewhere Condition**), and a machinery for stipulating precedence where the Elsewhere Condition fails or needs to be overridden (**disjunctive rule-blocks**).

The Elsewhere Condition is familiar from chapter 3, where we encountered it in the context of Kiparsky's Lexical Phonology (1982c). Anderson's informal statement of it is as follows (1986: 4): 'Whenever one rule is more specific than another in the sense that the forms subject to the first constitute a proper subset of those subject to the second, the application of the more specific rule precludes the later application of the more general, less specific one.' A stem which is lexically specified for a particular property behaves like a more specific rule, too, so the lexically Plural form *cattle* fails to get pluralised as **cattles*. But Anderson also proposes that the application of one rule can preclude that of another, even when there is no such proper subset relationship between the forms subject to them, if they belong to the same block of disjunctively ordered rules. The need for disjunctive rule-blocks, according to Anderson, is illustrated by the Georgian Person–Number agreement markers at (2). Recall that for most verbs in non-Perfect Tenses, the V-set affixes agree with the subject while the M-set ones agree with the direct object. But both sets include both prefixes and suffixes. What happens if the verb is to agree with a subject and an object whose agreement markers are both prefixes? For example, what is the Georgian for 'I see you (Singular)', which would seem to require the addition of both *v-* and *g-* to the stem *-xedav-* 'see'? Despite Georgian's notorious tolerance for consonant clusters, the actual form is not **g-v-xedav* or **v-g-xedav* but *g-xedav* (homonymous with the form meaning 'he sees you'). In fact, Georgian verbs do not permit more than one Person–Number affix on either side of the stem, so a mechanism has to be found which gives the 2nd Person Singular object marker *g-* priority over the 1st Person Singular subject marker *v-*. The Elsewhere Condition is no help here, so Anderson proposes that the *g-*rule simply precedes the *v-*rule within a disjunctive rule-block. Although morphological theory makes available the rule-block mechanism, the fact that *g-* precludes *v-* and not vice versa is not derivable from any general principle.

German verb inflection, as discussed by Anderson (1982; 1986) and Jensen and Stong-Jensen (1984), illustrates nicely the kinds of analysis which the Elsewhere Condition and the rule-block mechanism either impose or facilitate, and the problems which arise with them. Consider the data in (10), noting especially the distribution of the suffix *-t-* in the Past and of umlaut (stem-vowel change) in the Past Subjunctive:

(10)		Present Infinitive	Past Indicative	Past Subjunctive	Past Participle	
	a.	lob-en	lob-t-e	lob-t-e	ge-lob-t	'praise'
		mach-en	mach-t-e	mach-t-e	ge-mach-t	'make'
	b.	bring-en	brach-t-e	bräch-t-e	ge-brach-t	'bring'
		wiss-en	wuss-t-e	wüss-t-e	ge-wuss-t	'know'
	c.	sitz-en	sass	säss-e	ge-sess-en	'sit'
		sing-en	sang	säng-e	ge-sung-en	'sing'

Anderson expresses the spell-out rules for Past and Subjunctive as in (11) and (12) (1982: 607–8; 1986: 16):

(11) [+Past]
      /X/→/X+t/

(12) [+Past, +Subjunctive]
      /X   V   Y   (e)/
       1   2   3   4
→   1   2   3   e
           [−back]

But evidently the verbs of type (10c) do not undergo rule (11), since we do not find a Past form such as *sass-t-e*, and verbs of type (10a) do not undergo rule (12), since we do not find a Subjunctive form such as *löb-t-e*; only the 'mixed' verbs of type (10b) undergo both rules. How is this to be described and, if possible, explained?

For the (10c) verbs, the Elsewhere Condition seems relevant; the special Past stems *sass* and *sang*, with their distinctive vowels, will be lexically marked [+Past], and thus will be prevented by the Elsewhere Condition from undergoing rule (11). But then why does the Condition not also apply in (10b), so as to block the suffixation of -*t* to the special stem *brach-* (contrast non-Past *bring-*)? In answer, Anderson points out that the stem *brach-* occurs not only in the Past Indicative but also in the Past Participle and (with umlaut) the Past Subjunctive, so it is the non-Past stem *bring-* which stands out as 'special'; by contrast, in the (10c) verbs, the Past Participle has a stem of its own (-*sess-*, -*sung-*). Anderson therefore suggests that the (10b) verbs are unusual in that it is their non-Past stem which is lexically marked ([−Past]), not their Past stem. The stem *brach-* therefore has no lexical marking which might inhibit rule (11). The absence of the Past suffix -*t*- is therefore explained by the Elsewhere Condition in (10c) and at least compatible with it in (10b).[5]

The Past Subjunctive umlaut rule (12) applies straightforwardly to the strong verbs in (10c). But why does it not apply in (10a)? By the Elsewhere Condition, Past Subjunctive forms should not only undergo (12) but also fail to undergo (11), because [+Past, +Subjunctive] forms are a proper subset of the [+Past] forms. The Past Subjunctive of *loben* should therefore be not *lob-t-e* but *löb-e*! To overcome the fact that the Elsewhere Condition makes exactly the wrong prediction here, Anderson proposes (1982: 608) that (11) and (12) are stipulated to apply in this order within a disjunctive rule-block. Since the verbs of (10a) can undergo (11), they are then precluded by disjunctivity from undergoing rule (12); on the other hand, since the verbs of (10c) are precluded by the Elsewhere Condition from undergoing (11), they are free to undergo rule (12). Unfortunately, this analysis runs into difficulty with the (10b) verbs. These undergo rule (11), as we have just seen; but in this instance the stipulated disjunctivity of (11) and (12) gives the wrong result, since we do want them to receive umlaut in the Past Subjunctive. As it stands, Anderson's analysis incorrectly predicts nonumlauted Past Subjunctive forms *brachte* and *wusste*.

Quite apart from whether it successfully handles the German facts, a rule-block mechanism which can override the Elsewhere Condition is extremely powerful – too powerful, according to Jensen and Stong-Jensen (1984). To account for the distribution of umlaut in Past Subjunctives, they invoke instead the mechanism of level-ordering from Lexical Phonology (see chapter 3). They suggest that the 'regular' Past-formation rule (11) applies at a late level (specifically, Level 3), whereas the Past Subjunctive umlaut rule (12) applies at Level 1, along with other irregular inflection. Rule (12) can therefore apply only to those Past forms which already exist at Level 1, such as the lexically specified Past stems *sass* and *sang*; it cannot apply to Past stems such as *lob-t-* and *mach-t-*, which do not exist until Level 3. But, just like Anderson's, this analysis runs into trouble with the mixed verbs of (10b). If the stem *brach-t-* is not formed until Level 3, it will not be available for umlaut; on the other hand, if it is formed on Level 1, then the 'regular' *t*-suffixation rule for Past must apply on Level 1 as well as Level 3 – not impossible within the Lexical Phonology framework, but suspiciously *ad hoc*. The German facts thus remain uncomfortable for both the Extended Word-and-Paradigm and the Lexical Phonology frameworks.[6]

Zwicky's version of the Elsewhere Condition and of stipulated disjunctivity differ from Anderson's so as to be more restrictive in some respects, less restrictive in others. For example, Zwicky proposes (1985c) a very general rule (13) for the inflection of German adjectives in 'weak' contexts (that is, broadly speaking, where they are preceded by an inflected determiner):

(13) In the context of [CATEGORY:adjective, CLASS:weak], any bundle of CASE, GENDER and NUMBER values is realised by suffixation of /en/.

This looks as if it states that weak German adjectives always end in *-en*, which is incorrect; in the Singular, the Nominative and non-

Masculine Accusative forms end in *-e*. But (13) is a **default** rule, automatically **overridden** where necessary by more specific rules. In addition, stems which are lexically associated with particular properties override the subsequent spell-out of those properties by realisation rules (1986b), so the existence of a special Past stem for German (10c) verbs (*sass-*, *sang-*, etc.) precludes the formally compatible suffixation of *-t* by rule (11). On the other hand, between rules, 'overrides are predicted only when there are conflicts in the specification of phonological properties for forms. . . . When a more general rule is formally compatible with a more specific one, then both apply' (Zwicky 1990: 221); this allows, for example, a German form such as *Kind-er-n* 'children (Dative Plural)', in which the Plural ending *-er* appears alongside the more specific Dative Plural ending *-n*.

In place of Anderson's stipulated disjunctivity, Zwicky proposes a principle of **slot competition** (1987: 529). In Anderson's treatment of the Georgian form *g-xedav* 'I see you', the fact that the disjunctively ordered *g*-prefixing and *v*-prefixing rules both add a prefix directly to a stem is an accident, so far as the rule-block mechanism is concerned, since that mechanism could equally well be invoked if one of the rules happened to be suffixing rather than prefixing. But Zwicky disallows that possibility. One rule can preclude the application of another, morphosyntactically compatible, rule only if they both complete to fill the same positional 'slot'; in the Georgian example, this is a prefixal Person–Number slot which can be separated from the lexical stem of the verb only by a limited set of markers indicating something like Aspect (Aronson 1982). It remains to be seen whether Zwicky's more restrictive principle can be sustained generally.[7]

7.3.2 Extended exponence and the Peripherality Constraint

The Elsewhere Condition and the Adjacency Condition (chapter 3) both limit the circumstances under which a morphosyntactic property can be realised in more than one place within a word-form. So one can regard both as proposals about constraints on extended exponence, or Deviation I. In addition, the Lexical Phonology framework, within which words are built up from the root outwards by successive applications of morphological and phonological processes, implicitly claims that a process on one level cannot be affected by a process on a 'later' level or a 'later' process within the same level. Simpson and Withgott (1986) call this the **No Lookahead** principle.

But do the Elsewhere and Adjacency Conditions constitute the only constraints on extended exponence, and is No Lookahead always observed?

Simpson and Withgott (1986), discussing clusters of pronominal clitics in the Australian languages Warlpiri and Warumungu and in French, suggest that two fundamentally different types of morphology should be distinguished: **layered morphology** and **template morphology**. Layered morphology, as found in most Indo-European languages, is hierarchically structured in the fashion emphasised by, for example, Lieber (1981b) and Selkirk (1982) (see chapters 2 and 4 above), and observes the Adjacency Condition and No Lookahead. Template morphology, on the other hand, is characterised by a flat, nonhierarchical structure, with individual elements (affixes or clitics) grouped into classes associated with particular 'slots' or 'positions' in linear sequence. But how do we tell whether a given set of morphological phenomena belongs in the layered or the template category? Without clear criteria, there is a risk that the template category may become merely a dump for counterexamples to the Elsewhere and Adjacency Conditions. One language whose elaborate affixal morphology has traditionally been described in terms of a matrix of slots or positions is Quechua (Yokoyama 1951), so it would seem to be a prime candidate for template status. Yet Muysken (1986) argues that Quechua morphology is not, after all, describable entirely in terms of a flat structure with a fixed order of slots. Instead, he proposes tentatively that Quechua's many affixes must be divided among three morphological **modes** (lexical, syntactic and inflectional), each with its own characteristics, as summarised in (14) (1986: 640):

(14)

	Order	Meaning	Number	Position
lexical	fixed	idiosyncratic	limited	internal
syntactic	variable	independent	no limit	intermediate
inflectional	fixed	no lexical meaning	limited	external

Any of these modes may be unrepresented in any language; what is unusual about Quechua, Muysken suggests, is that all three modes are represented, although to a different extent in different dialects. So, even if not all morphology is of the kind that Simpson and Withgott call 'layered', there is no consensus about where nonlayered morphology occurs, let alone what its characteristics are.

Even within layered morphology, is No Lookahead always ob-

served, as Simpson and Withgott assume? Carstairs (1987a) proposes
a **Peripherality Constraint** which, in effect, specifies conditions under
which violations of No Lookahead are possible.[8] To get a clear
idea what such a violation would look like, let us consider first an
inflectional process which 'looks back' rather than 'ahead'. In (15a)
and (15b) are given the Present Imperfective and Perfective forms
respectively of the Latin verb *amo*: 'love':

(15)			a. Imperfective	b. Perfective
Singular	1		am-o:	am-a:-v-i:
	2		am-a:-s	am-a:-v-isti:
	3		am-a-t	am-a:-v-it
Plural	1		am-a:-mus	am-a:-v-imus
	2		am-a:-tis	am-a:-v-istis
	3		am-a-nt	am-a:-v-erunt

All these forms except the 1st Person Singular Imperfective contain
a 'theme vowel' *-a:-* or *-a-*. But what concerns us are the Person–
Number endings, which follow the last hyphen in each form. The
Perfective endings differs from the Imperfective endings, and, being
unique to the Perfective Indicative, they can be said to help realise
the property Perfective. Yet the lion's share of the task of realising
Perfective goes to the suffix *-v-*, which shows up not only in all
the forms of (15b) but in all other Active Moods and Tenses of
the Perfective. We can therefore call *-v-* the **principal exponent** of
the Perfective in these forms. Clearly, the Person–Number suffixes
in (15b) 'look back' to the Perfective, whose principal exponent is
more central (closer to the root) than they are. But can one find a
situation where some property 'looks ahead' in its realisation to a
property whose principal exponent is less central (further from the
root)?

The No Lookahead principle denies this possibility. Indeed, if it
did occur, it would seem hard to reconcile not only with the kind of
layering explicit in Lexical Phonology but also with that implicit in
Anderson's and Zwicky's ordering of spell-out rules. But Carstairs
(1987a: 165–7) points out that just this kind of lookahead seems to
occur in the Possessed forms of Hungarian nouns. The Plural suffix on
unpossessed nouns is *-k*, *-ok*, *-ak* or *-ek*, depending partly on lexical,
partly on phonological characteristics of the noun stem; thus, *ruha*
'dress' has a Plural form *ruhá-k*.[9] Possessed forms ('my dress', 'your
dress', etc.) also involve suffixes: 1st Person Singular *-m*, *-om*, *-am*
or *-em*, etc. The paradigm in (16) illustrates the combination of these
with *ruha* in the Singular:

(16)		Singular	Plural
	1	ruhá-m	ruhá-nk
	2	ruhá-d	ruhá-tok
	3	ruhá-ja	ruhá-juk

On the basis of this, one might expect the 1st Person Singular Possessed form of *ruha* in the Plural to involve simply adding *-am* or *-om* to *ruhá-k*: **ruhá-k-am* or **ruhá-k-om*. But, as the asterisks indicate, this is wrong. Instead, we find *ruhá-i-m* 'my dresses', with a Plural suffix *-i-* replacing the usual *-k*. We can be confident in calling *-i-* a realisation of Plural because it occurs in all Possessed forms, and in the 1st and 2nd Persons there is a clear principal exponent of the Possessor identical with that in (16), as (17) shows:

(17)		Singular	Plural
	1	ruhá-i-m	ruhá-i-nk
	2	ruhá-i-d	ruhá-i-tok
	3	ruhá-i	ruhá-i-k

It seems, then, that the realisation of Plural in Hungarian nouns violates No Lookahead by looking ahead to properties in the Possessor category, realised more peripherally. But one thing which is striking about (17) is that this lookahead is consistent; the exponent of Plural is *-i-* when followed by not just some but all Possessors. We can say that Plural looks ahead not to some property or properties (e.g. 1st Person Singular) but to a whole category, namely Possessor. Discussing a variety of similar examples, Carstairs argues that this categorial consistency is a common feature. He therefore proposes a Peripherality Constraint which in effect licenses lookahead in specific circumstances (1987a: 168):

> The realisation of a property may be sensitive inwards, i.e. to a property realised more centrally in the word-form . . . but not outwards to an individual property realised more peripherally. . . . It may, however, be sensitive outwards consistently to all the properties within a given category.

The Peripherality Constraint can be thought of as a constraint on Deviation II involving the syntagmatic dimension of word structure, in other words involving Deviation I also, to some degree. It is still not clear how even this limited lookahead can be accommodated within layered morphology; but at least the problem is circumscribed.

Carstairs accounts for certain apparent counterexamples to the Peripherality Constraint by appealing to the Systematic Homonymy

Claim (section 7.2.2) and by the distinction between morphological and phonological lookahead (since the Peripherality Constraint bears only on the former, not the latter). But the greatest challenge relating to the Peripherality Constraint at present is to anchor it more securely in inflectional theory as a whole. Given that the existence of lookahead of any kind is problematic, it is not surprising that it should be subject to some constraint; but why precisely this constraint? It is as if inflectional realisation operates on the basis of precise information about what has already been spelled out (subject perhaps to 'forgetting' some material that is no longer 'adjacent'), but only vague information about what has yet to be spelled out.[10] What is needed, perhaps, is a more sophisticated account of what morphosyntactic representations look like after they have been linearised, roughly as proposed by Warburton (1973) – an account which will be needed anyway, if the Systematic Homonymy Claim is on the right lines. At the same time, if the distinction between template and layered morphology can be made more precise, it will be important to investigate whether template morphology is as free of constraints on lookahead as Simpson and Withgott tentatively suggest, or whether some version of the Peripherality Constraint applies here too.

8 Natural Morphology and related approaches

8.1 INTRODUCTION

Natural Morphology (NM) is an approach to morphology developed in Germany and Austria since the late 1970s by, in particular, Wolfgang Ullrich Dressler, Willi Mayerthaler and Wolfgang Ullrich Wurzel.[1] This choice of label has irked some linguists outside the Natural Morphology circle; but the label has stuck, so it is necessary to continue using it, while consciously rejecting any evaluative connotation. It was in fact adopted in imitation of the title 'Natural Phonology' chosen by Stampe for his approach to phonology in the early 1970s (see e.g. Donegan and Stampe 1979). Stampe's central suggestion is that acquiring the phonology of one's native language is a matter of suppressing phonological processes rather than learning them. The innate language faculty with which every normal child is equipped includes a repertoire of 'natural' phonological processes. There are conflicts between different kinds of naturalness, however. Within phonology, processes favouring ease of production may conflict with ones favouring ease of perception, such as the aspiration of initial voiceless stops (which English fails to suppress). And, if we look beyond phonology, it is clear that if in some language all 'natural' processes favouring ease of production were to apply quite freely, so as to reduce all sounds to some kind of undifferentiated low-mid vowel, that 'language' would be useless for communication because it would be incapable of expressing any lexical, syntactic or morphological contrasts.

Developing Stampe's idea, Natural Morphologists see much of what goes on in language in terms of the need to find a balance, or trade-off, when conflicts arise between what is natural on one dimension and what is natural on another. The dimensions concerned may involve distinct components of grammar (phonology, word formation, inflectional morphology, syntax) or different aspects of one component (such as ease of production and ease of perception within phonology). For all components, determining what is 'natural' involves principally, though not exclusively, 'external' and typological evidence. External evidence is that which goes beyond individual *états de langue*, seen as static and homogeneous systems, or descriptions of adult idiolectal competence; it includes facts about acquisition, language change, speech disorders, and pidgins and creoles. Typological evidence includes implicational universals (or statistical generalisations) based on more or less wide surveys of languages, in the tradition of Greenberg (1963). At the same time, Natural Morphologists are concerned to develop some explanatory theory of morphology (and of language generally) from which their decisions about naturalness based on external and typological evidence can be derived as consequences.

From this sketch of the NM programme, it is evident that there is plenty of scope for differences of emphasis within it. Investigators may focus on different intercomponential or intracomponential conflicts, on different kinds of evidence, or on different kinds of explanatory theory. The work of Dressler, Mayerthaler and Wurzel does in fact diverge in all these ways; but it has enough in common to justify the claim that they are working within a common framework.

The universals that Natural Morphologists tend to propose involve semiotic principles or aspects of the human organism which are not specific to language, in contrast to the Chomskyan assumption of a relatively self-contained innate 'language organ'. Moreover, in its emphasis on diachronic evidence, NM has more in common with the approaches of some generativists of a decade or more ago (e.g. Kiparsky 1968; Lightfoot 1979) than with Chomskyan Principles-and-Parameters theory today. On the other hand, the increasing relevance attributed by contemporary Chomskyans to the actual stages of language development in early childhood (as opposed to, or alongside, the 'logical problem' of language acquisition) parallels the importance which NM assigns to it, at least nominally. Both approaches are modular in the sense that they see grammars as, at least in part, products of the interaction between more-or-less independent sets of principles. This resemblance is superficial, however. In Principles-and-Parameters linguistics, broadly speaking, any well-formed sentence must comply with the requirements applicable to it at each level of representation (D-structure, S-structure, Logical Form and Phonological Form); there is usually no question of, for example, sacrificing some principle of LF in order to secure easier compliance with some principle of PF. In Natural Morphology, however, precisely this kind of trade-off can occur, and almost everything which happens is described in terms of conflicts between different principles of naturalness, whereby one or more principles are complied with in less than optimal fashion.

The two approaches may still be compatible, however. One could see Principles-and-Parameters theory as emphasising the absolute boundaries within which linguistic variation is possible (resembling in this respect Carstairs's approach to inflectional morphology, discussed in chapter 7) while NM (or 'Natural Grammar' generally) deals with the reasons why some options within these boundaries are more preferred and others less preferred. But whether this sort of division of labour is feasible will emerge clearly only when 'Natural Grammarians' have ventured further into syntax, the principal terrain of Chomskyan linguistic theory, and when Chomskyans have begun to tackle allomorphic and morphophonological aspects of morphology more seriously.

8.1.1 Explanatory principles: universal

Like Carstairs, the Natural Morphologists are concerned with the relationship between expression and meaning in morphology – or, to use the Latin terms that they prefer, the relationship between **signantia** (singular **signans**) and **signata** (singular **signatum**). As we saw in chapter 7, Carstairs seeks constraints on the extent and nature of deviation from an ideal one-to-one relationship between signantia and signata. For the Natural Morphologists, on the other hand, the emphasis is not on deviation from some ideal relationship but on conformity with a 'natural' relationship. Admittedly, naturalness is seen as a matter of degree, not an absolute, and in many *états de langue* a relatively unnatural piece of morphological patterning may be imposed or sustained through interference from other components of grammar, particularly phonology. But, even with these qualifications, the central claim of all versions of NM is at least in appearance very strong: the relationship between signans and signatum is always 'natural'. Establishing the validity of NM therefore involves devising a model of naturalness with which as many actual morphological phenomena as possible are consistent, and suggesting plausible, nonarbitrary explanations for any phenomena which seem at first sight 'unnatural'.

Does morphology have to comply with universal principles of naturalness directly, or is this compliance filtered through inter-mediate typological or language-particular principles? We will examine Mayerthaler's direct-compliance framework (1981)[2] before noting problems of the kind which led Dressler (1985b) and Wurzel (1984) to deviate from it.

For Mayerthaler, naturalness is the inverse of an all-pervasive notion of **markedness** (Markiertheit). Markedness applies both to morphological content (the relationship of one morphological signatum to another) and to morphological symbolisation or **coding** (the relationship of a morphological signatum to its signans). An unmarked, or natural, coding for a pair of signata A and B, of which A is more marked than B, is a coding such that the signans of A is more **markerful** (merkmalhaft) than the signans of B – that is, such that A has an overt realisation whereas B has none, or A's realisation is phonologically more substantial than B's. This kind of coding is said to be (**constructionally**) **iconic**.[3] (The background to this choice of terminology will emerge presently.)

An example of a markedness relationship on the plane of content is that between the inflectional properties Singular (relatively unmarked) and Plural (relatively marked). Plural is more marked than Singular because it is textually less frequent and because in many languages the Singular may be used freely in reference to sets or collectivities (e.g. *the elephant is the largest land mammal*) whereas the Plural is never freely used to refer to individuals; apparent exceptions such as pluralia tantum (English *trousers* or Latin *castra* 'camp') and the 'royal plural' *We* are lexically or pragmatically restricted. It follows that a (relatively) natural coding for Singular and Plural will be one in which Plural is realised by an overt marker while Singular is not; that is, where Plural but not Singular has markerful coding. English Singular *dog* and Plural *dogs* exhibit coding of this kind. By contrast, *sheep* (Plural *sheep*) exhibits less natural (hence more marked) coding, since the Plural form is **markerless** (merkmallos). In *dog/dogs* the Number coding is constructionally iconic, wherease in *sheep/sheep* it is **noniconic**. Less natural still is **countericonic** coding, in which it is the less marked signatum Singular which is realised by an overt marker while the more marked Plural has none; a possible illustration is Welsh *coeden* 'tree', Plural *coed*. These examples illustrate the importance of distinguishing between 'marked' (in Mayerthaler's sense) and 'markerful'; the markerless Plural *sheep* is relatively marked so far as its coding of Number is concerned. Unfortunately, in English-speaking linguists' usage the term 'marked' tends to vacillate in sense between Mayerthaler's 'markiert' (our 'marked') and 'merkmalhaft' (our 'markerful').

Iconicity is not the only factor relevant to markedness in coding.

Where two codings are equally iconic, the more **uniform** is less marked (more natural). A signatum is coded in maximally uniform fashion when there is only one signans corresponding to it; for example, the coding of the verbal property Progressive in English is maximally uniform, since it is always realised by the suffix *-ing*. The well-known tendency for children at a certain stage of language learning to overgeneralise the 'regular' verbal Past inflection (*comed, bringed*, etc.) can be seen in Mayerthaler's terms as an attempt to increase the uniformity of verbal inflection. This overgeneralisation increases iconicity too, because *comed*, with **additive** coding (suffixation), is constructionally more iconic than *came*, with purely **modulatory** coding (vowel change).

A third relevant factor is **transparency**. Transparency is the inverse of uniformity, involving not a signatum with a unique signans but rather a signans with a unique signatum. In English adjectival inflection, the Comparative is not maximally uniformly coded, because although many adjectives have a Comparative in *-er*, many have no inflectional Comparative at all and a few display partial or total suppletion (*better, worse*). It is also not maximally transparently coded, since *-er* can code agent (*writer*) and instrument (*cooker*) as well as Comparative. On the other hand, the Superlative suffix *-est* is maximally transparent, since it codes nothing else except superlative (assuming that the 2nd Person Singular *-est* of *writest, knowest*, etc. is obsolete).

Uniform transparent coding in inflection corresponds to the one-to-one relationship between expression and content which is the starting-point for Carstairs's search for constraints on deviations (see chapter 7). It also represents what could be called a **biunique** relationship between signans and signatum, borrowing here a term from phonology; and in Dressler's version of NM, biuniqueness replaces uniformity and transparency (Dressler 1985b). Dressler also favours the term **diagrammatic** in lieu of Mayerthaler's 'constructionally iconic' (see also Kilani-Schoch 1988). We will return to Dressler's version in the next section.

A clear *prima facie* problem for Mayerthaler's use of constructional iconicity as a criterion for naturalness arises from examples such as Welsh *coeden/coed* 'tree/trees', already mentioned. But in some languages there is evidence in favour of treating not the Singular but the Plural form of some nouns as unmarked (in Mayerthaler's sense). Nouns which are most typically used to refer to a collection of objects may display additive inflection for a Singular, or 'Singulative', form. This phenomenon occurs in many nouns in Turkana, for example

(Dimmendaal 1987), and is clearly related to the choice of the Plural stem rather than the Singular as the basis for analogical levelling for some nouns in Frisian (Tiersma 1982). In Welsh, other nouns which behave like *coed* in this respect are *pysgodyn/pysgod* 'fish/fishes' and *plentyn/plant* 'child/children'. Should we perhaps regard the usual markedness relationship between Singular and Plural as reversed for these nouns? Local **markedness inversion** (Markiertheitsumkehrung) is indeed what Mayerthaler proposes for handling instances of this kind. His own principal illustration also involves the Singular–Plural contrast. In Latin nouns with stems originally ending in /Vs/ (where V is any vowel), the /s/ underwent rhotacism (*s*>*r*) when a vowel-initial suffix followed, e.g. Nominative Singular *hono:s* 'honour', Genitive Singular *hono:r-is* (<**hono:s-is*). In later Latin, the stem alternant in -*r* was extended in polysyllables to the Nominative Singular too (e.g. *honor*, with regular shortening of the vowel in the final syllable) – a change which, in Mayerthaler's terms, reduces coding markedness by increasing uniformity – while monosyllables retained their Nominatives in -*s*: *flo:s* 'flower', *mu:s* 'mouse'. An exception to this exception was the noun *lar* 'household deity' (Plural *lare:s*), whose earlier Nominative Singular was *las*. Why this divergence from the other monosyllables in -*s*? Mayerthaler's explanation (1981: 49) hinges on the fact that *lar* occurs much more frequently in the Plural than in the Singular, especially in the collocation *lares et penates* 'household deities and ancestors'. Because of this, the lexical item *lar* constitutes a **marked context** within which the usual markedness relationship between Singular and Plural is inverted; consequently, the stem of the locally less-marked Plural can naturally be extended to the Singular – a change which would not be natural for nouns such as *flo:s* and *mu:s*, for which the Singular is less marked than the Plural.

Markedness inversion is persuasive as an explanation for apparently countericonic coding only to the extent that there are clear independent criteria for identifying the 'marked contexts' within which the inversion is to be expected. In the examples which we have looked at so far, the independent criteria are the semantic grounds (more or less strong) for regarding Plural as less marked than Singular for a certain class of nouns. But the instance of alleged markedness inversion which Mayerthaler discusses at most length is of a different kind. All Romance languages except Romanian have lost Case as a morphosyntactic category in nouns. The question therefore arises: of the Latin Case-forms for any noun, which survives as the ancestor of the sole Case-less form in each Number (Singular and Plural)? On various grounds, Mayerthaler argues that the Nominative is a less marked signatum than the other cases. It is therefore the signans of the Nominative which ought to survive when Case distinctions are lost. Yet in most nouns in the western Romance languages (French, Spanish, Portuguese, Catalan, Italian), the form which has survived is generally taken to have descended from a non-Nominative form (or, more specifically, the Accusative form). How can we reconcile this with Mayerthaler's universal markedness principles?

Mayerthaler's response is to claim, first, that the evidence does not in fact support the received opinion among Romance scholars that it is the Accusative which survives predominantly. An Italian form such as the disyllabic *monte* 'mountain' is usually analysed as descended from the Classical Latin Accusative *montem* via Vulgar Latin *monte*, rather than from the monosyllabic Nominative *mons*. Mayerthaler disputes this analysis on philological grounds, citing the Vulgar Latin Nominative form *montis* as a likely source for *monte*. But this kind of explanation cannot account for the following pattern in French, where, as indicated, the modern French forms appear to descend from the Accusative forms in Old French:

(1)		Classical Latin	Old French	Modern French	
Sg.	Nom.	du:rus	durs		
	Acc.	du:rum	dur	>dur	'hard'
Pl.	Nom.	du:ri:	dur		
	Acc.	du:ro:s	durs	>durs	

This pattern of development is exemplified in nearly all the many nouns and adjectives derived from the so-called 'second declension' in Latin. If the Nominative forms had survived, we would have a modern Singular *durs* and Plural *dur*. (It is true that the two are pronounced identically in modern French; however, the relevant phonological change was not firmly established until after the loss of the Nominative–Accusative contrast.) How can this be reconciled with the claim that it is the less marked of the two Old French Case-forms which should survive?

Mayerthaler invokes markedness inversion here in an ingenious way. The coding of the Cases in the Singular in Old French is countericonic, since the Nominative has an additive marker -*s* while the Accusative is markerless. But, he says, the marked coding pattern itself constitutes a 'marked context', in which the usual markedness relationship between Nominative and Accusative is inverted; in this context, Accusative is less marked than Nominative. The survival of the Accusative Singular form is therefore consistent after all with the expectation that, when two signata merge, it is the signans of the less marked signatum which should survive. There are two problems with this analysis, however, one factual and one conceptual.

The factual problem is that the predictions which this analysis generates are frequently incorrect. In general, Mayerthaler predicts that, if Nominative and Accusative are coded iconically (i.e. if Nominative is markerless and Accusative has additive marking), then the Nominative form should survive into Romance, but if the coding is counericonic (as in Old French *durs/dur*) then the Accusative should survive. This implies that, in the case of the many Latin agentive and abstract nouns with Nominative in *-or* and Accusative in *-orem*, it should be the Nominative which survives. This prediction is consistent with a few French nouns such as *soeur* 'sister', *ancêtre* 'ancestor' and *peintre* 'painter', from Latin *sóror*, *antecéssor* and *pínctor* respectively (where the accent indicates stress) (Mayerthaler 1981: 67); on the other hand, it is not consistent with the great majority of French nouns from Latin sources in *-or*, such as *auteur, empereur, honneur, couleur* from *auctóre(m), imperatóre(m), honóre(m), colóre(m)*. Conversely, an Italian Nominative survival is *re* 'king', derived from Latin Nominative /reːk-s/ rather than Accusative /reːg-em/; yet this additive coding of the Nominative is noniconic and so might be considered, by Mayerthaler's criteria, to create a marked environment in which the Accusative form, not the Nominative, should have survived. This is not to say that the form which survives is entirely random (it is probably no coincidence that the clear instances of Nominative survivals are nearly all nouns denoting humans); but the pattern of survival which Mayerthaler predicts does not occur.

The conceptual problem with Mayerthaler's analysis is that it 'legitimises' a large class of possible coding patterns which would otherwise be classified as unnatural, and thus weakens the empirical force of his theory. Consider the class of French nouns and adjectives in *-al* or *-ail* (/al/ or /aj/) with Plurals in *-aux* (/o/), including *cheval* 'horse', *travail* 'work', *international*. The coding of Number here is countericonic, in that the Plural is shorter than the Singular. This looks like a straightforward instance where a phonological change (no longer active) has created a less than optimal situation from the morphological point of view, in other words an instance of an intercomponential naturalness conflict. Without markedness inversion, NM will lead us to expect (a) that the conflict will be mitigated by diminution of the class of stems or affixes which form their Plurals in this fashion as individual items defect to the majority pattern for spoken French, with no overt Number marking, and (b) that the signans which survives should be that of the less marked signatum, namely Singular. And this is indeed what happens, as Mayerthaler himself points out (1981: 6, 55–6). Yet exactly the opposite expectation emerges from an argument precisely analogous to the one which Mayerthaler applies to the Accusative survivals in Romance. Because Number is coded counericonically in *cheval* (/-al/) and *chevaux* (/-o/), they constitute a 'marked context' in which Plural is less marked than Singular; consequently, it should be the old Plural forms which gradually replace the old Singular ones, not vice versa. Markedness inversion is thus a two-edged sword. It may suggest a useful way of looking at Number marking in Welsh and Turkana; but, if it is combined with too great a readiness to recognise 'marked contexts', it leads us to predict that counericonic and therefore highly marked coding patterns, so far from being levelled out of existence, should actually be perpetuated and spread.

Can one find a way out of Mayerthaler's difficulty with the Romance data while preserving the spirit of NM? Reasonably promising avenues suggests themselves for at least some of the data; for example, since maintenance of the Old French Nominative forms in (1) would lead to counericonic coding of Number (Singular *durs*, Plural *dur*), the preservation of the Accusative forms in words of this type leads to a more 'natural' outcome, so far as the (in Bybee's terms) more relevant category of Number is concerned, than the preservation of the Nominative forms would. But other Natural Morphologists have not (so far as I am aware) tried to repair Mayerthaler's analysis on these lines. What they have done, rather, is attribute Mayerthaler's difficulties to his determination to apply universal naturalness principles to morphological data directly, without qualification; and they have suggested that these principles must be 'filtered' through subsidiary nonuniversal principles. In other words, what is 'natural' on universal grounds may fail to occur in some *état de langue* because certain characteristics of either that *état de langue* itself (section 8.1.3) or of the type to which it belongs (section 8.1.2) conspire to overrule the expectation derived from the universal principles.

8.1.2 Explanatory principles: typological

Dressler (1985a; 1985b) emphasises the role of linguistic types in mediating between universal principles and language-particular behaviour. The morphological typology which he assumes is that of Skalička (1979) (section 5.3), and the types which mainly interest him are the agglutinating and the fusional (Skalička's 'inflecting'). An apparent puzzle for any proponent of universal naturalness principles including diagrammaticity and biuniqueness is why fusional languages should exist at all. To illustrate the problem, Dressler (1985a: 4) cites the Latin and Turkish Ablative Plural forms of the phrase meaning 'our islands':

(2)   a.   insul-iːs   nostr-iːs
           island-Abl.Pl.   our-Abl.Pl.
      b.   ada-lar-ımız-dan
           island-Plural-our-Ablative

The Turkish version at (2b), with agglutination of markers for Plural, Ablative and 1st Person Plural Possessive, exhibits coding which is not only diagrammatic but also perfectly transparent (none of the markers *-lar*, *-ımız* and *-dan* ever encodes a signatum other than the one it encodes here) and almost perfectly uniform (neither Plural nor Ablative is ever encoded differently, if we ignore the effects of vowel harmony and voicing assimilation). On the other hand, the Latin version at (2a) has none of these virtues. Being fused, the realisation of Ablative and Plural is obviously not diagrammatic. Nor is it transparent, because, as we noted in chapter 7, the suffix *-iːs* also encodes Dative Plural with these same lexical items, as well as many other signata with other items, such as Accusative Plural (*host-iːs* 'enemies') and 2nd Person Singular (*aud-iːs* 'you hear'). And it is not uniform either, because for the combined signata Ablative and Plural a widespread rival signans is *-ibus* (*urbibus* 'to/from cities'). It scarcely seems plausible to attribute all this 'unnaturalness' to phonological interference. Yet the fusional pattern illustrated by the Latin example is hardly unique or even unusual. What accounts for the persistence of a morphological type which seems so grossly 'unnatural' by Mayerthaler's main criteria?

Dressler's solution is to invoke two dimensions of naturalness which Mayerthaler ignores: word-size and indexicality. The dimension of word-size is straightforward. Indexicality is less straightforward, and explaining it will involve discussing the threefold classification of signs into icons, indices and symbols which the Natural Morphologists borrow from the American philosopher and pioneer of semiotics, Charles Sanders Peirce.[4]

Calculating the average length of the words in sample texts from forty-two languages, Dressler (1985a) arrives at a figure of between two and three syllables (which coincides with the optimal size of a prosodic foot in phonology). If this constitutes the optimal (least marked, most natural) word-size, it is evident that the Latin example at (2) is more natural on this dimension than the Turkish one. And, in general, given a certain number of morphological signata (lexical meanings, derivational concepts or morphosyntactic properties) to be packed into one word-form, cumulative or fusional packing is bound to be more economical (i.e. shorter) than agglutinative packing, because fusional packing allows two or more signata to share one signans whereas pure agglutinative packing does not. It follows that in agglutinating languages derivationally or inflectionally complex word-forms are more likely to be 'unnaturally' large than in fusional languages.

An **icon** is a sign whose signans directly resembles its signatum in some respect. Few individual linguistic signs are iconic to any degree and none is perfectly so. As is well known, even onomatopoeic words differ considerably from one language to another. But iconicity does show up regularly in the ways in which combinations of signata are related to their signantia. *Cats* has 'more' content than *cat* in an intuitive sense, and this 'moreness' is diagrammed (so to speak) by the construction of *cats* out of two morphs, *cat* and *-s*. Here we have the motivation for the already familiar terms 'constructionally iconic' and 'diagrammatic'. By contrast, this diagrammatic relationship is absent in the Plural form *mice*, because it consists of only one morph, just like the Singular *mouse*. Individual linguistic signs are typically **symbols**, displaying only an arbitrary and conventional relationship between signans and signatum. But, according to Dressler, it is an oversimplification to analyse the *-s* of *cats* as signifying only Plural. Because *-s* is an affix, it cannot occur except bound to some noun stem. It therefore signifies that noun stem too, in some sense; it points towards it, rather as a signpost points towards a neighbouring town. In Peircean terms, a signpost is an **index**, and likewise the Plural suffix is an index of any noun stem which it is suffixed to. But, just as there are degrees of iconicity, so there are degrees of indexicality. The highest degree belongs to those indices which locate most precisely the signata which they point to. Let us compare in this respect the Latin Ablative Plural suffix *-i:s* in (2a) with the Turkish Ablative suffix *-dan* in (2b). The Latin suffix locates the noun stem *insul-* with maximal precision, in that nothing can intervene between the stem and the suffix. On the other hand, the Turkish suffix locates the noun stem relatively vaguely. The stem must precede the suffix somewhere in the same word, but there is scope for a variety of material to intervene; in (2b) two suffixes intervene, but the number could equally well have been zero (*ada-dan* 'from (the) island') or one (e.g. *ada-lar-dan* 'from (the) islands', *ada-mız-dan* 'from our island').

The greater indexicality of the coding pattern serves a communicative function (Dressler says) by rendering Latin words more cohesive and easier to pick out of the spoken continuum than Turkish words. This relative deficiency of Turkish is remedied to some extent by vowel harmony, which helps to locate word boundaries; so it is perhaps not an accident that vowel harmony is quite a widespread phenomenon in agglutinative languages (e.g. Finnish, Hungarian, Mongolian). The Case–Number concord illustrated in *insuliːs nostriːs* is indexical in another respect too; the *-iːs* of *nostriːs* points towards not only its own stem *nostr-* but also towards the *-iːs* of *insuliːs*. From the point of view of NM, concord is a way of enhancing naturalness on the dimension of indexicality at the phrase or clause level, rather than at the word level.

A language in which all morphological coding is consistently diagrammatic is conceivable; it would be like Esperanto, or Turkish without even the degree of fusion exhibited by a form such as *gel-méz* 'he/she does not come', where the suffix *-méz* is joint signans for 'Aorist' (i.e. habitual aspect), Negative and 3rd Person Singular. But could a language have morphological coding which is perfectly indexical? It is not so easy to visualise what this would mean. If closeness to the stem enhances indexicality, then perfect indexicality would presumably require in every word-form the total fusion of the lexical stem with the realisations of all its associated derivational processes and morphosyntactic properties, yielding inflectional paradigms consisting entirely of unsegmentable suppletive 'stems'. Even with only the few inflectional categories of English, such a language would impose a totally implausible burden on the memory. There is therefore a clear psychological reason why indexicality must be, in some sense, subordinate to diagrammaticity. For Dressler, there is also a reason grounded in Peircean semiotics; 'icons are more natural signs than indices' (Dressler 1985a: 5), so one will expect to find iconic traits in even the most consistently fusional languages. A quite subtle and intriguing example of this is the fact that, in Russian nouns, more central (i.e. less marked) morphosyntactic properties tend to be coded with more sonorous sounds – a kind of phonological iconicity (Shapiro 1969; Plank 1979). A similar picture emerges in the fusional Case–Number inflection of Classical Latin nouns and adjectives, if one calculates the ratio of sounds at the more sonorous end of the spectrum (vowels) to sounds at the less sonorous end (consonants) in the Singular and in the Plural of each declension-type. The exact ratios differ according to whether one includes relatively marginal Cases (Vocative, Locative) and whether one counts long vowels as two for the purpose; but in all but one declension-type the vowel–consonant ratio emerges as consistently higher in the Singular than in the Plural (Dressler 1985a).

Our comparison of Latin with Turkish shows that diagrammaticity and biuniqueness, on the one hand, and indexicality and word-size, on the other, cannot be optimised simultaneously. This is an instance of a 'naturalness conflict', not between components but within one component, namely morphology. The typological filter provides a way of resolving the conflict, according to Dressler. A language may choose (so to speak) to give more weight to the first two dimensions by joining the agglutinative type, or to optimise the second two by joining the fusional type. In the latter case, it will tend also to exhibit other characteristics of the fusional type, such as a variety of distinct inflection classes (e.g. the four conjugations and five declensions of traditional Latin grammar). With the typological filter, therefore, NM permits iconically marked codings which are not attributable to phonological interference, and even predicts that such codings should occur.

The argument presented so far in this section illustrates fairly, I hope, both the appeal of Dressler's typological version of NM and its current limitations. Many questions are raised but left unanswered. Can all languages really be assigned relatively unequivocally to one of the five morphological types listed by Skalička? If so, are all these types 'natural' according to the kind of criteria that Natural Morphologists recognise? For example, if phonological developments do not intervene, does all morphological change lead towards, rather than away from, typological consistency, and do infants learn most easily those aspects of their mother tongue's morphology which conform to its (predominant) type? And, even if we grant that the agglutinative and fusional types are motivated by fundamental semiotic principles of iconicity and indexicality respectively, what semiotic principles (if any) underlie the isolating, introflexive and polysynthetic types?[5] In any case, two characteristics generally associated with fusional languages, namely the existence of distinct inflection classes and inflectional syncretism (see chapter 7), are not obviously motivated by optimisation of indexicality or word-size; so does some other semiotic principle come to the rescue here?

The fact that these questions arise is not necessarily a drawback. They can be seen as constituting the NM research programme. But to some of them at least partial answers are already available, and not always answers favourable to NM. For example, psycholinguistic research on the learning of inflectional systems seems to suggest that agglutinative patterns are always learned more quickly and accurately than fusional ones, irrespective of the 'type' of the language being learned (Slobin 1971; Dressler 1988: 202). Is this really (as Dressler speculates) because small children and their mothers use only word-forms involving relatively short and simple combinations of signata, so that the indexical drawbacks of diagrammaticity are temporarily concealed? Clearly, for typologically oriented Natural Morphologists there is much to do in answering the detailed factual questions which their approach provokes. But they need to make sure that these detailed answers are not *ad hoc*; in other words, they need to define the relationships and priorities between the various potentially conflicting dimensions of naturalness more precisely, so that an appeal to interference from some other dimension is not invariably available as a way of accounting for any imaginable piece of 'unnatural' behaviour.

8.1.3 Explanatory principles: system-dependent

In addition to typology, Dressler acknowledges another 'filter' mediating between universal principles of naturalness and actual morphological behaviour, namely language-particular or **system-dependent** naturalness (Dressler 1985b: 292–4). This facet of NM has been studied most extensively by Wurzel, particularly in reference to inflectional morphology (1984). At first sight, naturalness criteria which are meant to apply not to all languages nor even to all languages of a certain type but only to one individual language may seem like an all too convenient device for reconciling any morphological behaviour whatever with NM. But it is not simply an excuse for arbitrarily labelling as 'natural' anything which is highly marked by universal or typological criteria. Rather, the central idea of system-dependent naturalness is that the speakers and, more especially, the infant learners of each language pick out what constitutes 'natural' morphological behaviour along a number of parameters on the basis of what they observe to be the dominant pattern in that language for each parameter. These parameters relate to **system-defining structural properties** (SDSPs). For example, one parameter relates to whether inflectional markers attach to bound stems (the SDSP of 'stem inflection') or to free-form bases ('base-form inflection'). If we compare, say, the varieties of Plural formation in modern (demotic) Greek and English, we find that both languages exhibit both patterns, as (3) shows:

(3) a. Modern Greek

	Singular	Plural
Stem inflection	ánθrop-os 'person'	ánθrop-i
	élin-as 'Greek'	élin-es
	mér-a 'day'	mér-es
	vun-ó 'mountain'	vun-á
	spít-i 'house'	spít-ja
Base-form inflection	pséma 'lie'	pséma-ta
	garáz 'garage'	garáz

b. English

	Singular	Plural
Stem inflection	cris-is	cris-es
	formul-a	formul-ae
	radi-us	radi-i
Base-form inflection	cat	cat-s
	beach	beach-es

But the two languages differ as to which is the normal pattern; most Greek nouns exhibit stem inflection, whereas nearly all English nouns exhibit base-form inflection. Base-form inflection therefore constitutes a SDSP of English, and coding via stem inflection, not being **system-congruent**, is vulnerable to erosion (cf. *formulas, radiuses*); in Greek, on the other hand, stem inflection is system-congruent and therefore stable.

The parameters which relate to SDSPs operate differently from the dimensions of iconicity and indexicality. Whether one coding pattern is more iconic than another can be settled just by reference to the immediate data; but whether one pattern is more system-congruent than another depends crucially on the system (hence the language) in question. Some of Wurzel's parameters are in fact quite close in spirit to those of Chomskyan Principles-and-Parameters syntax. One can think of the choice between stem inflection and base-form inflection as part of Universal Grammar; a child has to learn only which of the two settings is appropriate for his or her mother tongue. But Wurzel's SDSPs are considerably less abstract in content than the Chomskyan ones, and it is not clear to what extent Wurzel himself would welcome the comparison. Wurzel lists the parameters applicable to inflection as follows (1984:82 1989:75):

(a) 'an inventory of categorial complexes [i.e.morphosyntactic categories] and categories [i.e. morphosyntactic properties] assigned to them';[6]
(b) base-form inflection versus stem inflection;
(c) separate versus combined coding of properties belonging to different categories (i.e. absence versus presence of cumulation);
(d) absence versus presence of inflectional homonymies, or syncretisms, and their location within inflectional paradigms;
(e) the marker types (additive, modulatory, subtractive, etc.) associated with each morphosyntactic category;
(f) absence versus presence of inflection classes.[7]

Clearly, not all of these are 'parameters' of the kind which one can visualise as a dial or an on–off switch with a clear-cut choice of possible settings. But they all represent aspects of inflection for which a majority pattern may in principle be discerned in any inflected language. For example, in respect of (e), German presents a pattern of consistent additive (suffixal) marking for nominal and adjectival Case and adjectival Number, but a combination of additive and modulatory marking for nominal Number, adjectival Comparison and verbal Tense–Aspect and Person–Number (e.g. *Wolf* 'wolf', Plural *Wölfe*; *gross* 'big', Comparative *grösser*; *helfen* 'help', 3rd Person Singular Present (*er*) *hilft* '(he) helps', Past Indicative (*er*) *half*, Past Subjunctive (*er*) *hülfe*). It follows that a change in the direction of modulatory marking for Plural in adjectives (e.g. **grösse* 'big (Plural)', with umlaut) would not be system-congruent and therefore should not occur, despite the fact that umlaut has spread in recent centuries as a marker of Plural in some classes of nouns (e.g in Neuters such as *Wort* 'word', for which a Plural *Wörter* has replaced an earlier markerless *wort*).

Wurzel does not explicitly propose any connections between the seven parameters (a)–(f); that is, he does not suggest any ways in which the setting for one parameter may influence the setting for another. He also denies explicitly that the SDSPs of a language can change except through the interference of extramorphological (e.g. phonological) factors. But the claim that connections between SDSPs exist is implicit in Dressler's typological version of NM (for example, alleged characteristics of the fusional type include stem inflection, cumulation, syncretisms and inflection classes, implying links between parameters (b), (c), (d) and (f)); and if this is correct, then changes in SDSPs could well come about to increase typological consistency.[8]

8.1.4 Inflection classes, paradigm structure conditions and paradigm economy

The aspect of inflectional morphology which most concerns Wurzel is the nature and organisation of **inflection classes**, that is inflectionally contrasting subclasses of one word-class such as the 'conjugations' and 'declensions' familiar in the traditional descriptions of many languages. Here he confronts another *prima facie* embarrassment for universal principles of NM; the very existence of inflection classes implies lack of uniformity in morphological coding. Wurzel seeks to reconcile inflection classes with NM by two strategies: linking them to extramorphological factors wherever possible, and devising for ones which cannot be so linked criteria of naturalness which will generate predictions about inflectional change and the treatment of loan-words. In this way, although inflection classes imply failure to achieve 'natural' coding on the dimension of uniformity, they can still be shown to conform to markedness principles of their own.

The breach of uniformity implied by the existence of two or more inflectional markers for one morphosyntactic property is mitigated if their distribution is at least partly motivated, or predictable, by extramorphological factors, whether phonological, lexical, syntactic or semantic. These factors take the markers concerned out of direct competition with one another, so to speak. For nouns, one relevant factor may be Gender; this is 'extramorphological' because it is an inherent, lexically determined characteristic, unlike Number and Case. In German all Feminine nouns have an identical form (the base form) for all Cases in the Singular, so the distribution of the base form as a realisation of Singular Case-forms is to that extent motivated by Gender. The semantic factor of animacy plays a role in motivating the Accusative Case markers in most Slavic languages, inasmuch as several pairs of distinct inflection classes are differentiated only in that in one class in each pair, containing animate nouns, the Accusative is homophonous with the Genitive, while in the other class, containing only inanimates, the Accusative is homophonous with the Nominative. Or the motivating factor may be phonological; Italian nouns choose between four distinct Plural suffixes (*-i*, *-e*, zero, and in a few nouns *-a*), but for nouns ending in stressed syllables only the zero realisation is available (e.g. *città* 'city', *caffè* 'coffee', *film* 'film', Plurals *città*, *caffè*, *film*). Sometimes several extramorphological factors combine; for example, German nouns ending in *-er* with umlautable vowels and denoting close relatives all form their Plurals with umlaut and no suffix (*Mutter* 'mother',

Vater 'father', *Tochter* 'daughter', *Bruder* 'brother' and *Schwager* 'brother-in-law', Plurals *Mütter* etc.; contrast *Schwester* 'sister', Plural *Schwestern*, with no umlautable vowel) (D. Bittner 1988). In all these instances, the extramorphological links render the inflectional system less arbitrary and therefore more natural.

Not all inflection-class membership is motivated in this way, however. Two or more classes whose membership cannot be distinguished extramorphologically are called **complementary classes**. But even here naturalness comes into play. On external grounds such as changes in class membership, the treatment of loan-words and errors made in first-language acquisition (Wurzel claims), one can always identify one of a set of complementary classes as the **unmarked class** in that set. This will be the class into which members of the other classes tend to drift, and to which loan-words will be assigned (provided that they meet the relevant extramorphological requirements). For example, German nouns ending in unstressed vowels other than schwa exhibit a number of distinct Plural endings and for that reason belong to a number of complementary classes: *Firma* 'firm', *Auto* 'car', *Cello* 'cello', *Schema* 'schema', Plurals *Firm-en*, *Auto-s*, *Cell-i*, *Schema-ta*. Of these, however, the *Auto* class is clearly the unmarked one, as evidenced by the fact that Plurals such as *Firmas*, *Cellos*, *Schemas* are in many instances acceptable as alternative 'standard' Plural forms and are in any case frequent in child language, whereas drifts in other directions (replacement of Plural *Kino-s* 'cinemas' by *Kin-en or *Kin-i, for example) do not occur. This drift also supports Wurzel's claim that base-form inflection (as opposed to stem inflection) is a SDSP for nouns in German as well as English; *Auto-s* displays base-form inflection whereas *Firm-en* and *Cell-i* do not.

In Wurzel's framework, the proliferation of complementary classes is 'unnatural', but he places no absolute limit on such proliferation. Carstairs, by contrast, has explored inflection-class behaviour with the specific aim of identifying, if possible, an upper bound for the number of distinct inflection classes, or inflectional paradigms, which is compatible with a given array of inflectional resources. Consider, for example, the inflectional resources for nouns in a hypothetical language L represented schematically in (4):

(4)	Singular	Plural
Nominative	a	f,g,h
Accusative	b,c	i,j
Genitive	d,e	k

The phonological shape of the inflections represented as *a*, *b*, etc.

does not matter; all that matters is that they are distinct. What are the mathematical minimum and maximum for the number of distinct inflection classes into which the nouns of L can be organised? This question has a clearcut answer. The minimum is three, because fewer than three classes could not accommodate the inflectional diversity of the Nominative Plural. The maximum is twenty-four, because the total number of distinct ways of selecting one of the available inflections for each of the six Case–Number combinations is got by multiplying together the number of distinct inflections for each combination: $1 \times 2 \times 2 \times 3 \times 2 \times 1$. But is there a linguistic maximum, which L could not exceed without ceasing to be a possible human language? On the basis of evidence from various languages, Carstairs (1983; 1987a) claims that there is *prima facie* evidence for a linguistic maximum at or close to the mathematical minimum; in other words, that inflectional behaviour is subject to an extremely tight requirement of what he calls **paradigm economy**. If this is correct, then inflectional theory is constrained in a highly desirable fashion. It is therefore of interest to investigate carefully any apparent breaches of paradigm economy, to see whether they point towards refinements of Carstairs's claim which are consistent with its spirit.[9]

Establishing whether a given inflectional system obeys paradigm economy presupposes clear criteria for establishing whether two lexical items are inflected in the same way or differently. For example, what of the English Past Participle forms *given* and *spoken* (with the same suffix but different patterns of ablaut), or the Dyirbal Ergative suffixes -*ŋgu* (added to disyllabic vowel-final stems, as in *yaṭa-ŋgu* 'man (Ergative)') and -*gu* (added to longer vowel-final stems, as in *yamani-gu* 'rainbow (Ergative)') (Dixon 1972: 42)? Carstairs concludes that only affixal inflection is relevant to paradigm economy, not nonaffixal processes such as ablaut (1988b), so that *given* and *spoken* count as inflectionally identical. He therefore suggests that, when partially similar paradigms differ only in respect of inflections whose distribution correlates with phonological, semantic or lexically determined syntactic factors, these paradigms should all count as the same **macroparadigm**, the contrasting inflections constituting a single **macroinflection**; *yaṭa-ŋgu* and *yamani-gu* therefore both count as inflectionally identical, whether or not -*gu* and -*ŋgu* can be argued to have the same underlying phonological representation in Dyirbal. Whether these decisions improve a basically sound proposal or shore up a basically unsound one depends on further investigation of how inflection-class systems work. For the moment, what concerns us is how Carstairs's proposals relate to Wurzel's.

In inflectional systems with affixation as the only method of coding, the fact that two classes are complementary by Wurzel's criteria will nearly always mean that they adhere to distinct macroparadigms by Carstairs's criteria. A macroparadigm can be seen as a pattern of inflection shared by a set of inflectionally similar noncomplementary classes. In Carstairs's terms, therefore, Wurzel's ideal pattern of inflection classes – one in which all inflection-class membership is extramorphologically motivated and no complementary classes remain – is a situation in which all superficially distinct paradigms can be lumped together into one grand macroparadigm.

Not surprisingly, German noun inflection has figured prominently in the development of Wurzel's version of NM (Wurzel 1984; D. Bittner 1988), and it has also been discussed by both Lieber (1981b) and Carstairs (1986; 1987a: 234–51), so it provides a useful arena in which to compare various approaches to a moderately complex inflectional pattern. As an illustration of the kind of problem which arises in Wurzel's framework, consider the Plural of monosyllabic Masculine nouns (*Tag* 'day', *Hund* 'dog', *Baum* 'tree', *Wolf* 'wolf', *Wald* 'forest', etc.). In Wurzel's terms, these belong to several complementary classes including one with Plural in -e (*Tage, Hunde*), one with Plural in umlaut plus -e (*Bäume, Wölfe*) and one with Plural in umlaut plus -er (*Wälder*). The *Wälder* class is small, but the other two are quite large and about equally numerous. Which of them is the sole unmarked class that Wurzel's framework requires us to identify? The evidence from membership drift in the past is equivocal, since there has been movement in both directions; and although there is vacillation in contemporary German (e.g. *Schlucke/Schlücke* 'gulps', *Schalke/Schälke* 'jokers'), it is not clear whether it is the umlauted or the umlaut-free variants which are consistently gaining the upper hand (D. Bittner 1988: 49–50). One possibility is that Wurzel is wrong in assuming that there is just one unmarked class in any set of complementary classes. But another possibility is suggested by Carstairs's distinction between affixal and nonaffixal inflection for paradigm-economy purposes. Could it be that markedness relationships hold only between complementary classes which differ affixally? If so, the *Tage* and *Bäume* classes may perhaps both be unmarked relative to the *Wälder* class, without either being unmarked relative to the other. This suggestion clearly has implications for other sets of complementary classes, in German and elsewhere, which have yet to be investigated.

If some inflection classes are more marked than others, then we will expect the lexical entries for members of marked classes to be more complex than those for members of unmarked classes. This is indeed what Wurzel proposes. All morphosyntactic properties (signata) are spelled out (coded) by means of **paradigm structure conditions** (PSCs), some of which are more general than others. When two distinct PSCs can apply to the same grammatical word, the more specific PSC takes precedence, according to a version of the familiar Elsewhere Condition (see chapters 3 and 7). In any set of complementary classes (sharing by definition the same set of extramorphological characteristics), the unmarked class will comply with the **dominant PSC** for that set. Members of this class will need no special lexical specification to ensure compliance, because it will be an automatic consequence of their extramorphological characteristics. Members of the marked classes, however, must be specified lexically in a fashion which may override the dominant PSC, at least in part, and which may in turn trigger the application of more specific 'marked' PSCs.

Let us see how this might work in the Plural of German monosyllabic Masculine nouns, discussed above. The first point to note is that, like all German nouns without exception, these have the same form in all Plural cases except the Dative; in Wurzel's terms, this represents a SDSP under parameter (d) above. This can be expressed fairly informally by a PSC on the following lines, where the arrow represents an implication ('if . . ., then . . .'):

(5)   Noun→[Nom=Acc=Gen in Plural]

These nouns also mark the Dative Plural by suffixing *-n* to the non-Dative Plural form, as nearly all German nouns do:

(6)   Noun$_{Pl}$→[*-n* in Dative]

But what about the non-Dative Plural form itself? Let us assume, for the sake of argument, that it is the class with *-e* but without umlaut which is unmarked. Then the dominant PSC for monosyllabic Masculines will be on these lines:

(7)   [Noun, Masc, monosyll]→[*-e* in Plural]

This PSC will apply automatically to nouns such as *Tag* and *Hund*, because it will be evident from their lexical entries that they are masculine and monosyllabic. It will also apply to nouns belonging to the marked complementary class with umlaut, such as *Wolf*; these nouns, however, must be lexically specified [umlaut in Plural], because this characteristic is not predictable by rule. As for nouns like

Wald, these must be lexically specified [-*er* in Plural] so as to override (7); they need not be lexically specified for umlaut, however, because this characteristic is common to all nouns with Plural in -*er* (provided that the stem vowel is umlautable). In Wurzel's terms, the marked Plural suffix triggers a marked PSC, as in (8):

(8)   [-*er* in Plural]→[umlaut in Plural, if umlautable].

For *Wald*, the non-Dative Plural form *Wälder* constitutes a **reference form** (Kennform), in that it is on the strength of this form that we can tell which parts of which PSCs it conforms to, and it is aspects of this form which are lexically specified. In general, all German nouns outside the unmarked classes will have the non-Dative Plural form as a reference form.

This is hardly a definitive or complete analysis. But it illustrates the range of generality of the PSCs which Wurzel posits, from the very specific, such as (8), to the very general, such as (6). The dominant PSC for a set of complementary classes, such as (7), occupies an intermediate position. It also illustrates how a lexical specification can both block and trigger the application of PSCs.

It may seem that 'paradigm structure condition' is rather a grand term for what look much like morphological spell-out rules of a kind which have been posited more or less informally since the earliest days of generative grammar. But the term seems more appropriate when applied to conditions such as (9) and (10), which Wurzel claims to apply to certain nouns in Latin (1984: 120 (1989: 116)):

(9)   [-*im* in Acc Sg]→[-*i:* in Abl Sg]→[-*i:s* in Acc Pl]→[-*ium* in Gen Pl]

(10)   [-*um* in Gen Pl]→[-*e:s* in Acc Pl]→[-*e* in Abl Sg]→[-*em* in Acc Sg]

The form of (9) and (10) shows that they must be marked PSCs, since they are not triggered by any extramorphological factors. The idea is that a noun may 'join in' at any point, as determined by its lexical specification; for example, a noun such as *auris* 'ear', lexically specified [-*i:s* in Acc Pl] and [-*e* in Abl Sg], will join (9) at the third point, so acquiring -*ium* as its Genitive Plural suffix, and will also join (10) at the third point, so acquiring -*em* as its Accusative Singular suffix. Wurzel claims that, thanks to their 'knowledge' of complex multi-stage PSCs such as this, native speakers can cope relatively easily even with complex patterns of distinct but partially similar paradigms – 'mixed paradigms' in the terminology of Carstairs (1987a). A. Bittner (1985) proposes a similar multi-stage PSC to account for the various subclasses of German strong verbs. But both Wurzel's analysis of Latin and Bittner's analysis of German have been challenged, and Carstairs (in press) proposes that the distinction between affixal and nonaffixal inflection is once again relevant; multi-stage PSCs apply only to the latter. Again, more investigation is needed to resolve the matter.

Wurzel's proposals about system-dependent naturalness have the great merit, by comparison with some other work in NM, of yielding relatively clear empirical predictions, relatively uncomplicated by intersecting dimensions of naturalness, conflicting semiotic preferences and so on. Moreover, he has developed his ideas in relation to data for which his predictions can readily be checked, particularly diachronic data from the Germanic languages. But his claims about inflection-class behaviour, and Carstairs's partly conflicting claims, need to be tested against a wider range of data, particularly non-Indo-European; and it remains to be seen whether equally rich results will follow from investigations of Wurzel's other system-defining parameters in comparable depth.

8.1.5 Morphological and phonological naturalness

In section 8.1 we mentioned the idea that the achievement of naturalness in one component of grammar (say, phonology) may obstruct the achievement of naturalness in another (say, morphology), and this idea resurfaced briefly in our discussions of Mayerthaler and Wurzel; but we have not so far looked at any intercomponential conflicts in detail. This issue has been attacked with gusto by Dressler (1985b). His central proposal is that the whole domain of morphophonology, which dominated generative 'phonology' until the mid-1970s, involves naturalness conflicts between phonology and morphology. Proper to phonology are **phonological rules** (PRs), which can have no lexically marked or grammatically conditioned exceptions. Included within morphology are **allomorphic morphological rules** (AMRs), which effect phonologically unnatural changes in the shapes of morphs. In between is the realm of **morphonological rules** (MPRs), which are more or less phonologically natural in their effects but which are subject to lexical or grammatical restrictions. Dressler prefers the term **morphonology** to 'morphophonology' or 'morphophonemics' because the last of these terms, in particular, has often been used to embrace all allomorphy, including alternations which are clearly suppletive or due to AMRs (e.g. *go* versus *went*) and alternations due to phonological neutralisation (e.g. German /pfaːt/

in *Pfad* 'path', with syllable-final /t/, versus /pfaːd/ in *Pfades* 'path (Genitive)', with non-syllable-final /d/). Morphonology also covers the phonological structure of morphemes; for example, if most major-class morphemes consist of precisely three consonants (as in Semitic languages), this is a morphonological fact about the language in question.

At first sight it may seem that Dressler has in effect created a distinct morphonological component by designating a class of rules (MPRs) which belong to neither morphology nor phonology. But he denies this, on the ground that morphonology has no organising principles or naturalness dimensions of its own. Besides, the boundaries between the three types of rule are intrinsically fuzzy; a given rule may be more or less natural in phonological terms according to how closely it reflects one of Stampe's universal phonological processes, and also, in its capacity as an index of the morphological signs which it affects, it may be more or less natural in morphological terms, according to its degree of uniformity and transparency. One can illustrate Dressler's spectrum of rule types by reference to English examples, as in (11) (based on Dressler 1985b: 316–17):

(11) Rule type	Example (relevant segments in bold)
PRs, non-neutralising	exci**t**e ~ exci**t**ement
	exis**t** ~ exis**t**ence
PR, neutralising	ri**d**e ~ ri**d**er (American English, with 'Flapping')
MPR without fusion	electri[**k**] ~ electri[**s**]ity
MPR with fusion	conclu**d**e ~ conclu**s**ion
AMR	dec[**ai**]d ~ dec[**ɪ**]sion
Weak suppletion	chil**d** ~ chil**dr**en
Strong suppletion	**Glasgow** ~ **Glaswegian**
	am ~ **are** ~ **is** ~ **was** ~ **be**

The residue of the English vowel shift exhibited by *decision* versus *decide* (Trisyllabic Laxing, in the terminology of Lexical Phonology) is deemed an allomorphic morphological rule (AMR), because the vowel alternation is quite unnatural in Stampean terms; on the other hand, the consonant alternation in the same words still preserves enough phonological naturalness to be considered a morphonological rule (MPR). This illustrates the fuzziness of the boundaries between the rule types.

Ideally, the drift of rules from phonological to morphonological status and from morphonological to allomorphic status should be

consistent with basic semiotic principles. But we immediately encounter a paradox. Icons are more natural signs than indices are
(Dressler 1985b: 301); yet MPRs, by blurring the boundaries between
one morph and another, tend to reduce constructional iconicity.
Dressler acknowledges this paradox (321), but points out that MPRs
increase morphological indexicality (that is, they cause morphs
to point towards their neighbours more effectively). This in turn
is said to be semiotically desirable because of 'the precedence
of morphology over phonology' (336). But that does not explain
why morphological icons are disrupted in order to facilitate the
development of morphological indices. Typological factors, as discussed in section 8.1.2, may come into play here. But a central
difficulty remains. If intercomponential naturalness conflicts were
as straightforward as NM leads us to expect, then a sound change
(such as German umlaut) which loses its phonological motivation and
so becomes phonologically less natural should always simultaneously
acquire a clear compensating morphological function, preferably by
becoming a relatively transparent and uniform signans for some
morphological signatum. But this does not normally happen. In
German noun inflection, umlaut has indeed become transparent in
this way; in those nouns which display it, it unambiguously encodes
Plural. In verb inflection, however, umlaut has been left in a semiotic
limbo. The paradigm in (12) illustrates a common pattern in strong
verbs:

(12)			No umlaut	Umlaut
Singular		1	wasch-e	
		2		wäsch-est
		3		wäsch-t
Plural		1	wasch-en	
		2	wasch-t	
		3	wasch-en	

As can be seen, umlaut correlates neither with Number nor with
Person. One can of course attribute to it an indexical function,
as 'pointing towards' the affixes *-est* and *-t*; but this looks here
suspiciously like a semiotic *deus ex machina*, capable of rendering
any morphological behaviour whatever 'natural'.

These somewhat negative comments are not meant to imply that
Dressler's project is not worthwhile. The subject-matter is of central
importance to linguistic theory, and has exercised some of the best
linguists of each generation since Baudouin de Courtenay. Almost
certainly, however, assumptions such as the primacy of icons over

indices and of morphology over phonology will need to be re-examined if a model of morphophonology is to be developed which is not only consistent with the facts but also explains them. The best prospect for progress within the NM approach seems to lie in refining and tightening the morphological end of the theory, particularly with regard to the balance between typological and language-particular (system-dependent) principles, as demanded by the critics of NM discussed in the next section. This refinement should provide a more secure morphological anchor for morphophonological investigations than Peircean semiotics can provide on its own.

8.2 A RIVAL TO NM: MORPHOLOGICAL ECONOMY

Increasingly sophisticated typological and system-specific filters have been superimposed on Mayerthaler's original 'universal' criteria of constructional iconicity and biuniqueness. But all versions of NM agree in seeing phonological rather than morphological factors as the main triggers for morphological change, and for all versions of NM suppletion constitutes a more or less embarrassing residuum of extreme morphological unnaturalness – all the more embarrassing for being in some languages quite persistent.[10] But there has developed among German-speaking linguists a rival view of morphology, under the label **Morphological Economy**, which sees iconicity and biuniqueness as 'ideal' only for word-forms with low token-frequency. It follows that, for word-forms with high token-frequency, a historical drift towards fusion and even suppletion can be motivated morphologically, and not just phonologically, as a by-product of sound change. The main recent exponent of this viewpoint is Werner (e.g. 1987; 1989), but the central idea is not new; token-frequency as a factor in linguistic change has been emphasised for many years by Mańczak (e.g. 1957–8; 1980).[11]

Consider a pair of forms like Old Norse Singular *barn* 'child', Plural *börn* 'children', descended from Proto-Norse **barn*, **barn-u*. (The asterisks here indicate reconstructed, not ungrammatical, forms.) The Proto-Norse forms clearly score higher on the NM scales of diagrammaticity and uniformity, but this pattern has been disrupted by two phonological developments, *u*-umlaut and apocope. The result, however, is a more condensed and, in that sense, more economical word-form. As Werner (1987: 596) puts it:

An obvious advantage of this is the shortness of expression involving low articulatory effort. It would, however, demand considerable encoding-work before the articulation can start and decoding-work before full comprehension is possible . . . From this it follows that these morphological devices [of fusion and suppletion] are useful and tolerable only in the case of inflectional forms which have a relatively high frequency in usage.

Werner cites the German 'strong' Past Subjunctive forms (*ich*) *wäre, hätte, bräuchte, hielte, schöbe* '(I) was, had, needed (to), held, pushed'. These all display stem alternations in comparison with the present stems in (*ich*) *bin, habe, brauche, halte, schiebe*. In this respect they contrast with the pattern of 'weak' verbs, which is productive or 'dominant' in Wurzel's sense, and in which there is no stem alternation. But these strong forms are not all equally 'normal'. Given that German provides a choice in Past Subjunctive coding between a pattern with stem allomorphy and one without, the stem-allomorphy choice exemplified in the extremely common form *wäre* is appropriate, whereas the same choice exempified in the rare form *schöbe* is not. Conversely, the choice of a less fused, more agglutinative coding may be inappropriate for an extremely common word-form; that is why the standard German weak forms *sagst, machst* '(you) say, do' are replaced in some dialects by strong forms with umlaut: *sägst, mächst* (Harnisch 1988: 430). The frequency 'threshold' below which suppletion ceases to be normal is not the same for all speech communities, however; there is evidence that large-scale stem alternations, including suppletion, are especially characteristic of the languages of small, relatively isolated and linguistically homogeneous communities, such as Faeroese and some Frisian dialects (Braunmüller 1984).

In Dressler's version of NM, cumulation and stem allomorphy are 'natural' in languages of the fusional type, and in Wurzel's version, incorporating system-dependent naturalness, there is scope for more precise language-particular stipulation of domains in which noniconic, nontransparent coding shall be deemed natural. It may seem, therefore, that not too much compromise will be needed on either side in order to reconcile Morphological Economy with at least some versions of NM (See Harnisch 1988; Ronneberger-Sibold 1988). But the two models still differ in their attitude to token-frequency.

The NM approach to language change, as exemplified especially in the work of Wurzel, emphasises system-congruity as a source of pressure for change; for example, *Radiusse* gains at the expense of *Radii* as the Plural of German *Radius* 'radius' because it conforms with the system-defining preference in German for base-form inflection over stem inflection. In this approach, the language-as-system is closely analogous to Chomskyan competence, and the framework of naturalness principles and filters which organise morphology can perfectly well be seen in Chomskyan terms as a contribution to Universal Grammar. The frequency with which competing word-forms (such as *Radii* and *Radiusse*) occur in actual usage, which is clearly a performance phenomenon, is merely a by-product of their system-congruity, not itself an instigator of change. In the Morphological Economy model, on the other hand, frequency in usage plays a direct part in explaining certain aspects of morphological organisation, and even sociolinguistic considerations may be relevant, as for Faeroese and Frisian.

The implications of this disagreement are considerable. If Morphological Economy is right, there seem to be two alternatives. On the one hand, we can maintain the competence–performance (or langue–parole) distinction, with the theory of morphology as part of the theory of competence, but concede that morphological change tells us less than we might have hoped about morphological theory. On the other hand, we can maintain the relevance of morphological change to morphological theory, at the cost of abandoning the widespread assumption that performance is not directly relevant to Universal Grammar. Neither of these courses is to be embarked on lightly. Not surprisingly, therefore, some adherents of NM are determined to resist token-frequency as a factor in accounting for suppletion. A. Bittner (1988b) argues instead that there is a semantic **suppletion domain** within which suppletion is not merely tolerated but actually desirable. This domain includes basic verbal concepts such as coming, going, giving, taking, saying, doing, eating, drinking, being born and dying. Verbs with suppletive stems often have high token-frequency, but it is not their token-frequency that makes them suppletive, as Werner claims; rather, it is because verbs in the suppletion domain designate basic concepts that they tend to be used frequently.

For Bittner's argument to be convincing, he must first provide independent justification for the existence of a semantic suppletion domain, and then demonstrate that there is a clear difference in stability between suppletions within this domain and suppletions which arise outside it (as the residue of sound changes, for example). Drawing the boundary of the suppletion domain is difficult, he admits. Nevertheless, he argues that, if we compare pairs of verbs with suppletive or more-or-less irregular stem alternations, such that the two verbs in each pair are identical in frequency but differ in that one can plausibly be considered to belong to the suppletion domain while the other does not, we will consistently find that the stem alternation in the former remains stable whereas the stem alternation in the latter is replaced by a more regular pattern. For example, German *essen* 'eat' (Past *ass*) and *hauen* 'chop' (old Past form *hieb*) have roughly equal token-frequency (he claims), but the former, belonging to the suppletion domain, retains its 'irregular' Past form whereas the latter, outside the domain, acquires a new 'regular' Past *haute*; and *sterben* 'die', within the suppletion-domain, retains its Past stem alternant *starb* whereas the equally frequent *hören* 'hear', outside the domain, has lost its old 'reverse-umlaut' Past stem *hor-*, replacing *horte* '(he/she) heard' with *hörte*.

The issue is by no means settled. But it is an issue which deserves continued investigation, because it has implications far outside morphology. At the outset of generative grammar, Chomsky argued that statistics was irrelevant to grammaticality, because within a given sentence frame one word-form could yield a clearly acceptable sentence while another word-form could yield a clearly unacceptable one, even though the probability of these word-forms appearing in that sentence-frame was identical, namely zero; his examples were *whale* and *of* in the sentence-frame *I saw a fragile___* (Chomsky 1957: 16). This amounts to saying that it is a fruitless exercise to compare the frequency of the strings *I saw a fragile whale* and *I saw a fragile of* in any text, now matter how long, because almost certainly neither string will ever occur. But it is not a fruitless exercise to compare the frequency of (say) the two verbs *essen* and *hauen*, and find out which of them more consistently maintains its suppletive Past form; so one cannot dismiss out of hand the possibility of discovering that the relative frequency of two words is directly relevant to some aspect of their morphological analysis. If so, this reinforces the possibility that statistics may be relevant also to the well-formedness and analysis of sentences, in ways not envisaged by Chomsky in 1957.

Although it does not make sense to count occurrences of individual sentences, it is feasible to count the relative frequency of sentence-types (for example, active and passive, or with and without 'Dative Movement'). It is therefore feasible to assess changes in relative frequency over time. But is it realistic to classify all such changes as merely matters of performance – of stylistic fashion, perhaps? If not, at what point does a change in relative frequency indicate a corresponding change in competence? And if no clear-cut answer can be given, does this mean that the competence–performance distinction is undermined? These are large questions, and they arise independently of morphological suppletion (see e.g. Chung 1977; Kroch 1989). But the issue between NM and Morphological Economy is relevant, in that if it is settled in favour of Morphological Economy, there is clear support outside syntax for the view that frequency considerations have a bearing on grammatical theory.

8.3 AUTONOMOUS FORMS AND THE ORGANISATION OF PARADIGMS

Alongside her work on inflectional categories and their expression, discussed in chapter 6, Bybee, with her colleagues, has developed a theory of the organisation of inflectional paradigms. She has done so independently of both the Natural Morphologists and the Morphological Economists; but she addresses many of the same questions as them and her approach is methodologically quite similar, so it is appropriate to discuss it alongside theirs. She shares with the Natural Morphologists an interest in 'external' evidence, not only from historical change and developmental psycholinguistics but also from psycholinguistic experimentation with adults; on the other hand, she shares with the Morphological Economists a view of suppletion as a central, well-integrated characteristic of inflectional systems, not as a more or less 'unnatural' fringe phenomenon.

Bybee's starting-point is the observation that 'in inflectional paradigms, it often happens that a form can be described by taking another form as a base and adding a marker to it. . . . Furthermore, there is a great deal of cross-linguistic agreement about which form it is: most often [in verbs] the 3s [i.e. 3rd Singular] of the present indicative' (1985b: 50).[12] Moreover, this **base form** is typically markerless, or, in Bybee's terms, has **zero expression**. In her sample of fifty languages, she finds that the Present Tense has zero expression in 63 per cent of the languages, the Indicative Mood in 60 per cent, the Singular Number in 78 per cent and the 3rd Person (subject) in 54 per cent (1985b: 54). Bybee's observation suggests an empirical hypothesis to the effect that (a) any 3rd Singular form will tend to be analysed by native speakers as having zero expression for Person and Number, and (b) this zero-expression analysis will cause other Person–Number forms of the same Tense and Mood to be restructured on the basis of the 3rd Singular. As an instance of this, Bybee cites the Person–Number forms of the Preterite in certain modern Provençal dialects by comparison with Old Provençal (1985b: 55; cf. Bybee and Brewer 1980):

(13)			Old Provençal	Charente dialect
Singular	1		cantéi 'I sang'	cantí
	2		cantést	cantétei
	3		cantét	cantét
Plural	1		cantém	cantétem
	2		cantétz	cantétetz
	3		cantéren	cantéton

The extension of -*t*- to all the Charente dialect forms except the 1st Person Singular is due to the reanalysis of the Old Provençal form *cantét* as containing a zero expression for 3rd Person Singular, with -*t* as a marker not of Person–Number but of Tense (Preterite) alone. After this reanalysis, other Person–Number endings are added to the new stem *cantét*.

Two aspects of this reanalysis are central for Bybee. Firstly, the 3rd Person Singular Preterite form is the basis for the formation of new Person–Number forms in the Preterite, not new Tense forms in the 3rd Person Singular. Secondly, the 1st Person Singular in the Charente dialect resists innovation. For Bybee, these facts highlight two ways in which the various forms within an inflectional paradigm can differ: in degrees of relatedness and in relative autonomy. We will define these terms directly.

Relatedness involves the notion of relevance, discussed in section 6.2. Consider the two inflectional categories (or category combinations) Tense and Person–Number. Of these, Tense is the more relevant to the verb stem, in Bybee's sense, because it affects the meaning of the verb stem more than Person–Number does; moreover, where it is expressed separately from Person–Number, its expression is nearly always closer to the stem. Now, let us say that two forms which differ only in a less relevant category (say, Person–Number) are more closely related than two forms which differ only in a more relevant category (say, Tense). It follows that the 3rd Person Singular Preterite Indicative form is more closely related to the 2nd Singular Preterite Indicative, for example, than it is to the 3rd Singular Present Indicative. Bybee's main hypothesis concerning the relationship between basic forms and the forms derived from them can now be stated: basic forms influence other forms to which they are closely related rather than other forms to which they are less closely related. This hypothesis is consistent with the innovations in the Charente dialect; the Old Provençal 3rd Person Singular Preterite form *cantét* is the basis for new Person–Number forms in the Preterite, not for new 3rd Singular forms in other tenses. The hypothesis is confirmed also by research on the order of acquisition of verb forms in Brazilian Portuguese, and in errors made during their acquisition (Simões and Stoel-Gammon 1979; cf. Bybee 1985b: 51, 59). The 3rd Person Singular Present (i.e. the most basic form) is learned first, followed by the 3rd Singular Preterite, and the 1st Singular forms are then built on the 3rd Singular forms of the same Tense; one does not find, for example, a 1st Singular Preterite form derived from the corresponding 1st Singular Present.

As we saw in (13), the 1st Person Singular form *cantí* in the Charente dialect resists innovation based on the 3rd Singular; it alone is not replaced by a new form incorporating the stem *cantét-*. In this respect, the Charente dialect differs from some other modern Provençal dialects, and Bybee does not claim to be able to explain precisely why Charente should stand out. But, given that one Preterite form is not replaced, it is not an accident, she suggests, that it is the lst Person Singular rather than, say, the 2nd Plural. This is because 1st Person Singular forms are second only to 3rd Singular forms in frequency of usage (Bybee 1985b: 71), and are hence relatively **autonomous** within their paradigms. The factors contributing to autonomy are (a) token-frequency, (b) semantic basicness and (c) morphophonological irregularity (1985b: 57).

Autonomy and relatedness help to account for suppletion, according to Bybee (1985b: 91–6). A morphophonologically irregular stem must be relatively frequent in usage; it is usually also character-istic of some relatively basic forms within the paradigm, from which it will naturally spread to other closely related forms (e.g. other Person–Number forms of the same Tense). That is why suppletive stems are not scattered randomly in inflectional paradigms; rather, we find that one stem is shared by all forms which also share a single semantic element relatively high in the hierarchy of relevance. In verbal suppletion, for example, there are suppletive Tense stems but not suppletive Person–Number stems (Rudes 1980). Suppletion thus provides a kind of litmus-test for the way in which paradigms are structured by intersecting inflectional categories, and (Bybee claims) supports the hierarchy of relevance propounded on other grounds. Even without stem suppletion, the relevance-based paradigm struc-ture for which Bybee argues shows up in some *prima facie* breaches of paradigm economy, in Carstairs's terms. For example, there is a class of 'mixed' German nouns which display a mixture of so-called 'strong' and 'weak' endings (e.g. *Staat* 'state', Genitive Singular *Staat-s*. Plural *Staat-en*). But these endings are not scattered randomly through the paradigm; rather, Singular endings are consistently strong and Plural endings are consistently weak. So, for paradigm-economy purposes, relatively autonomous subparts of paradigms may perhaps operate independently.

Autonomy also constitutes the main link in Bybee's framework between typological generalisations and psycholinguistics; the more autonomous a form is, she claims, the more likely it is to be learned and stored as a unit.[13] Her image of a paradigm is of a set of one or more autonomous forms connected more or less strongly in various ways (phonologically, syntactically and semantically) to other, non-autonomous, forms (Bybee 1988).[14] Indeed, forms connected in this way need not be members of the same paradigm, in conventional terms; *cat* is connected to *kitten* quite strongly semantically but less strongly phonologically, whereas *cat* is connected to *cats* very strongly in both ways, but there is no fundamental difference in the nature of the relationship. The *cat/cats* connection of course has innumerable parallels in English morphology while the *cat/kitten* connection has not; even so, Plural formation is not a 'rule' but rather a representational schema with very wide application and hence with the power to attract new lexical items (including neologisms) into its scope. Bybee thus sympathises with the 'connectionist' model of the lexicon and of grammar in general which is exemplified in Rumelhart and McClelland's simulation of the learning of English verb morphology (1986; 1987).[15]

Like the Morphological Economists, Bybee emphasises frequency of use as a factor in determining how a complex word-form should be analysed. In addition, she goes further than most theoretical morphologists towards equating the task of morphological theory with that of modelling the psychological and even neurological processes whereby words are stored, produced and perceived. Clearly, these are issues with implications for the whole of linguistic theory. But, because morphology appears to provide a more manageable domain in which to begin to tackle them than syntax does, it is sure to continue to figure in the controversy about connectionist models of language.

Part IV
Conclusions

9 What morphology can contribute to general linguistic theory

In chapter 1 I distinguished two target audiences: linguists who are already morphologists and linguists who are merely inquisitive. There is no need for any special summing-up addressed to the first audience. What has emerged is a picture of considerable variety in the questions which morphologists ask, alongside quite frequent lack of communication between morphologists asking closely related questions. I hope this book may encourage this variety and help to remedy this lack of communication. As to priorities, I have argued that two topics which deserve more attention than they get presently in the Chomskyan tradition are (a) allomorphy and (b) the relationship between morphology and lexical semantics.

To the second audience, there is more to say. Morphology poses certain problems of its own for general linguistic theory, quite unlike any posed by syntax. These problems involve both substance and method. In the course of describing some language, two questions which syntacticians never ask are 'What are the other forms of this sentence?' and 'How frequent is this sentence?', and one which they seldom ask is 'How frequent is this construction?' Yet the morphological analogues to these questions are asked constantly. Given any sentence, one can of course list other sentences related to it in various ways, as interrogatives are related to declaratives, passives to actives and so on, but one does not habitually characterise these as different 'forms' of 'the same' sentence; by contrast, the notion that 'the same' word can have more than one form crops up in one guise or another in almost every approach to morphology. In other words, the paradigmatic dimension of language structure looms larger in morphology than in syntax. The issue of 'construction-frequency' in morphology is the issue of productivity, in all its ramifications, which has no obvious syntactic analogue. And, as we saw in chapter 8, the token-frequency of words is claimed by some linguists to be relevant to the peculiarly morphological problem of suppletion. The fact that these problems arise does not, of course, guarantee that they are soluble in interesting ways; but parts II and III of this book has shown (I hope) that at least partial solutions of some interest have been proposed.

The special problem of method posed by morphology helps to explain the relative unpopularity of morphological research, even now, in the Chomskyan tradition. As is well known, Chomsky lays great stress on the 'poverty of stimulus' argument in justifying the principles and parameters hypothesised as part of Universal Grammar. Many of the things which native speakers 'know' about the syntax of their language could not possibly have been learned by induction or analogy from the data to which they were exposed in infancy (it is claimed). These aspects of syntax must therefore be 'wired in', constraining in advance the way infants will react to what they hear. Evidence from just one language can therefore justify conclusions about the syntactic aspect of Universal Grammar, provided that this evidence is of the intrinsically unlearnable kind. The trouble is that, in morphology as opposed to syntax, this kind of evidence is absent, as Spencer (1990) points out. There are few aspects of the morphology of any language that could not be simply learned through humdrum practice, without help from Universal Grammar. The subtle facts about sentence interpretation which are adduced in favour of the innate element in syntax have no analogue in word interpretation – at least, not in the languages best known to most linguists.

It would be a mistake to conclude from this that there is no morphological element in Universal Grammar, and I know of no linguist who has drawn that conclusion explicitly. The fact that we cannot deduce any morphological universals from looking at just English or Russian (say) does not mean that no morphological universals exist, or that all morphology belongs (in Chomskyan terms) to the 'periphery' of grammars, outside the 'core' determined by the interaction between linguistic data and Universal Grammar. But the inadequacy of the single-language approach to morphological universals does mean that in morphological theory-construction there is no alternative to detailed comparison of a wide variety of languages. Accepting this conclusion may go against the grain for some Chomskyan linguists, however. There is a strong tradition of generativist hostility towards 'typological' approaches to language universals (see e.g. Smith 1982; Coopmans 1983). A generative linguist is therefore tempted to decide in advance, as it were, that most of morphology must belong to the periphery – indeed, Chomsky (1986b: 147) picks 'irregular verb morphology in English' to illustrate 'departures from the core principles' – and so must be relatively barren terrain for the investigator of Universal Grammar.

It is not surprising, given this background, that every morphological study discussed in part II draws on data from only a limited range of languages, and that most of them emphasise issues which arise in either syntax or phonology as well as morphology: argument structure, headedness, the X-bar hierarchy, adjacency (compare 'subjacency' in syntax), the cycle and autosegmental tiers. Implicit here is the idea that all or most of what is universal about morphology is a by-product of principles and parameters governing other areas of grammar. Of the three aspects of morphology mentioned earlier (the paradigmatic dimension, productivity and frequency), only productivity has attracted much attention within the Chomskyan tradition. In contrast, the paradigmatic dimension and (to a lesser extent) the token-frequency of word-forms are prominent in part III, along with issues of morphological 'meaning'. And it seems fair to say that results achieved so far by these 'non-Chomskyan' initiatives justify the hope that universals can be found even in areas where the poverty-of-stimulus argument is inapplicable.

This in turn raises the question whether in other areas of grammar too there may not be 'deep' universals of the Principle-and-Parameters variety which poverty-of-stimulus considerations leave hidden – in lexical semantics, for example, and even in syntax. The only way to answer this question is through wide-scale comparisons, looking for features which are common to many languages even though on the basis of learnability they may seem 'peripheral'. This kind of investigation will be not a mere goodwill gesture to typologists but an essential part of the generative enterprise – and one in which morphologists will have taken the lead.

Notes

1 AIMS AND SCOPE

1 The two collections *Readings in Linguistics I* and *II* (Joos 1966; Hamp *et al.* 1966) offer excellent selections of twentieth-century pregenerative work on morphology, in America and Europe respectively. The former includes the classic articles by Harris (1942), Hockett (1947) and Nida (1948), while the latter includes Jakobson (1935) and Kuryłowicz (1945–9). For an extensive pedagogical introduction to the pregenerative American approach, see Nida (1949).
2 There are also references to the first of these authors under Hooper; my own earlier works are cited as Carstairs.
3 For an elaborate network of morphological definitions, see Mel'čuk (1982).

2 MORPHOLOGY AND THE LEXICON

1 Scalise (1984) discusses from a mainstream generative point of view most of the issues covered in this chapter, as well as some of those covered in chapters 3 and 4, and Toman (1987) discusses many of them. But their treatment is now dated, in that they do not take account of the recent resurgence of interest in syntactic word formation (see chapter 4 below).
2 The varieties of English compared in this section are ones in which either *shoat* or *piglet* occurs but not both. I ignore varieties in which both *shoat* and *piglet* exist, with slightly different meanings ('newborn pig' versus 'young pig').
3 On the prolonged struggle between generative semantics and the Chomskyan '(Extended) Standard Theory', see Newmeyer (1980). The classic transformational analysis of nominalisations is by Lees (1960). For more recent work in a similar spirit, see Levi (1978).
4 In more recent work done in cooperation with Sylvain Bromberger, unpublished at the time of writing, Halle departs from his 1973 view that derivational and inflectional morphology are handled alike. He now believes, along with several other scholars (see chapter 4), that most inflectional word formation is handled syntactically.
5 For early generative discussion of phonological constraints on word formation, including verb-forming -*en*, see Siegel (1979) (a MIT thesis completed in 1974).

6 Selkirk's *The Syntax of Words* (1982) is another important contribution to lexicalist morphology, particularly in relation to issue III, but discussion of it will be deferred to chapter 4. Allen's *Morphological Investigations* (1979), which addresses in particular issues I and II as well as some morphological implications of current phonological theory (see chapter 3), has unfortunately never been published in book or article form and has therefore not achieved the currency that it deserves; see, however, the comments by Scalise (1984) and Botha (1984).

7 In discussing whether the lexicon 'contains' this or that class of items, we use a spatial metaphor, visualising the lexicon as a sort of box. Pesetsky (1985) in effect suggests that the box metaphor is inappropriate; instead, he proposes rules which assign idiosyncrasies (semantic or other) to any constituent or pair of sister constituents (see section 4.7.1).

8 Facts of the kind which run counter to Lieber's expectation that affixes should have consistent meanings are the inspiration for Beard's Lexeme–Morpheme-Based Morphology (see section 6.4).

9 For a brief outline of Corbin's model, see Corbin (1989).

10 See Hoeksema (1985) and Hoeksema and Janda (1988) for a categorial-grammar approach to morphology which is explicitly associative, in Corbin's sense.

11 Blocking is related to the Unique Entry Condition of Pinker (1984) and to the Inflectional Parsimony Hypothesis of Carstairs (1987a). See also Di Sciullo and Williams (1987: 10–14).

12 Lieber implies that the distribution of umlauted and nonumlauted stems in German adjectives with the suffixes -*lich* and -*ig* is relatively unsystematic. For a generativist exposition of the opposite view, see Wurzel (1970).

13 Jackendoff's approach to morphology as involving rules which 'relate' words rather than 'form' them, and moreover rules which may cost more or less to refer to, parallels in interesting ways some more recent 'connectionist' views of the relationships between complex words (see section 8.3).

14 The issues of productivity and lexicalisation in English word formation is discussed at length by Bauer (1983), although in my view he confuses the three types of productivity which Corbin distinguishes.

15 Lieber's thesis (1981b) has never been published, only 'semi-published' by the Indian University Linguistics Club. For published summaries of her lexical-structure framework, see Lieber (1981a: 162–72) and (1983: 252–6); on percolation, see Lieber (1989).

16 Defending 'process morphology' against 'affix morphology', Wurzel (1989) criticises both Lieber's view of affixes as lexical items and also any application of McCarthy's (1981) autosegmental framework so as to analyse as 'morphemes' the kind of vowel alternations found in German or English strong verbs (e.g. *sing/sang/sung*).

17 Within morphology as Di Sciullo and Williams (1987) see it ('the science of word-form', in principle independent of both syntax and the lexicon), there is room for only one question about derivation and inflection: 'Are derivational and inflectional affixes formally different?' Their answer is no (1987: 69–71).

18 Lieber has more recently rejected her original view (1981b) that all word formation takes place 'in the lexicon' in favour of the view that all (productive) word formation takes place 'in the syntax' (1988b); only words which are in some way idiosyncratic are listed in the lexicon. In this, she is influenced by recent trends in syntactic theory (see chapter 4 below).

19 The fact that derivational affixes are generally 'inside' inflectional ones is also important for Bybee's view of the kinds of meaning which are typically expressed by morphological means (chapter 6) and for Anderson's view of inflection as 'outside' the lexicon (chapter 7).

20 Relevant to the issue of productivity and lexical-semantic matrices is the distinction proposed by Carstairs (1988a) between 'meaning-driven' and 'expression-driven' morphology.

3   MORPHOLOGY AND PHONOLOGY

1 Dell (1980) made the point that to constrain the phonological component one must constrain the readjustment component also, if the two exist side by side. However, generative phonologists did not take up the challenge.

2 Most morphologically relevant work in the framework of NGP proper (rather than its later, more morphologically oriented, offshoots) antedates Hooper's textbook (1976) and is cited there. Typical of Vennemann's contributions are his 1972 and 1974 articles.

3 Apart from his 1975 Ph.D. thesis, Hudson's major contribution is his 1980 article.

4 Something like the behaviour of the hypothetical language E2, which we cite below as problematic for the Hudson–Hooper suppletion analysis of alternations, may in fact occur in English; *knife*, *proof* and *house* all have alternants with voiceless and voiced final obstruents, but their distributions differ:

Noun singular	naif	pruf	haus
Noun plural	naiv	pruf	hauz
Verb	naif	pruv	hauz

(see Spencer 1988c).

5 Kenstowicz and Kisseberth (1977), although not attacking NGP by name, criticise a variety of proposed constraints on the abstractness of underlying representations.

6 Apart from Kiparsky, generative linguists who experimented with paradigmatic explanations for phonological 'misbehaviour' in the early 1970s included Wanner (1972) and Harris (1973).

7 Criticism of the Siegel–Allen level-ordered framework as applied to English has taken two forms: (a) denial that affixes can be divided into two clearly distinguishable classes, and (b) denial that the classes are related in level-ordered fashion. Position (b), taken by e.g. Aronoff and Sridhar (1987), does not entail the more radical position (a), which is espoused by e.g. Fabb (1988b). For a defence of the Siegel–Allen position involving the assignment of some affixes (such as *un-* and *-able*) to both classes, see Selkirk (1982).

8 The idea of deriving the (Revised) Alternation Condition from cyclicity originated with Mascaró (1976). On the extent to which cyclic rules and neutralisation rules coincide, see Rubach's summary (1984: 17, 238) of the rival views of Mascaró and of Pesetsky (1979), and the more extended discussion by Harris (1983: 71–84). Rubach offers a clear account of the theoretical background of cyclic phonology and its relation to Lexical Phonology (section 3.1.4).

9 Kiparsky's discussion of Spanish is based on work by Harris, although Harris's published analysis (1983: 54–5) is somewhat different from Kiparsky's. (Harris attributes the deletion of the theme vowel in *desdeñes* to a 'morphological operation', which, unfortunately for Kiparsky, seems to imply that it is unmotivated phonologically.)

10 Levin (1988) illustrates how morphological conclusions may be drawn from phonological arguments in a level-ordered framework, using a variety of non-Indo-European material.

11 On the suggestion that 'agglutinating' languages have special phonological characteristics, see Lehmann (1973: 61–2) and Neustupný (1978: 113–46).

12 Broselow (1983) explores the relevance of the Adjacency Condition to reduplication in some Salish languages, and compares it with the Bracketing Erasure Convention and Williams's (1981a) Atom Condition (see section 4.3.2).

13 One might argue that *utebantur* should be bracketed [[[[uːt]eːb]ant]ur], [[[[[uːt]eːb]a]nt]ur] or even [[[[[[uːt]eː]b]a]nt]ur]. But these analyses leave unaffected or exacerbate the difficulty of reconciling this form with the Adjacency Condition.

14 The clearest introduction to Lexical Phonology is found not in Kiparsky's writings but in Kaisse and Shaw (1985); however, it is Kiparsky (1982b; 1982c) who discusses its morphological implications most extensively. For an assessment of Lexical Phonology by one of the pioneers of autosegmental phonology, see Goldsmith (1990: 217–73).

15 Kiparsky (1983) attempts to deal with the apparent English counterexamples to level-ordering.

16 Kiparsky (1983) suggests replacing the Elsewhere Condition, at least in its morphological role, by a principle that he calls Avoid Synonymy. Janda and Sandoval (1984) seek to show that all the morphological facts which have been attributed to the Condition can be accounted for in other ways. Iverson and Wheeler (1988) point out technical difficulties in its formulation, and favour return to the Revised Alternation Condition. Anderson's and Zwicky's use of the Elsewhere Condition in their models of inflection will be discussed in chapter 7.

The Elsewhere Condition is usually invoked in inflection rather than in derivation. One might regard as its derivational counterpart either Aronoff's principle of blocking (see section 2.3 and the associated notes) or van Marle's Domain Hypothesis (section 6.5).

17 Paulissen and Zonneveld (1988) discuss the extent to which the Lexical Phonology framework can explicate some differences between English and Dutch in the inflection of compound verbs.

18 Szpyra (1989), on the basis of Polish and English material, agrees that some morphological processes can depend on the outcome of

phonological rules, yet rejects both Lexical Phonology and the Strict Cyclicity Principle. Instead, she argues that a word-form which has undergone all word-level phonological rules can 'loop back' to be the input to further word formation. The main empirical issue here is whether a morphological process ever crucially needs to refer to an 'intermediate' phonological representation of its base rather than to (what would be) its 'surface' representation; Lexical Phonology permits this but Szpyra's model forbids it.

19 Goldsmith (1990) offers a thorough but not always elementary account of the autosegmental framework, including its application to morphology (83–102, 309–18). For briefer introductions, also covering morphology, see van der Hulst and Smith (1982b; 1984b). Hudson (1986) mounts an NGP-based attack on McCarthy's treatment of Arabic morphology, to which Haile and Mtenje (1988) respond. For an application of the autosegmental framework to syntax (the 'surface' case of noun phrases), see Yip, Maling and Jackendoff (1987).

20 For a fundamentally different view of why metathesis is rare as a morphological process, see Janda (1984). In some Semitic language games, consonants are permuted with effects superficially similar to the crossing of association lines; however, McCarthy argues (1982; 1984) that the permutation takes place on the root tier, 'before' association with the CV-template.

21 Considerable effort has been devoted in the autosegmental framework to phonological aspects of reduplication; see, for example, Marantz (1982) and Davis (1988).

22 For the Temiar data, McCarthy (1982: 208) cites Benjamin (1976). For typographical convenience I have simplified the transcription of the vowels, which do not enter into the argument.

4   MORPHOLOGY AND SYNTAX

1 For an explicit statement of the Lexical Integrity Hypothesis by an exponent of it, see Lapointe (1981: 230): 'No syntactic rule can refer to an element of morphological structure.' The editors' introduction to Hoekstra *et al*. (1981) discusses the impact of 'lexicalism' on syntax and phonology as well as morphology.

2 The relevance of lexical semantics to bracketing paradoxes is mentioned by Fanselow (1988), although he does not develop the point as explicitly as Spencer does. For further comment on lexical-semantic pressure as a factor in morphology, see Carstairs (1988a).

3 The fundamental work on X-bar syntax is Jackendoff (1977). In her extension of X-bar theory into W-syntax, Selkirk originally envisaged a level Stem intermediate between Word and Root, and the existence of such a level is assumed by Williams (1981a).

4 Botha (1981) argues that the No Phrase Constraint does not apply in Afrikaans.

5 In some recent work (e.g. Abney 1987) *all that sour milk* is classified as a determiner phrase rather than a noun phrase, but that issue is not relevant to the present argument.

6 On the complex variety of criteria which have been or might be

used to identify heads, see Zwicky (1985a) and Bauer (1990). Allen (1979) discusses semantic characteristics of compounds, including the characteristic that in endocentric compounds the whole 'is an' instance of its head.

7 For a defence of Williams's Right-hand Head Rule against Selkirk and Lieber, see Trommelen and Zonneveld (1986).

8 Di Sciullo and Williams (1987: 45) claim a role for 'heads', in their sense, in the determination of the argument structure of compounds and phrases (see section 4.4). But affixal 'heads' behave differently in this area from the heads of compounds, so it is again doubtful what purpose the common label serves.

9 Within the Chomskyan tradition, the most thorough discussion of root compounds is probably that of Allen (1979), who also questions whether there is any fundamental distinction between them and synthetic compounds.

10 For a rigorous (not to say merciless) critique of the treatment of synthetic compounds by Roeper and Siegel (1978), Allen (1979), Selkirk (1982) and Lieber (1983), see Botha (1984).

11 Objections to structure-based accounts of the 'inheritance' of argument structure, somewhat similar to those raised in our discussion of examples (51) and (52), are put forward by Hoekstra and van der Putten (1988).

12 Examples (54)–(62), (65) and (66) are all taken directly from Baker (1988a: 21, 229, 407), except that (56) and (57) have been constructed with different lexical material on the basis of other example sentences given by Baker.

13 Despite Baker's claim that all applied objects can become subjects in the passive, it seems that instrumental applied objects in the west African language Fula cannot (Marantz 1984: 245, 251–5). In classifying the applicative suffix in Chichewa as a preposition, Baker follows the example of Marantz, who classifies similarly the applicative suffix in Chi-Mwi:ni, another Bantu language (1984: 231–75). But Marantz adjoins the suffix to the verb stem not by Move-Alpha but rather by his process of 'merger' (see section 4.7.2); and in some languages he analyses the applicative affix as a 'verb' rather than a 'preposition'.

14 Baker's argument for word formation in syntax (including what we may call 'syntactic affixation') is based mainly on Move-Alpha and the Empty Category Principle. The question arises whether any other devices of Principles-and-Parameters syntax have been invoked in support of syntactic affixation. The answer is yes. Fabb (1988b) argues on the basis of a version of Case Theory that the English verbal inflectional suffixes -*s*, -*ing* and past-tense -*ed* must be present as terminal elements in S-structure (though not D-structure), while passive -*en* (or an allomorph of it) is present as a noun phrase in both D- and S-structure.

15 Marantz (1988b: 223–4) considers but rejects the possibility of using Pesetsky's QR to account for causative constructions in Chi-Mwi:ni. To explain the partly verbal, partly nominal characteristics of Dutch infinitival phrases, Reuland (1988) considers but rejects string-vacuous reattachment of the Dutch infinitive suffix -*en* higher up the S-structure tree.

Lieber (1988a) explores the extent to which 'nonconcatenative' morphological processes such as reduplication can be viewed as 'con-figurational' i.e. as involving linearly ordered and hierarchically structured 'morphemes', and proposes an application for Pesetsky's morphological QR in Tagalog. But there are big differences; Lieber's rule is not string-vacuous, and it maps a morphological structure not into LF but into another morphological structure closer to, rather than further from, PF.

16 Di Sciullo and Williams (1987: 74) criticise Pesetsky's idea that idiosyncratic interpretation depends on sisterhood at LF, on the ground that idioms may be broken up at LF (e.g. *What kind of tabs$_i$ do you keep t$_i$ on Bill?*). One might answer this by suggesting that the trace of the moved idiom-part is sufficient to license idiomatic interpretation. But this in turn requires that, if we want to maintain Pesetsky's explanation for the lack of an idiomatic interpretation for *unrarity*, we must posit that 'morphological QR' does not leave traces.

17 The status of clitics has attracted considerable discussion since Zwicky's (1977) monograph. For a variety of views on morphological and phonological aspects of their behaviour, see e.g. Zwicky and Pullum (1983), Kaisse (1985), Zwicky (1985b), Carstairs (1987b).

18 Marantz (1984) proposes Morphological Merger to account for the syntax and morphology of causative and applicative constructions in Bantu languages and elsewhere.

19 Zubizarreta and van Haaften (1988) propose a coanalysis treatment for English *-ing* nominalisations; under one analysis, the N' *singing of the national anthem* appears as [[-ing]$_N$ [sing (of) the national anthem]$_{V'}$]$_{N'}$.

20 Bok-Bennema and Groos (1988), in an analysis of Eskimo data similar to Sadock's, agree with Baker in permitting 'syntactic word-formation', but agree with Sadock and Di Sciullo and Williams that syntactic units obey different principles from morphological ones. Their approach has much in common with Borer's (1988), although it has evidently been developed independently.

21 It is not true, as Sproat implies, that NOM spells itself out in only one way with each verb stem; cf. *commission, commitment, committal* and other examples discussed in section 2.7.

22 The kinds of morphological alternation displayed by the suffixes *-ion*, *-ment* and *-ance* and by the participles *dropped, broken* and *sung* are central to the concerns of several of the morphologists discussed in chapters 6, 7 and 8.

5   TYPOLOGICAL AND DIACHRONIC ISSUES

1 For a general survey of typology within linguistics, see Greenberg (1974).

2 Important collections of papers stimulated by Greenberg's work have been edited by Li (1975; 1977). Vennemann's Natural Serialisation Principle (1975 and elsewhere) represents an attempt to improve on Greenberg's universals while retaining their spirit. Vennemann, like Lehmann, emphasises the diachronic implications of typology.

3 The goal of explaining change by reference to typology has been criticised by e.g. Smith (1981) from the point of view of Chomskyan Universal Grammar.

4 For further criticisms of morphology as a tool in syntactic reconstruction, see Comrie (1980; 1989) and Kefer (1985). For more sympathetic assessments of Givón's claims, see Disterheft (1987) and Hall (1988).

5 For nineteenth-century morphological typology, see any history of linguistics such as Robins (1979) as well as Greenberg (1974) or Hagège (1986: 3–9). Despite its datedness, Jespersen's (1922) lively and provocative survey of the preoccupations and enthusiasms of nineteenth-century linguists, in morphology as well as other areas, is still worth reading.

6 Our statement of Skalička's characterisations of the morphological types is based on Skalička (1951) and (1966); see also Neustupný (1978). We substitute 'fusional' for the unfortunate but traditional term 'inflecting' (used by Skalička), in order to avoid suggesting that only 'inflecting' languages have inflectional morphology.

7 Somewhat parallel to the Zyryan developments described by Korhonen are certain radical morphological reanalyses in the eastern Nilotic language Turkana (Dimmendaal 1987).

6 MEANING-BASED APPROACHES TO MORPHOLOGY

1 The approaches outlined in this chapter are distinctive in giving central importance to meaning, but they do not exhaust the range of conceivable semantico-morphological questions. For example, Plank (1980) suggests necessary semantic conditions for certain homonymies within noun paradigms (see chapter 7).

2 In this chapter, and throughout the rest of the book, we will generally adopt Matthews's practice (1972; 1974) of giving capital initials to the names of morphosyntactic categories, such as Case and Tense, and the properties which belong to them, such as Accusative and Past.

3 For more discussion of relevance, morpheme order and fusion, see Bybee (1985a). Bybee's suggestion that derivational morphology should be more fusional (in Matthews's sense) than inflectional morphology resembles Dressler's claim that inflection ought to be morphotactically more transparent (i.e. more agglutinative) than derivation. Dressler acknowledges, however, that in some languages the pattern is exactly the reverse – an embarrassing 'typological mix' (1985b: 324, 342–3). On Dressler's morphonology, see section 8.1.5 below.

4 On meaning change in grammaticalisation, see also e.g. Aijmer (1985) and Conradie (1987).

5 For debate on Beard's separation hypothesis in relation to agent nouns in Dutch, see Booij (1986) and Beard (1990).

6 For a summary of Szymanek's approach to morphology in terms of cognitive categories and for some extended application to English, see Szymanek (1989), chapters 3–6.

7 Diminutives are a puzzle not only for Beard and Szymanek but also in some respects for 'lexicalist' morphology (see section 4.3.2).

8 For more discussion of van Marle's approach to word formation and of the implications of female nouns and deverbal nominalisations, see Carstairs (1988a). Van Marle shares Beard's view (1982) that plural formation is derivational rather than inflectional in English (and Dutch); but the issue

is important in the context of this section only if one regards it as crucial
to exclude inflection from the scope of the Domain Hypothesis.

7   MORPHOSYNTACTIC PROPERTIES AND THEIR REALISATION

1   The label 'Extended Word-and-Paradigm' was introduced in Thomas–
Flinders (1981), a collection of papers applying Anderson's (1982) model
in various languages.

2   The layering which Anderson posits for some morphosyntactic representations is quite independent of the 'layering' imposed by the successive
application of morphological processes or spell-out rules or by level-
ordering. The prefixes *g-* of the M-set and *v-* of the V-set are associated
with different layers in the first sense but the same layer in the second
sense (see section 7.3.1). The term 'layered morphology' used by Simpson
and Withgott (1986) (section 7.3.2) relates to the second sense.

   Lieber (1989) discusses layered morphosyntactic representations like
Anderson's from the point of view of feature percolation (see section
2.4).

3   Carstairs (1987a) uses the term **take-over** for a referral such that, in some
context, property A is referred to property B and the realisation of the two
properties A and B looks like that of B alone in other contexts. In such
circumstances, B can be said to 'take over' A. The Systematic Homonymy
Claim in effect states that noncumulative homonymies must be take-overs
of a certain kind.

   Plank (1986) proposes that there is an absolute upper limit of 'about
30' on the number of distinct exponents available for nominal inflection
in any language. This means that a language which has an elaborate
Case-system, cumulation of Case and Number, and more than one
declension-type must inevitably display some inflectional homonymy.

4   Anderson (1982) regards inflectional spell-out as taking place 'outside' the
lexicon, and Zwicky's modular approach commits him to a similar view.
They therefore claim that morphology is split into lexical (derivational)
and nonlexical parts, and implicitly that derivational processes cannot
follow inflectional ones. For discussion of this 'split-morphology hypothesis', see Lieber (1981b), Jensen and Stong–Jensen (1984), Bochner
(1984), Perlmutter (1988).

5   Rule (12) as it stands is insufficient to account for all stem-vowel changes
in the Past Subjunctive, because sometimes more than just 'ordinary'
umlaut is involved; for example, *helfen* 'help', Past Indicative *half*, has
in standard written German a Past Subjunctive form *hülfe*, not *hälfe*. Like
Anderson, we will ignore this difficulty. Rule (11) implicitly denies that
the *-e* of *lobte*, *brachte*, etc. is introduced by the same rule that introduces
-t-; the correctness of this assumption does not matter for our purposes.
Anderson's suggestion that the stem *bring-* is marked [−Past] has affinities
with Mayerthaler's 'markedness reversal' (see chapter 8).

6   Another problem for the Elsewhere Condition is double Plural marking
in Breton nouns; see Anderson (1986) and Stump (1989).

7   Constraints similar in appearance to the Elsewhere Condition have been
proposed for reasons to do with the syntactic rather than the phonological
end of morphology. These are the No Vacuous Affixation Principle

(Marantz 1984: 128): 'For a certain class of features F, an [alpha F_i] affix may attach only to a [−alpha F_i] root', and the Principle of Morphological Nonredundancy (Zubizarreta 1985: 278): 'Attachment of redundant morphology is prohibited'. The No Vacuous Affixation Principle is meant to ensure, for example, that the English Passive suffix -*en*, which is marked [−transitive], is attached only to [+transitive] verbs.

8 Carstairs's Peripherality Constraint has nothing to do with the Peripherality Condition proposed in metrical phonology. The coincidence of terminology is unfortunate.

9 The acute accent in the Hungarian examples indicates a long vowel.

10 For some thoughts on reconciling phonological lookahead with layered morphology, see Carstairs (1990).

8 NATURAL MORPHOLOGY AND RELATED APPROACHES

1 There is a useful introduction to NM, biased towards Dressler's version, by Kilani–Schoch (1988). A pioneer work on 'natural syntax' is Haiman (1985a); see also Haiman (1985b).

Many articles in the NM framework have appeared in journals not widely read by English-speaking linguists, such as *Wiener Linguistische Gazette, Zeitschrift für Phonetik, Sprachwissenschaft und Kommunikationsforschung*, and the series *Linguistische Studien (Reihe A: Arbeitsberichte)* published by the Academy of Sciences of the German Democratic Republic. However, *Leitmotifs in Natural Morphology* (Dressler *et al.* 1987) provides a useful summary of the approach in English by its three main protagonists. This can serve as an introduction to the three main monographs (Mayerthaler 1981; Wurzel 1984; Dressler 1985b), all of which can now be read in English too. In addition, almost every article by Dressler contains an extensive bibliography of earlier NM work.

2 Mayerthaler's *Morphologische Natürlichkeit* (1981) has been translated into English (1988), but the standard of translation, proof-reading and typography is bad, and the German original should be used if possible. 'Markerful' and 'markerless' are my own suggestions for terms to translate 'merkmalhaft' and 'merkmallos'; the terms 'featured' and 'featureless' used in the English version of Mayerthaler's book and in Mayerthaler (1987) seem likely to lead to confusion.

3 The notion of constructional iconicity is anticipated in a short but important article by Jakobson (1966).

4 The Natural Morphologists are not the first linguists to bring Peircean semiotics into the discussion of morphology. The Peircean notion of 'abduction' is applied to morphological change by Andersen (1973; 1980), while Anttila (1975) anticipates in many respects Dressler's view of allomorphy as indexical. Shapiro (1969; 1983; 1990) has developed a largely independent 'semeiotic' approach.

5 For an attempt to accommodate the introflexive morphology of Tunisian Arabic within NM, see Kilani–Schoch and Dressler (1985). Mithun (1988) discusses the polysynthetic type in relation to NM.

6 In discussing Wurzel's framework, we use 'category' and 'property' in

Matthews's (1972) senses. Wurzel's own terms are 'Kategoriengefüge' and 'Kategorie' respectively. As English glosses for 'Kategoriengefüge', Wurzel himself uses 'set of categories' (1984: 205), 'categorial system' (1987b) and 'categorial complex' (in the 1989 translation of his 1984 book).

7 For an illustration of how diachronic evidence can be applied to the analysis of inflection-class relationships, see Wurzel (1987a) on Icelandic.

8 For a discussion of the relationship between language-particular SDSPs and the typological filter, see A. Bittner (1988a).

9 Inflectional changes in certain Latin 'third-declension' nouns have been extensively discussed from the point of view of whether or not they illustrate the repair of a breach of paradigm economy brought about by independent developments (Carstairs 1984a; 1985; 1988c; Nyman 1987; 1988).

10 Dressler (1985c) offers one NM view of suppletion.

11 For a book-length presentation of a view similar to Werner's, with criticism of various earlier typologically based accounts of language change, see Ronneberger–Sibold (1980).

12 Although she does not mention Kuryłowicz's article 'La Nature des procés dits "analogiques"' (1945–9), Bybee's 'basic forms' and 'derived forms' resemble closely Kuryłowicz's 'formes de fondation' and 'formes fondées'.

13 For experimental psycholinguistic evidence in English which Bybee cites in support of her model of lexical organisation, see Bybee and Slobin (1982). De Bleser and Bayer (1988) and Stemberger and MacWhinney (1988) also discuss psycholinguistic evidence on whether inflection is 'in the lexicon' or not, and draw somewhat conflicting conclusions.

14 Diachronic evidence for the idea that some inflected word-forms are stored as wholes while some are not is cited by Vincent (1980). He contrasts the development of certain verb-forms in Italian (e.g. *sappiamo* 'we know' < Vulgar Latin *sapiamu(s)*, with -*pp*-, versus *capiamo* 'we understand' < *capiamu(s)*, with -*p*-); the former displays a regular phonological development while the phonology of the latter, with lower token frequency, suggests that it is constantly recreated from its elements.

15 'Connectionism' in general and Rumelhart and McClelland's article on English verbs (1986) in particular have provoked considerable controversy. For more or less favourable reactions, see Sampson (1987), Derwing and Skousen (1989) and Derwing (1990); for a hostile reaction, see Pinker and Prince (1988).

References

Abney, S. (1987) 'The English noun phrase in its sentential aspect', Ph.D. dissertation, Cambridge, MA: MIT.

Ahlqvist, A. (ed.) (1982) *Papers from the Fifth International Conference on Historical Linguistics*, Amsterdam: Benjamins.

Aijmer, K. (1985) 'The semantic development of *will*', in Fisiak (ed.), 11–21.

Aitchison, J. (1987) *Words in the Mind: an Introduction to the Mental Lexicon*, Oxford: Blackwell.

Allen M. (1979) 'Morphological investigations', Ph.D. thesis, University of Connecticut; Ann Arbor: University Microfilms.

Andersen, H. (1973) 'Abductive and deductive change', *Language* 49: 567–95.

—— (1980) 'Morphological change: towards a typology', in Fisiak (ed.) 1–50.

Anderson, J.M. and Jones, C. (eds) (1974) *Historical Linguistics I*, Amsterdam: North Holland.

Anderson, S.R. (1977) 'On the formal description of inflection', *Chicago Linguistic Society Papers* 13: 15–44.

—— (1982) 'Where's morphology?', *Linguistic Inquiry* 13: 571–612.

—— (1984) 'On representations in morphology: case marking, agreement and inversion in Georgian', *Natural Language and Linguistic Theory* 2: 157–218.

—— (1986) 'Disjunctive ordering in inflectional morphology', *Natural Language and Linguistic Theory* 4: 1–31.

Anderson, S.R. and Kiparsky, P. (eds) (1973) *A Festschrift for Morris Halle*, New York: Holt Rinehart.

Anshen, F. and Aronoff, M. (1989) 'Morphological productivity, word frequency and the *OED*', in Fasold and Schiffrin (eds), 197–202.

Anttila, R. (1975) *The Indexical Element in Morphology* (Innsbrucker Beiträge zur Sprachwissenschaft, 12), Innsbruck: Institut für Sprachwissenschaft.

Aronoff, M. (1976) *Word Formation in Generative Grammar* (Linguistic Inquiry Monographs, 1), Cambridge, MA: MIT Press.

—— (1980) 'The relevance of productivity in a synchronic description of word formation', in Fisiak (ed.), 71–82.

Aronoff, M. and Sridhar, S.N. (1987) 'Morphological levels in English and

Kannada', in Gussmann (ed.), 9–22.

Aronson, H.I. (1982) *Georgian: a Reading Grammar*, Columbus, OH: Slavica.

Baker, M. (1985) 'The Mirror Principle and morphosyntactic explanation', *Linguistic Inquiry* 16: 373–415.

—— (1988a) *Incorporation: a Theory of Grammatical Function Changing*, Chicago: University of Chicago Press.

—— (1988b) 'Morphology and syntax: an interlocking interdependence', in Everaert *et al.* (eds), 9–32.

—— (1988c) 'Morphological and syntactic objects: a review of A.M. Di Sciullo and E. Williams, *On the Definition of Word*', in Booij and van Marle (eds), 259–83.

Bauer, L. (1983) *English Word-Formation*, Cambridge: Cambridge University Press.

ᐯ —— (1988) *Introducing Linguistic Morphology*, Edinburgh: Edinburgh University Press.

—— (1990) 'Be-heading the word', *Journal of Linguistics* 26: 1–31.

Beard, R. (1981) *The Indo-European Lexicon: A Full Synchronic Theory*, Amsterdam: North-Holland.

—— (1982) 'The plural as a lexical derivation', *Glossa* 16: 133–48.

—— (1987) 'Lexical stock expansion', in Gussmann (ed.), 23–41.

—— (1988) 'On the separation of derivation from morphology: toward a Lexeme–Morpheme-Based Morphology', *Quaderni di Semantica* 9: 3–59.

—— (1990) 'The nature and origins of derivational polysemy', *Lingua* 81: 101–40.

Benjamin, G. (1976) 'An outline of Temiar grammar', in P. Jenner, L. Thompson and S. Starosta (eds), *Austroasiatic Studies (Part I)*, 129–87, Honolulu: University of Hawaii Press.

Bergenholtz, R. and Mugdan, J. (1979) *Einführung in die Morphologie*, Stuttgart: Kohlhammer.

Bierwisch, M. (1967) 'Syntactic features in morphology: general problems of the so-called pronominal inflection in German', in *To Honour Roman Jakobson: Essays on the Occasion of his Seventieth Birthday*, 239–70, The Hague: Mouton.

Bittner, A. (1985) 'Implikative Hierarchien in der Morphologie: das "Stark-Schwach-Kontinuum" der neuhochdeutschen Verben', *Acta Linguistica Academiae Scientiarum Hungaricae* 35: 31–42.

—— (1988a) 'Is anything "more natural"? Considerations on establishing a hierarchy of naturalness principles (NP)', *Linguistische Studien* (Series A: *Arbeitsberichte*) 188: 23–35.

—— (1988b) 'Reguläre Irregularitäten: zur Suppletion im Konzept der natürlichen Morphologie', *Zeitschrift für Phonetik, Sprachwissenschaft und Kommunikationsforschung* 41: 416–25.

Bittner, D. (1988) 'Motivationsstrukturen im Flexionsverhalten der neuhochdeutschen Substantive – Vorschlag eines Modells', *Linguistische Studien* (Series A: *Arbeitsberichte*) 188: 36–52.

Bleser, R. de and Bayer, J. (1988) 'On the role of inflectional morphology in agrammatism', in Hammond and Noonan (eds), 45–69.

Bloomfield, L. (1933) *Language*, New York: Holt.

Bochner, H. (1984) 'Inflection within derivation', *Linguistic Review* 3: 411–21.

Bok-Bennema, R. and Groos, A. (1988) 'Adjacency and incorporation', in Everaert *et al.* (eds), 33–56.

Booij, G. (1986) 'Form and meaning in morphology: the case of Dutch "agent nouns" ', *Linguistics* 24: 503–18.

—— (1988) 'The relation between inheritance and argument linking: deverbal nouns in Dutch', in Everaert *et al.* (eds), 57–73.

Booij, G. and van Haaften, T. (1988) 'On the external syntax of derived words: evidence from Dutch', in Booij and van Marle (eds), 29–44.

Booij, G. and van Marle, J. (eds) (1988) *Yearbook of Morphology 1988*, Dordrecht: Foris.

—— (eds) (1989) *Yearbook of Morphology 2*, Dordrecht: Foris.

Borer, H. (1984) 'The Projection Principle and rules of morphology', *NELS* 14: 16–33.

—— (1988) 'On the morphological parallelism between compounds and constructs', in Booij and van Marle (eds), 45–65.

Botha, R. (1981) 'A base rule theory of Afrikaans synthetic compounding', in Moortgat *et al.* (eds), 1–77.

—— (1984) *Morphological Mechanisms*, Oxford: Pergamon.

Braunmüller, K. (1984) 'Morphologische Undurchsichtigkeit – ein Charakteristikum kleiner Sprachen', *Kopenhagener Beiträge zur Germanistischen Linguistik* 22: 48–68.

Bresnan, J. (1981) 'Polyadicity: part I of a theory of lexical rules and representations', in Hoekstra *et al.* (eds), 97–121.

Broselow, E. (1983) 'Salish double reduplications: subjacency in morphology', *Natural Language and Linguistic Theory* 1: 317–46.

Bybee, J. (1985a) 'Diagrammatic iconicity in stem-inflection relations', in Haiman (ed.), 11–47.

—— (1985b) *Morphology: a Study of the Relation between Meaning and Form*, Amsterdam: Benjamins.

—— (1988) 'Morphology as lexical organization', in Hammond and Noonan (eds), 119–41.

Bybee, J. and Brewer, M.A. (1980) 'Explanation in linguistics: changes in Provençal and Spanish preterite forms', *Lingua* 52: 201–42.

Bybee, J. and Pagliuca, W. (1985) 'Cross-linguistic comparison and the development of grammatical meaning', in Fisiak (ed.), 59–83.

Bybee, J. and Slobin, D. (1982) 'Rules and schemas in the development and use of the English past tense', *Language* 58: 265–89.

Carstairs, A. (1983) 'Paradigm economy', *Journal of Linguistics* 19: 115–28.

—— (1984a) 'Paradigm economy in the Latin third declension', *Transactions of the Philological Society* 117–37.

—— (1984b) 'Outlines of a constraint on syncretism', *Folia Linguistica* 18: 73–85.

—— (1985) 'Paradigm economy in Latin', in J. Fisiak (ed.) *Papers from the Sixth International Conference on Historical Linguistics*, 57–70, Amsterdam/Poznan: Benjamins/Adam Mickiewicz University.

—— (1986) 'Macroclasses and paradigm economy in German nouns', *Zeitschrift für Phonetik, Sprachwissenschaft und Kommunikationsforschung* 39:

3–11.

—— (1987a) *Allomorphy in Inflexion*, London: Croom Helm.

—— (1987b) 'Diachronic evidence and the affix–clitic distinction', in Ramat *et al.* (eds), 151–62.

—— (1988a) 'Some implications of phonologically conditioned suppletion', in Booij and van Marle (eds), 67–94.

—— (1988b) 'Nonconcatenative inflection and paradigm economy', in Hammond and Noonan (eds), 71–7.

—— (1988c) 'Paradigm economy: a reply to Nyman', *Journal of Linguistics* 24: 489–99.

—— (1990) 'Phonologically conditioned suppletion', in Dressler *et al.* (eds), 16–23.

—— (in press) 'Inflection classes: two questions with one answer', in F. Plank (ed.) *Paradigms: The Economy of Inflection*, Berlin: Walter de Gruyter.

Carstairs, A. and Stemberger, J. (1988) 'A processing constraint on inflectional homonymy', *Linguistics* 26: 601–17.

Chomsky, N. (1957) *Syntactic Structures*, The Hague: Mouton.

—— (1965) *Aspects of the Theory of Syntax*, Cambridge, MA: MIT Press.

—— (1970) 'Remarks on nominalization', in R.A. Jacobs and P.S. Rosenbaum (eds) *Readings in English Transformational Grammar*, 184–221, Waltham, MA: Ginn.

—— (1986a) *Barriers*, Cambridge, MA: MIT Press.

—— (1986b) *Knowledge of Language: its Nature, Origin and Use*, New York: Praeger.

Chomsky, N. and Halle, M. (1968) *The Sound Pattern of English*, New York: Harper & Row.

Chung, S. (1977) 'On the gradual nature of syntactic change', in Li (ed.), 3–55.

Clark, E.V. (1987) 'The Principle of Contrast: a constraint on language acquisition', in Mac Whinney (ed.), 1–33.

Comrie, B. (1980) 'Morphology and word order reconstruction: problems and prospects', in Fisiak (ed.), 83–96.

—— (1989) *Language Universals and Linguistic Typology* (2nd edn), Oxford: Blackwell.

Conradie, C.J. (1987) 'Semantic change in modal auxiliaries as a result of speech act embedding', in M. Harris and P. Ramat (eds) *Historical Development of Auxiliaries*, 171–80, Berlin: Mouton de Gruyter.

Coopmans, P. (1983) Review of B. Comrie *Language Universals and Linguistic Typology*, *Journal of Linguistics* 19: 455–73.

Coopmans, P. and Everaert, M. (1988) 'The simplex structure of complex idioms: the morphological status of *laten*', in Everaert *et al.* (eds), 75–104.

Corbett, G. (1983) *Hierarchies, Targets and Controllers: Agreement Patterns in Slavic*, London: Croom Helm.

—— (1987) 'The morphology/syntax interface: evidence from possessive adjectives in Slavonic', *Language* 63: 299–345.

—— (1988) 'Agreement: a partial specification based on Slavonic data', in M. Barlow and C. A. Ferguson (eds) *Agreement in Natural Language*, 23–53, Stanford: CSLI.

Corbin, D. (1987) *Morphologie dérivationnelle et structuration du lexique* (2 vols), Tübingen: Niemeyer.

—— (1989) 'Form, structure and meaning of constructed words in an associative and stratified lexical component', in Booij and van Marle (eds), 31–54.

Davis, S. (1988) 'On the nature of internal reduplication', in Hammond and Noonan (eds), 305–23.

Dell, F. (1980) *Generative Phonology*, Cambridge: Cambridge University Press.

Derwing, B. (1990) 'Morphology and the mental lexicon: psycholinguistic evidence', in Dressler *et al.* (eds), 249–65.

Derwing, B. and Skousen, R. (1989) 'Morphology in the mental lexicon: a new look at analogy', in Booij and van Marle (eds), 55–71.

Di Sciullo, M. and Williams, E. (1987) *On the Definition of Word* (Linguistic Inquiry Monographs, 14), Cambridge, MA: MIT Press.

Dimmendaal, G. (1987) 'Drift and selective mechanisms in morphological changes: the Eastern Nilotic case', in Ramat *et al.* (eds), 193–210.

Disterheft, D. (1987) 'The diachronic relationship of morphology and syntax', in Ramat *et al.* (eds), 211–20.

Dixon, R.M.W. (1972) *The Dyirbal Language of North Queensland*, Cambridge: Cambridge University Press.

Doke, C.M. (1961) *Textbook of Zulu Grammar* (6th edn), Cape Town: Longmans.

Donegan, P.J. and Stampe, D. (1979) 'The study of Natural Phonology', in D.A. Dinnsen (ed.) *Current Approaches to Phonological Theory*, 126–73, Bloomington: Indiana University Press.

Dressler, W.U. (1985a) 'Typological aspects of natural morphology', *Wiener Linguistische Gazette* 35–6: 3–26. Also in *Acta Linguistica Academiae Scientiarum Hungaricae* 35: 51–70. (Page references are to the *WLG* version.)

—— (1985b) *Morphonology: the Dynamics of Derivation*, Ann Arbor: Karoma.

—— (1985c) 'Suppletion in word-formation', in Fisiak (ed.), 97–112.

—— (1985d) 'On the definite Austrian and Italian articles', in Gussmann (ed.), 35–47.

—— (1988) 'Zur Bedeutung der Sprachtypologie in der Natürlichen Morphologie', in J. Lüdtke (ed.) *Energeia und Ergon, III: Das sprachtheoretische Denken Eugenio Coserius in der Diskussion (2)*, 199–208, Tübingen: Narr.

Dressler, W.U., Luschützky, H., Pfeiffer, O. and Rennison, J. (eds) (1990) *Contemporary Morphology*, Berlin: Mouton de Gruyter.

Dressler, W.U., Mayerthaler, W., Panagl, O. and Wurzel, W.U. (eds) (1987) *Leitmotifs in Natural Morphology*, Amsterdam: Benjamins.

Everaert, M., Evers, A., Huybregts, R. and Trommelen, M. (eds) (1988) *Morphology and Modularity: in Honour of Henk Schultink*, Dordrecht: Foris.

Evers, A. (1988) 'Non-finite verb forms and subject theta assignment', in Everaert *et al.* (eds), 105–28.

Fabb, N. (1988a) 'Doing affixation in the GB syntax', in Everaert *et al.* (eds), 129–45.

—— (1988b) 'English suffixation is constrained only by selectional restrictions', *Natural Language and Linguistic Theory* 6: 527–39.

Fanselow, G. (1988) ' "Word syntax" and semantic principles', in Booij and van Marle (eds), 95–122.

Fasold, R.W. and Schiffrin, D. (eds) (1989) *Language Change and Variation*, Amsterdam: Benjamins.

Fisiak, J. (ed.) (1980) *Historical Morphology*, The Hague: Mouton.

—— (ed.) (1985) *Historical Semantics, Historical Word-Formation*, Berlin: Mouton.

Fleischman, S. (1982) *The Future in Thought and Language: Diachronic Evidence from Romance*, Cambridge: Cambridge University Press.

Gabelentz, G. von der (1901) *Die Sprachwissenschaft: ihre Aufgaben, Methoden und bisherigen Ergebnisse*, Leipzig: Tauchnitz.

Givón, T. (1971) 'Historical syntax and synchronic morphology: an archaeologist's field trip', *Chicago Linguistic Society Papers* 7: 394–415.

—— (1975) 'Serial verbs and syntactic change: Niger–Congo', in Li (ed.), 47–112.

Goldsmith, J. (1990) *Autosegmental and Metrical Phonology*, Oxford: Blackwell.

Greenberg, J.H. (1963) 'Some universals of grammar with particular reference to the order of meaningful elements', in J.H. Greenberg (ed.) *Universals of Language*, 58–90, Cambridge, MA: MIT Press.

—— (1974) *Language Typology: a Historical and Analytic Overview*, The Hague: Mouton.

Gussmann, E. (ed.) (1985) *Phono-Morphology: Studies in the Interaction of Phonology and Morphology*, Lublin: Redakcja Wydawnictw Katolickiego Uniwersytetu Lubelskiego.

—— (ed.) (1987) *Rules and the Lexicon: Studies in Word-Formation*, Lublin: Redakcja Wydawnictw Katolickiego Uniwersytetu Lubelskiego.

Hagège, C. (1986) *La Structure des langues* (2nd edn), Paris: Presses Universitaires de France.

Haile, A. and Mtenje, A. (1988) 'In defence of the autosegmental treatment of nonconcatenative morphology', *Journal of Linguistics* 24: 433–55.

Haiman, J. (1985a) *Natural Syntax*, Cambridge: Cambridge University Press.

—— (ed.) (1985b) *Iconicity in Syntax*, Amsterdam: Benjamins.

Hall, M.J. (1988) 'Integrating diachronic and processing principles in explaining the suffixing preference', in J.A. Hawkins (ed.) *Explaining Language Universals*, 321–49, Oxford: Blackwell.

Halle, M. (1973) 'Prolegomena to a theory of word-formation', *Linguistic Inquiry* 4: 3–16.

—— (1979) 'Formal and functional considerations in phonology', in B. Brogyanyi (ed.) *Studies in Diachronic, Synchronic and Typological Linguistics: Festschrift for O. Szemerényi*, 325–41, Amsterdam: Benjamins.

Halle, M. and Mohanan, K.P. (1985) 'Segmental phonology of modern English', *Linguistic Inquiry* 16: 57–116.

Hammond, M. and Noonan, M. (eds) (1988) *Theoretical Morphology: Approaches in Modern Linguistics*, San Diego: Academic Press.

Hamp, E.P., Householder, F.W. and Austerlitz, R. (eds) (1966) *Readings in Linguistics II*, Chicago: University of Chicago Press.

Harnisch, R. (1988) 'Natürliche Morphologie und morphologische Ökono-mie: ein Vermittlungsversuch angesichts der Morphologien natürlicher Sprachen', *Zeitschrift für Phonetik, Sprachwissenschaft und Kommuni-kationsforschung* 41: 426–37.

Harris, A. (1981) *Georgian Syntax*, Cambridge: Cambridge University Press.

Harris, J.W. (1973) 'On the order of certain phonological rules in Spanish', in Anderson and Kiparsky (eds), 59–76.

—— (1983) *Syllable Structure and Stress in Spanish: a Nonlinear Analysis*, Cambridge, MA: MIT Press.

Harris, Z.S. (1942) 'Morpheme alternants in linguistic analysis', *Language* 18: 169–80. Reprinted in Joos (ed.) (1966), 109–15.

Hawkins, J.A. (1983) *Word Order Universals*, New York: Academic Press.

Hjelmslev, L. (1935) *La Catégorie des cas*, Aarhus: Universitetsforlaget. Reprinted (1972), Munich: Wilhelm Fink.

Hockett, C.F. (1947) 'Problems of morphemic analysis', *Language* 23: 321–43. Reprinted in Joos (ed.) (1966), 229–42.

—— (1954) 'Two models of grammatical description', *Word* 10: 210–31. Reprinted in Joos (ed.) (1966), 386–99.

Hoeksema, J. (1985) *Categorial Morphology*, New York: Garland.

—— (1987) 'Relating word structure and Logical Form', *Linguistic Inquiry* 18: 119–26.

Hoeksema, J. and Janda, R. (1988) 'Implications of process-morphology for categorial grammar', in R.T. Oehrle, E. Bach and D. Wheeler (eds) *Categorial Grammars and Natural Language Structures*, 199–247, Dordrecht: Reidel.

Hoekstra, T., van der Hulst, H. and Moortgat, M. (eds) (1981) *Lexical Grammar*, Dordrecht: Foris.

Hoekstra, T. and van der Putten, F. (1988) 'Inheritance phenomena', in Everaert *et al.* (eds), 163–86.

Hooper, J.B. and Bybee, J. (1976) *Introduction to Natural Generative Phonology*, New York: Academic Press.

Hudson G. (1975) 'Suppletion in the representation of alternations', Ph.D. thesis, UCLA; Ann Arbor: University Microfilms.

—— (1980) 'Automatic alternations in non-transformational phonology', *Language* 56: 94–125.

—— (1986) 'Arabic root and pattern morphology without tiers', *Journal of Linguistics* 22: 85–122.

Hulst, H. van der and Smith, N. (eds) (1982a) *The Structure of Phonological Representations (Part I)*, Dordrecht: Foris.

—— (1982b) 'An overview of autosegmental and metrical phonology', in van der Hulst and Smith (eds) (1982a), 1–45.

—— (eds) (1984a) *Advances in Nonlinear Phonology*, Dordrecht: Foris.

—— (1984b) 'The framework of nonlinear generative phonology', in van der Hulst and Smith (eds) (1984a), 3–55.

Iverson, G. and Wheeler, D. (1988) 'Blocking and the Elsewhere Condition', in Hammond and Noonan (eds), 325–38.

Jackendoff, R. (1975) 'Morphological and semantic regularities in the lexicon', *Language* 51: 639–71.

—— (1977) *X' Syntax: A Study of Phrase Structure* (Linguistic Inquiry Monographs, 2), Cambridge, MA: MIT Press.

—— (1983) *Semantics and Cognition*, Cambridge, MA: MIT Press.

Jakobson, R. (1935) 'Beitrag zur allgemeinen Kasuslehre', *Travaux du Cercle Linguistique de Prague* 6: 240–88. Reprinted in Hamp *et al.* (eds) (1966), 51–95.

—— (1966) 'Quest for the essence of language', *Diogène* 51: 21–37. Also in (1971) *Selected Writings II*, 345–59, The Hague: Mouton.

Janda, R. (1984) 'Why morphological methathesis rules are rare: on the possibility of historical explanation in linguistics', *Berkeley Linguistics Society Proceedings* 10: 87–103.

Janda, R. and Sandoval, M. (1984) *'Elsewhere' in Morphology*, Bloomington: Indiana University Linguistics Club.

Jensen, J.T. and Stong-Jensen, M. (1984) 'Morphology is in the lexicon!', *Linguistic Inquiry* 15: 474–98.

Jespersen, O. (1922) *Language: its Nature, Development and Origin*, London: Allen & Unwin.

Joos, M. (ed.) (1966) *Readings in Linguistics I* (4th edn), Chicago: University of Chicago Press.

Kaisse, E. (1985) *Connected Speech: the Interaction of Syntax and Phonology*, Orlando: Academic Press.

Kaisse, E. and Shaw, P. (1985) 'On the theory of lexical phonology', *Phonology Yearbook* 2: 1–30.

Kefer, M. (1985) 'What syntax can we reconstruct from morphology?', *Lingua* 66: 151–75.

Kenstowicz, M. and Kisseberth, C. (1977) *Topics in Phonological Theory*, New York: Academic Press.

Kiefer, F. (1970) *Swedish Morphology*, Stockholm: Skriptor.

Kilani-Schoch, M. (1988) *Introduction à la morphologie naturelle*, Bern: Lang.

Kilani-Schoch, M. and Dressler, W.U. (1985) 'Natural Morphology and Classical vs. Tunisian Arabic', *Studia gramatyczne* 7: 27–47.

Kiparsky, P. (1968) 'How abstract is phonology?', Bloomington: Indiana University Linguistic Club. Reprinted in O. Fujimura (ed.) (1973) *Three Dimensions of Linguistic Theory*, 5–56, Tokyo: TEC and in Kiparsky (1982a), 119–63.

—— (1972) 'Explanation in phonology', in S. Peters (ed.) *Goals of Linguistic Theory*, 189–227, Englewood Cliffs: Prentice-Hall. Reprinted in Kiparsky (1982a), 81–118.

—— (1973) ' "Elsewhere" in phonology', in Anderson and Kiparsky (eds), 93–106.

—— (1982a) *Explanation in Phonology*, Dordrecht: Foris.

—— (1982b) 'Lexical morphology and phonology', in Linguistic Society of Korea (ed.) *Linguistics in the Morning Calm: Selected Papers from SICOL-1981*, 3–91, Seoul: Hanshin.

—— (1982c) 'From cyclic phonology to Lexical Phonology', in van der Hulst and Smith (eds), 131–75.

—— (1983) 'Word-formation and' the lexicon', in F. Ingemann (ed.) *Proceedings of the 1982 Mid-America Linguistics Conference*, 3–22, Lawrence: University of Kansas.

—— (1985) 'Some consequences of Lexical Phonology', *Phonology Yearbook* 2: 85–138.

Klavans, J. (1985) 'The independence of syntax and phonology in cliticization', *Language* 61: 95–120.

Koefoed, G. and van Marle, J. (1987) 'Requisites for reinterpretation', in W. Koopman, F. van der Leek, O. Fischer and R. Eaton (eds) *Explanation and Linguistic Change*, 121–50, Amsterdam: Benjamins.

Korhonen, M. (1969) 'Die Entwicklung der morphologischen Methode im Lappischen', *Finnisch-Ugrische Forschungen* 37: 203–362.

—— (1979) 'Entwicklungstendenzen des finnisch-ugrischen Kasussystems', *Finnisch-Ugrische Forschungen* 43: 1–21.

—— (1980) 'Über die struktural-typologischen Strömungen (Drifts) in den uralischen Sprachen', in O. Ikola (ed.) *Congressus Quintus Internationalis Fenno-Ugristarum, Pars I*, 87–110, Turku: Suomen Kielen Seura.

—— (1982) 'Reductive phonetic developments as the trigger to typological change: two examples from the Finno-Ugrian languages', in Ahlqvist (ed.), 190–5.

Koutsoudas, A., Sanders, G. and Noll, C. (1974) 'On the application of phonological rules', *Language* 50: 1–28.

Kroch, A.S. (1989) 'Function and grammar in the history of English: periphrastic *do*', in Fasold and Schiffrin (eds), 133–72.

Kuryłowicz, J. (1945–9) 'La Nature des procès dits "analogiques" ', *Acta Linguistica* 5: 121–38. Also in Hamp *et al.* (eds) (1966), 158–74.

Lakoff, G. and Johnson, M. (1980) *Metaphors We Live By*, Chicago: University of Chicago Press.

Lapointe, S.G. (1981) 'A lexical analysis of the English auxiliary verb system', in Hoekstra *et al.* (eds), 215–54.

Lees, R.B. (1960) *The Grammar of English Nominalizations*, Bloomington: Indiana University Press.

Lehmann, W.P. (1969) 'Proto-Indo-European compounds in relation to other Proto-Indo-European syntactic patterns', *Acta Linguistica Hafniensia* 12: 1–20.

—— (1973) 'A structural principle of language and its implications', *Language* 49: 47–66.

—— (1975) 'A discussion of compound and word order', in Li (ed.) 149–62.

Levi, J. (1978) *The Syntax and Semantics of Complex Nominals*, New York: Academic Press.

Levin, J. (1988) 'Bidirectional foot construction as a window on level ordering', in Hammond and Noonan (eds), 339–52.

Li, C.N. (ed.) (1975) *Word Order and Word Order Change*, Austin: University of Texas Press.

—— (ed.) (1977) *Mechanisms of Syntactic Change*, Austin: University of Texas Press.

Li, C.N. and Thomson, S.A. (1974) 'Historical change of word order: a case study in Chinese and its implications', in Anderson and Jones (ed.), 199–217.

—— (1975) 'The semantic function of word order: a case study in Mandarin', in Li (ed.) 163–95.

Lieber, R. (1981a) 'Morphological conversion within a restrictive theory of the lexicon', in Moortgat *et al.* (eds.), 161–200.

—— (1981b) *On the Organization of the Lexicon* (Ph.D. dissertation, MIT),

Bloomington: Indiana University Linguistics Club.
—— (1982) 'Allomorphy', *Linguistic Analysis* 10: 27–52.
—— (1983) 'Argument linking and compounds in English', *Linguistic Inquiry* 14: 251–85.
—— (1988a) 'Configurational and nonconfigurational morphology', in Everaert *et al.* (eds), 187–215.
—— (1988b) 'Phrasal compounding in English and the morphology-syntax interface', in D. Brentari, G. Larson and L. Macleod (eds), *Papers from the Parasession on Agreement in Grammatical Theory*, 202–22, Chicago: Chicago Linguistic Society.
—— (1989) 'On percolation', in Booij and van Marle (eds), 95–138.
Lightfoot, D.W. (1979) *The Principles of Diachronic Syntax*, Cambridge: Cambridge University Press.
Lüdtke, H. (ed.) (1980) *Kommunikationstheoretische Grundlagen des Sprachwandels*, Berlin: De Gruyter.
McCarthy, J. (1981) 'A prosodic theory of nonconcatenative morphology', *Linguistic Inquiry* 12: 373–418.
—— (1982) 'Prosodic templates, morphemic templates, and morphemic tiers', in van der Hulst and Smith (eds), 191–223.
—— (1984) 'Speech disguise and phonological representation in Amharic', in van der Hulst and Smith (eds), 305–12.
MacWhinney, B. (ed.) (1987) *Mechanisms of Language Acquisition*, Hillsdale: Erlbaum.
Malicka-Kleparska, A. (1985) 'Parallel derivation and Lexicalist Morphology: the case of Polish diminutivization', in Gussmann (ed.), 95–112.
Mańczak, W. (1957–8) 'Tendances générales des changements anal-ogiques', *Lingua* 7: 298–325, 387–420.
—— (1980) 'Frequenz und Sprachwandel', in Lüdtke (ed.), 37–79.
Marantz, A. (1982) 'Re reduplication', *Linguistic Inquiry* 13: 435–82.
—— (1984) *On the Nature of Grammatical Relations*, Cambridge, MA: MIT Press.
—— (1988a) 'Clitics, morphological merger, and the mapping to phonological structure', in Hammond and Noonan (eds), 253–70.
—— (1988b) 'Apparent exceptions to the Projection Principle', in Everaert *et al.* (eds), 217–32.
Marle, J. van (1985) *On the Paradigmatic Dimension of Morphological Creativity*, Dordrecht: Foris.
—— (1986) 'The domain hypothesis: the study of rival morphological processes', *Linguistics* 24: 601–27.
Mascaró, J. (1976) *Catalan Phonology and the Phonological Cycle* (Ph.D. dissertation, MIT), Bloomington: Indiana University Linguistics Club.
Matthews, P.H. (1972) *Inflectional Morphology*, Cambridge: Cambridge University Press.
—— (1974) *Morphology: an Introduction to the Theory of Word-Structure*, Cambridge: Cambridge University Press.
May, R. (1977) *The Grammar of Quantification* (Ph.D. dissertation, MIT), Bloomington: Indiana University Linguistic Club.
Mayerthaler, W. (1981) *Morphologische Natürlichkeit*, Wiesbaden: Athenaion. English translation (1988) *Morphological Naturalness*, Ann Arbor: Karoma.

—— (1987) 'System-independent morphological naturalness', in Dressler *et al.* (eds), 25–58.

Mel'čuk, I.A. (1973) 'On the possessive forms of the Hungarian noun', in F. Kiefer and N. Ruwet (eds) *Generative Grammar in Europe*, 315–32, Dordrecht: Reidel.

—— (1982) *Towards a Language of Linguistics: a System of Formal Notions for Theoretical Morphology*, Munich: Wilhelm Fink.

Mithun, M. (1988) 'System-defining structural properties in polysynthetic languages', *Zeitschrift für Phonetik, Sprachwissenschaft und Kommunikationsforschung* 41: 442–52.

Mohanan, K.P. (1986) *The Theory of Lexical Phonology*, Dordrecht: Reidel.

Moortgat, M., van der Hulst, H. and Hoekstra, T. (eds) (1981) *The Scope of Lexical Rules*, Dordrecht: Foris.

Muysken, P. (1986) 'Approaches to affix order', *Linguistics* 24: 629–43.

Neustupný, J.V. (1978) *Post-Structural Approaches to Language*, Tokyo: University of Tokyo Press.

Newmeyer, F.J. (1980) *Linguistic Theory in America*, New York: Academic Press.

—— (ed.) (1988) *Linguistics: the Cambridge Survey* (Volume I: *Linguistic Theory: Foundations*), Cambridge: Cambridge University Press.

Nida, E.A. (1948) 'The identification of morphemes', *Language* 24: 414–41. Reprinted in Joos (ed.) (1966), 255–71.

—— (1949) *Morphology: the Descriptive Analysis of Words* (2nd edn), Ann Arbor: University of Michigan Press.

Nyman, M. (1987) 'Is the Paradigm Economy Principle relevant?', *Journal of Linguistics* 23: 251–67.

—— (1988) 'Paradigm economy: a rejoinder to Carstairs', *Journal of Linguistics* 24: 501–13.

Paulissen, D. and Zonneveld, W. (1988) 'Compound verbs and the adequacy of Lexical Morphology', in Everaert *et al.* (eds), 281–302.

Perlmutter, D. (1988) 'The split morphology hypothesis: evidence from Yiddish', in Hammond and Noonan (eds), 79–100.

Pesetsky, D. (1979) 'Russian morphology and lexical theory', unpublished paper, MIT.

—— (1985) 'Morphology and Logical Form', *Linguistic Inquiry* 16: 193–246.

Pinker, S. (1984) *Language Learnability and Language Development*, Cambridge, MA: Harvard University Press.

Pinker, S. and Prince, A. (1988) 'On language and connectionism: analysis of a parallel distributed processing model of language acquisition', *Cognition* 28: 73–193.

Plank, F. (1979) 'Ikonisierung und De-Ikonisierung als Prinzipien des Sprachwandels', *Sprachwissenschaft* 4: 121–58.

—— (1980) 'Encoding grammatical relations: acceptable and unacceptable non-distinctness', in Fisiak (ed.), 289–325.

—— (1984) 'Romance disagreements: phonology interfering with syntax', *Journal of Linguistics* 20: 329–49.

—— (1986) 'Paradigm size, morphological typology, and universal economy', *Folia Linguistica* 20: 29–48.

Posner, R. (1985) 'Non-agreement on Romance disagreements', *Journal of*

Linguistics 21: 437–51.

Pranka, P. (1983) 'Syntax and word formation', unpublished Ph.D. dissertation, MIT.

Pulleyblank, D. (1988) 'Tone and the Morphemic Tier Hypothesis', in Hammond and Noonan (eds), 353–70.

Pullum, G. and Zwicky, A. (1988) 'The syntax–phonology interface', in Newmeyer (ed.), 255–80.

Ramat, A.G., Carruba, O. and Bernini, G. (eds) (1987) *Papers from the Seventh International Conference on Historical Linguistics*, Amsterdam: Benjamins.

Reuland, E. (1988) 'Relating morphological and syntactic structure', in Everaert *et al.* (eds), 303–37.

Robins, R.H. (1959) 'In defence of WP', *Transactions of the Philological Society*, 116–44.

—— (1979) *A Short History of Linguistics*, London: Longman.

Roeper, T. (1988) 'Compound syntax and head movement', in Booij and van Marle (eds), 187–228.

Roeper, T. and Siegel, M. (1978) 'A lexical transformation for verbal compounds', *Linguistic Inquiry* 9: 197–260.

Rohlfs, G. (1949) *Historische Grammatik der Italienischen Sprache und ihrer Mundarten* (Volume II: *Formenlehre und Syntax*), Bern: Francke.

Ronneberger-Sibold, E. (1980) *Sprachverwendung – Sprachsystem: Ökonomie und Wandel*, Tübingen: Niemeyer.

—— (1988) 'Entstehung von Suppletion und Natürliche Morphologie', *Zeitschrift für Phonetik, Sprachwissenschaft und Kommunikationsforschung* 41: 453–62.

Ross, R. (1972) 'A reanalysis of English word stress', in M.K. Brame (ed.) *Contributions to Generative Phonology*, 229–323, Austin: University of Texas Press.

Rubach, J. (1984) *Cyclic and Lexical Phonology: the Structure of Polish*, Dordrecht: Foris.

Rudes, B. (1980) 'On the nature of verbal suppletion', *Linguistics* 18: 655–76.

Rumelhart, D. and McClelland, J. (1986) 'Learning the past tenses of English verbs', in Rumelhart *et al.*, 216–71.

—— (1987) 'Learning the past tenses of English verbs: implicit rules or parallel distributed processing?', in MacWhinney (ed.), 195–248.

Rumelhart, D., McClelland, J. and the PDP Research Group (1986) *Parallel Distributed Processing: Explorations in the Microstructure of Cognition* (Volume II: *Psychological and Biological Models*), Cambridge, MA: MIT Press.

Sadock, J. (1985) 'Autolexical Syntax: a proposal for the treatment of noun incorporation and similar phenomena', *Natural Language and Linguistic Theory* 3: 379–439.

—— (1988) 'The autolexical classification of morphemes', in Hammond and Noonan (eds), 271–90.

Sampson, G. (1987) Review of Rumelhart *et al.* (1986), *Language* 63: 871–86.

Sapir, E. (1921) *Language*, New York: Harcourt Brace.

Scalise, S. (1984) *Generative Morphology*, Dordrecht: Foris.

—— (1988) 'The notion of "head" in morphology', in Booij and van Marle (eds), 229–45.

Selkirk, E.O. (1982) *The Syntax of Words* (Linguistic Inquiry Monograph, 7), Cambridge, MA: MIT Press.

Shapiro, M. (1969) *Aspects of Russian Morphology: a Semiotic Investigation*, Cambridge, MA: Slavica.

—— (1983) *The Sense of Grammar: Language as Semeiotic*, Bloomington: Indiana University Press.

—— (1990) 'On a universal criterion of rule coherence', in Dressler *et al.* (eds), 25–34.

Siegel, D. (1978) 'The Adjacency Constraint and the theory of morphology', *NELS* 8 (*Papers from the Eighth Annual Meeting of the North-Eastern Linguistic Society*): 189–97.

—— (1979) *Topics in English Morphology*, New York: Garland.

Simões M. and Stoel-Gammon, C. (1979) 'The acquisition of inflections in Portuguese: a study of the development of person markers on verbs', *Journal of Child Language* 6: 53–67.

Simpson, J. and Withgott, M. (1986) 'Pronominal clitic clusters and templates', in H. Borer (ed.) *The Syntax of Pronominal Clitics* (Syntax and Semantics 19), 149–74, Orlando: Academic Press.

Skalička, V. (1951) 'Das Erscheinungsbild der Sprachtypen', in Skalička (1979), 21–58.

—— (1966) 'Ein "typologisches Konstrukt" ', *Travaux linguistiques de Prague* 2: 157–64. Reprinted in Skalička (1979), 335–41.

—— (1979) *Typologische Studien*, Brunswick: Vieweg.

Slobin, D. (1971) 'Cognitive prerequisites for the development of grammar', in C. Ferguson and D. Slobin (eds) *Studies of Child Language Development*, 175–208, New York: Holt Rinehart.

Smith, E. and Medin, D. (1981) *Categories and Concepts*, Cambridge, MA: Harvard University Press.

Smith, N.V. (1981) 'Consistency, markedness and language change: on the notion "consistent language" ', *Journal of Linguistics* 17: 39–54.

—— (1982) Review of B. Comrie *Language Universals and Linguistic Typology*, *Australian Journal of Linguistics* 2: 255–61.

Spencer, A. (1988a) 'Bracketing paradoxes and the English lexicon', *Language* 64: 663–82.

—— (1988b) 'Morpholexical rules and lexical representation', *Linguistics* 26: 619–40.

—— (1988c) 'Arguments for morpholexical rules', *Journal of Linguistics* 24: 1–29.

—— (1990) 'The advantages of morpholexical phonology', in Dressler *et al.* (eds), 35–40.

—— (1991) *Morphological Theory: an Introduction to Morphology in Generative Grammar*, Oxford: Blackwell.

Sproat, R. (1985) 'On deriving the lexicon', unpublished Ph.D. dissertation, MIT.

—— (1988) 'Bracketing paradoxes, cliticization and other topics: the mapping between syntactic and phonological structure', in Everaert *et al.* (eds), 339–60.

Stemberger, J. and MacWhinney, B. (1988) 'Are inflected forms stored in the lexicon?', in Hammond and Noonan (eds), 101–16.

Strauss, S. (1982a) *Lexicalist Phonology of English and German*, Dordrecht: Foris.

—— (1982b) 'On "relatedness paradoxes" and related paradoxes', *Linguistic Inquiry* 13: 694–700.

Stump, G.T. (1989) 'A note on Breton pluralization and the Elsewhere Condition', *Natural Language and Linguistic Theory* 7: 261–73.

Szpyra, J. (1989) *The Phonology–Morphology Interface: Cycles, Levels and Words*, London: Routledge.

Szymanek, B. (1988) *Categories and Categorization in Morphology*, Lublin: Redakcja Wydawnictw Katolickiego Uniwersytetu Lubelskiego.

—— (1989) *Introduction to Morphological Analysis*, Warsaw: Panstwowe Wydawnictwo Naukowe.

Talmy, L. (1985) 'Lexicalization patterns: semantic structure in lexical forms', in T. Shopen (ed.) *Language Typology and Syntactic Description III: Grammatical Categories and the Lexicon*, 57–149, Cambridge: Cambridge University Press.

Thomas-Flinders, T. (ed.) (1981) *Inflectional Morphology: Introduction to the Extended Word-and-Paradigm Theory* (UCLA Occasional Papers in Linguistics, 4), Los Angeles: UCLA Department of Linguistics.

Tiersma, P. (1982) 'Local and general markedness', *Language* 58: 832–49.

Toman, J. (1987) *Wortsyntax* (2nd edn), Tübingen: Niemeyer.

Trommelen, M. and Zonneveld, W. (1986) 'Dutch morphology: evidence for the Right-hand Head Rule', *Linguistic Inquiry* 17: 147–69.

Vennemann, T. (1972) 'Phonetic analogy and conceptual analogy', in T. Vennemann and T.H. Wilbur (eds) *Schuchardt, the Neogrammarians and the Transformational Theory of Sound Change*, 181–204, Frankfurt: Athenäum.

—— (1974) 'Words and syllables in Natural Generative Grammar', in A. Bruck, R.A. Fox and M.W. LaGaly (eds) *Papers from the Parasession on Natural Phonology*, 346–74, Chicago: Chicago Linguistic Society.

—— (1975) 'An explanation of drift', in Li (ed.), 269–305.

Vincent, N. (1980) 'Words versus morphemes in morphological change: the case of Italian *-iamo*', in Fisiak (ed.), 383–98.

Wanner, D. (1972) 'The derivation of inflectional paradigms in Italian', in J. Casagrande and B. Saciuk (eds) *Generative Studies in Romance Languages*, 293–318, Rowley, MA: Newbury House.

Warburton, I.P. (1973) 'Modern Greek verb conjugation: inflectional morphology in a transformational grammar', *Lingua* 32: 193–226.

Werner, O. (1987) 'The aim of morphological change is a good mixture – not a uniform language type', in Ramat *et al.* (eds), 591–606.

—— (1989) 'Sprachökonomie und Natürlichkeit im Bereich der Morphologie', *Zeitschrift für Phonetik, Sprachwissenschaft und Kommunikationsforschung* 42: 34–47.

Williams, E.O. (1981a) 'On the notions "lexically related" and "head of a word" ', *Linguistic Inquiry* 12: 245–74.

—— (1981b) 'Argument structure and morphology', *Linguistic Review* 1: 81–114.

Wurzel, W.U. (1970) *Studien zur deutschen Lautstruktur* (Studia Grammatica, VIII), Berlin: Akademie-Verlag.

—— (1984) *Flexionsmorphologie und Natürlichkeit* (Studia Grammatica, XXI), Berlin: Akademie-Verlag. English translation (1989) *Inflectional Morphology and Naturalness*, Dordrecht: Kluwer.

—— (1987a) 'Paradigmenstrukturbedingungen: Aufbau und Veränderung von Flexionsparadigmen', in Ramat *et al.* (eds), 629–44.

—— (1987b) 'System-dependent morphological naturalness in inflection', in Dressler *et al.* (eds), 59–96.

—— (1989) 'Von der Inadäquatheit einer Affixmorphologie: weshalb morphologische Kategorienmarker nicht als eigene Einheiten im Lexikon repräsentiert sein können', *Linguistische Studien* (Series A), 194: 277–98.

Yip, M., Maling, J. and Jackendoff, R. (1987) 'Case in tiers', *Language* 63: 217–50.

Yokoyama, M. (1951) 'Outline of Kechua structure I: morphology', *Language* 27: 38–67.

Zubizarreta, M.L. (1985) 'The relation between morphophonology and morphosyntax: the case of Romance causatives', *Linguistic Inquiry* 16: 247–89.

Zubizarreta, M.L. and van Haaften, T. (1988) 'English -*ing* and Dutch -*en* nominal constructions: a case of simultaneous nominal and verbal projections', in Everaert *et al.* (eds), 361–93.

Zwicky, A. (1977) *On Clitics*, Bloomington: Indiana University Linguistics Club.

—— (1985a) 'Heads', *Journal of Linguistics* 21: 1–29.

—— (1985b) 'Clitics and particles', *Language* 61: 283–305.

—— (1985c) 'How to describe inflection', *Berkeley Linguistics Society Proceedings* 11: 372–86.

—— (1985d) 'Rules of allomorphy and phonology–syntax interactions', *Journal of Linguistics* 21: 431–6.

—— (1986a) 'Imposed versus inherent feature specifications, and other multiple feature markings', Bloomington: Indiana University Linguistics Club.

—— (1986b) 'The general case: basic form versus default form', *Berkeley Linguistic Society Proceedings* 12: 305–14.

—— (1987) 'Phonological and morphological rule interactions in highly modular grammars', *Eastern States Conference on Linguistics* 3: 523–32.

—— (1990) 'Inflectional morphology as a (sub)component of grammar', in Dressler *et al.* (eds), 217–36.

Zwicky, A. and Pullum, G. (1983) 'Cliticization vs. inflection: English -*n't*', *Language* 59: 502–13.

Author index

Subject index

Language index